NOODLES, RICE, AND EVERYTHING SPICE

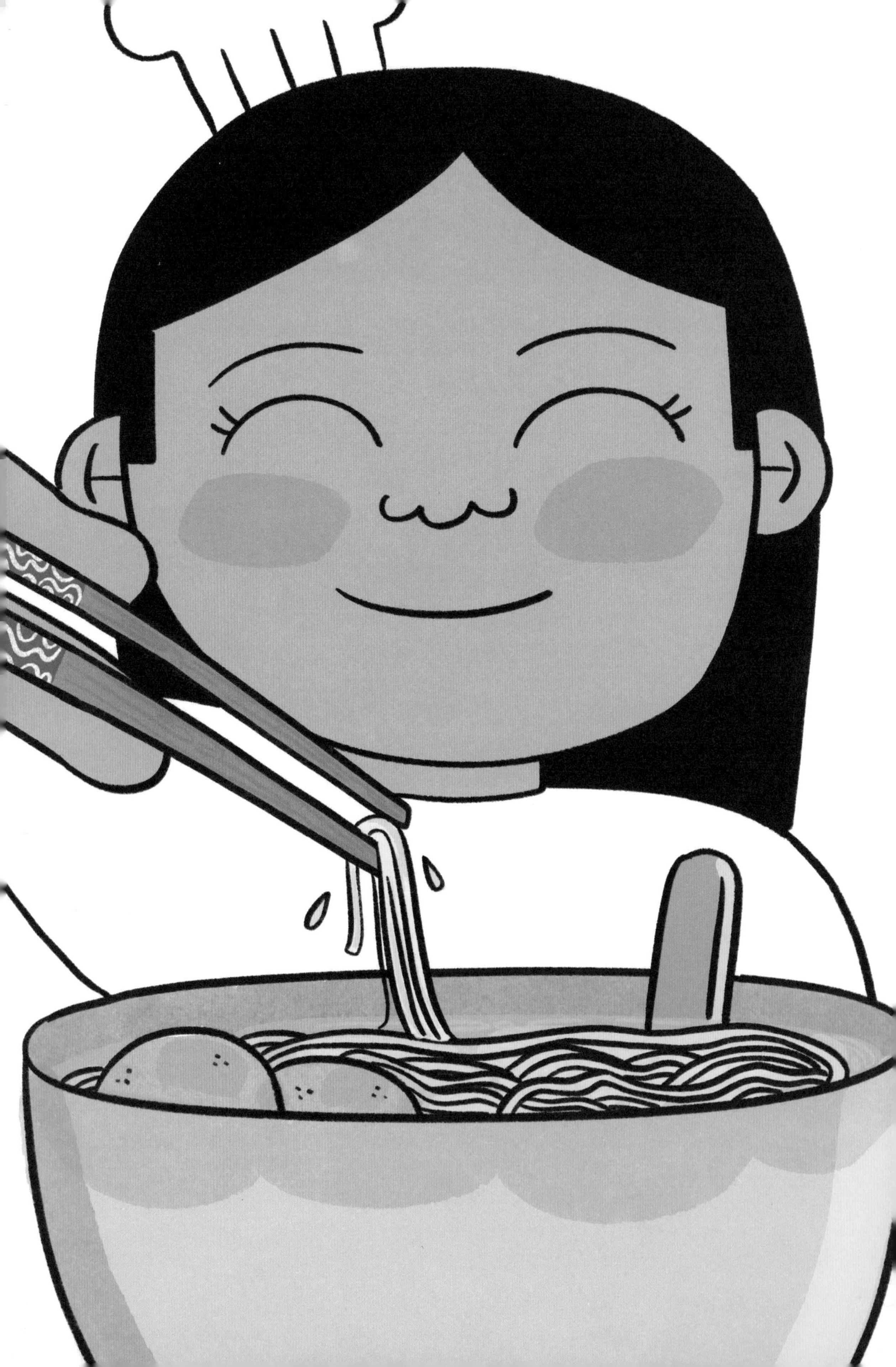

CHRISTINA DE WITTE
AND MALLIKA KAUPPINEN

NOODLES, RICE, AND EVERYTHING SPICE

A THAI COMIC BOOK COOKBOOK

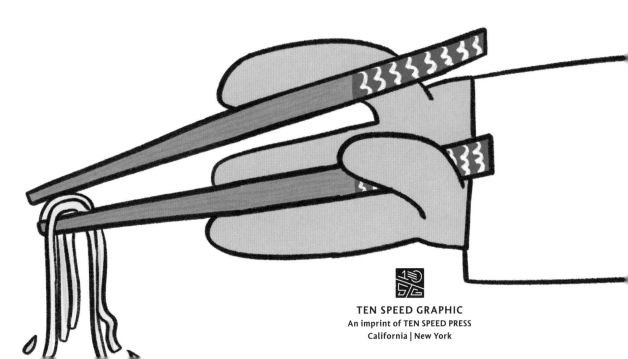

TEN SPEED GRAPHIC
An imprint of TEN SPEED PRESS
California | New York

CONTENTS

CURRIES & SOUPS 122

DESSERTS & DRINKS 145

STAPLES & ACCOMPANIMENTS 166

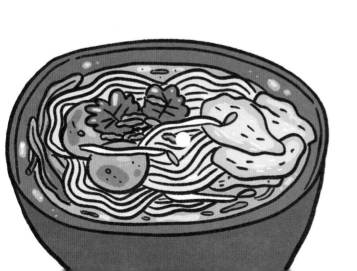

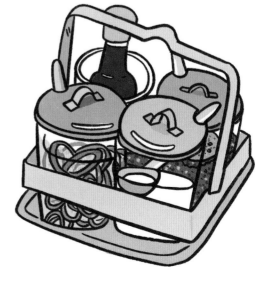

PROLOGUE

MALLIKA WAS RAISED IN A BIG FAMILY IN CHUMPHON, A SOUTHERN PROVINCE IN THAILAND. HER PARENTS LEFT EVERY MORNING TO WORK ON THEIR FRUIT PLANTATION WHILE SHE STAYED HOME TO HELP HER AUNT AND GRANDMOTHER AROUND THE HOUSE.

BY THE AGE OF SEVEN, MALLIKA WAS HELPING HER AUNT WITH ALL THE CHORES, ESPECIALLY IN THE KITCHEN.

MALLIKA AND HER AUNT MADE SURE THERE WAS FOOD READY WHEN HER PARENTS CAME BACK HOME. WHETHER THE MEAL WAS ON THE TABLE OR ON THE FLOOR, THE WHOLE FAMILY ALWAYS ATE TOGETHER. NO EXCEPTIONS.

SHE WAS ONLY TEN WHEN SHE MOVED TO BANGKOK TO GO LIVE WITH HER MATERNAL AUNTS.

HER AUNTS OWNED A SMALL GROCERY STORE, WHERE THEY MADE AND SOLD SOUTHERN THAI DISHES. EVERY DAY—EVEN ON WEEKENDS— MALLIKA WOULD START WORK AT 5 A.M. TO HELP PREPARE THE MANY INGREDIENTS.

BEEP! BEEP! 4:45

20฿

50฿

เจ้ ขายหมด Sold out

THEY PREPARED UP TO TEN DISHES EACH DAY, AND THEY ALWAYS SOLD OUT. PEOPLE WENT ABSOLUTELY WILD FOR THEIR FOOD, AND THERE WAS A REASON WHY IT WAS CALLED "THE BEST SOUTHERN FOOD OF THE NEIGHBORHOOD."

SINCE MALLIKA ALREADY HAD A TASTE OF HOME-COOKING EVERY SINGLE DAY, SHE STARTED EXPLORING THE CITY'S LOCAL STREET FOOD BY HERSELF. HER FAVORITE GUAY TIAW WAS ONLY A FIVE-MINUTE WALK AWAY.

DURING HER TIME IN COLLEGE, SHE INVITED EXCHANGE STUDENTS TO COME COOK THAI FOOD WITH HER AT HER AUNTS' PLACE.

SHE STILL REMEMBERS DANIEL, A STUDENT FROM SWITZERLAND, WHO LOVED THE GAENG KEOW WAN AND VOWED HE WOULD MAKE IT FOR HIS FAMILY.

THE JOY OF FOREIGNERS ENJOYING THAI FOOD SPARKED MALLIKA'S ENTHUSIASM FOR COOKING AND SHARING HER CULTURE.

LIVING IN BANGKOK, SHE WORKED AS A SECRETARY, WAS THE OWNER OF A SMALL TRAVEL AGENCY, AND SPENT HER SPARE TIME AS A SELF-PROCLAIMED THAI FOOD AMBASSADOR FOR HER FOREIGN COLLEAGUES AND FRIENDS.

IN 2015, MALLIKA TRAVELED TO FINLAND TO ENJOY A NEW ADVENTURE. SHE ENDED UP SETTLING DOWN WITH HER BELOVED FINNISH NOW-HUSBAND, AND THEY WELCOMED A LITTLE SON.

PAD THAI € 5!

IN FINLAND, MALLIKA COOKED MORE THAI FOOD THAN EVER, FOR FRIENDS AND STRANGERS ALIKE. THEY WOULD ASK, "SO WHEN ARE YOU OPENING A RESTAURANT?" MALLIKA WOULD REPLY, "I DON'T KNOW! AFTER MY TEACHING BUSINESS, MAYBE?"

MALLIKA BEGAN TEACHING THE THAI LANGUAGE ONLINE,
AND THAT'S WHERE SHE MET . . . CHRISTINA.

BORN AND RAISED IN A SMALL TOWN IN
BELGIUM, IT WAS NOT ALWAYS EASY
FOR CHRISTINA TO FIND A CONNECTION
WITH THE *OTHER PARTS* OF HERSELF.

ESPECIALLY WHEN THOSE PARTS REACHED
ALL THE WAY TO THE OTHER SIDE OF
THE WORLD. IT WASN'T UNTIL CHRISTINA
WAS IN HER EARLY TWENTIES THAT SHE
ADDRESSED THE FACT THAT BEING BIRACIAL
MEANT SHE WAS A LITTLE DIFFERENT
FROM THE FRIENDS SHE GREW UP WITH.

BUT EVEN THOUGH HER STORY WAS DIFFERENT, SHE WAS STILL EAGER TO FIND PEOPLE WITH RELATABLE AND SHARED EXPERIENCES.

WHEN CHRISTINA WENT TO STUDY IN BRUSSELS AND LIVE IN ANTWERP, SHE WAS ABLE TO EXPLORE MORE OF HERSELF BECAUSE SHE *SAW* MORE PEOPLE LIKE HERSELF. BEING DIFFERENT WAS THE NORM IN AN INTERNATIONAL, MULTIRACIAL CITY, AND BLENDING IN BECAME EASIER.

SHE MET PEOPLE LIKE HER WHO WERE FIRST-, SECOND-, OR THIRD-GENERATION IMMIGRANTS, GROWING UP IN AN ENVIRONMENT THAT LOOKED AND FELT DIFFERENT FROM WHERE THEIR ROOTS LAY.

SOME OF THEM HAVE NEVER SEEN THEIR FAMILY'S COUNTRY OF ORIGIN; OTHERS CAN'T WAIT TO GO BACK AGAIN. SOME HAVE NEVER SPOKEN A SINGLE WORD OF THEIR NATIVE LANGUAGE; OTHERS SPEAK NOTHING ELSE AT HOME.

MANY PEOPLE HAVE EXPERIENCED FEELING SPLIT BETWEEN TWO OR MORE "CLIFFS," BATTLING WITH HOW THEY LOOK VERSUS HOW THEY FEEL, AND REALIZING THERE WILL ALWAYS BE A DISCREPANCY BETWEEN THE TWO.

BUT IN THAT GAP BETWEEN THE CLIFFS, CHRISTINA FOUND PEACE IN THE AMBIGUITY OF BEING A LITTLE BIT FROM EVERYWHERE AND NOWHERE AT THE SAME TIME.

BELGIUM

THAILAND

SHE FOUND A PLACE FOR CULTURAL MISFITS WHERE SHE COULD FREELY ASK, "WHO AM I?" AND "WHO DO I WANT TO BE?"

HOWEVER, THE ONE GAP THAT SHE *COULDN'T* GET OVER WAS THE LANGUAGE BARRIER BETWEEN HER AND HER MOM. AT THE START OF 2020, CHRISTINA DECIDED IT WAS ABOUT TIME TO LEARN THE LANGUAGE THAT WAS SO CLOSE, YET SO FAR AWAY FROM HER.

CHRISTINA SEARCHED FOR ONLINE THAI CLASSES. BEFORE SHE EVEN FULLY PROCESSED HER DECISION, SHE WAS INTRODUCING HERSELF TO KHRUU* MALLIKA IN A PRIVATE ZOOM CLASS.

MALLIKA WAS KIND AND PATIENT, AND THEY QUICKLY NOTICED THEY HAD A LOT IN COMMON.

MALLIKA HAD A CLEAR MISSION: TO HELP OTHER THAI OR MULTIRACIAL KIDS LIVING ABROAD LEARN TO SPEAK, READ, AND WRITE THAI. SHE WAS DRAWN TO THIS WORK NOT ONLY BECAUSE SHE LOVES TEACHING BUT BECAUSE SHE KNOWS HOW IT FEELS TO BE FAR REMOVED FROM ONE'S HERITAGE AND THE PRIDE THAT RESULTS FROM BEING ABLE TO UNITE THROUGH BASIC COMMUNICATION.

*TEACHER

SHE WANTED TO MAKE SURE THAT PEOPLE WHO'VE LOST THEIR CONNECTION TO THAI CULTURE AND LANGUAGE KNOW IT'S NEVER TOO LATE TO RESTORE THAT LINK. CHRISTINA WAS ONE OF THOSE PEOPLE, AND QUICKLY A NEW WHOLESOME FRIENDSHIP—ALTHOUGH ONLY ONLINE—SPROUTED.

YOU'RE HOLDING IN YOUR HANDS THE RESULT OF THAT FRIENDSHIP. CHRISTINA AND MALLIKA HAVE WORKED CLOSELY TOGETHER ON MULTIPLE PROJECTS BEFORE, BUT THIS IS BY FAR THE MOST EXCITING ONE.

CHRISTINA IS A STORYTELLER AND MALLIKA HAD A STORY THAT NEEDED TELLING. THIS OPENED THE DOOR TO THE SAME STORY SHARED BY THOUSANDS OF PEOPLE LIKE THEM ACROSS THE WORLD. THEY SET OUT TO CREATE SOMETHING THAT WAS UNIQUE AND YET SO ORDINARY AT THE SAME TIME.

ONE OF THEIR COMMON INTERESTS HAS ALWAYS BEEN FOOD. IT SOON MADE SENSE TO MAKE A COOKBOOK TOGETHER—AND TO LEARN ABOUT CULTURE, LANGUAGE, AND FOOD AT THE SAME TIME.

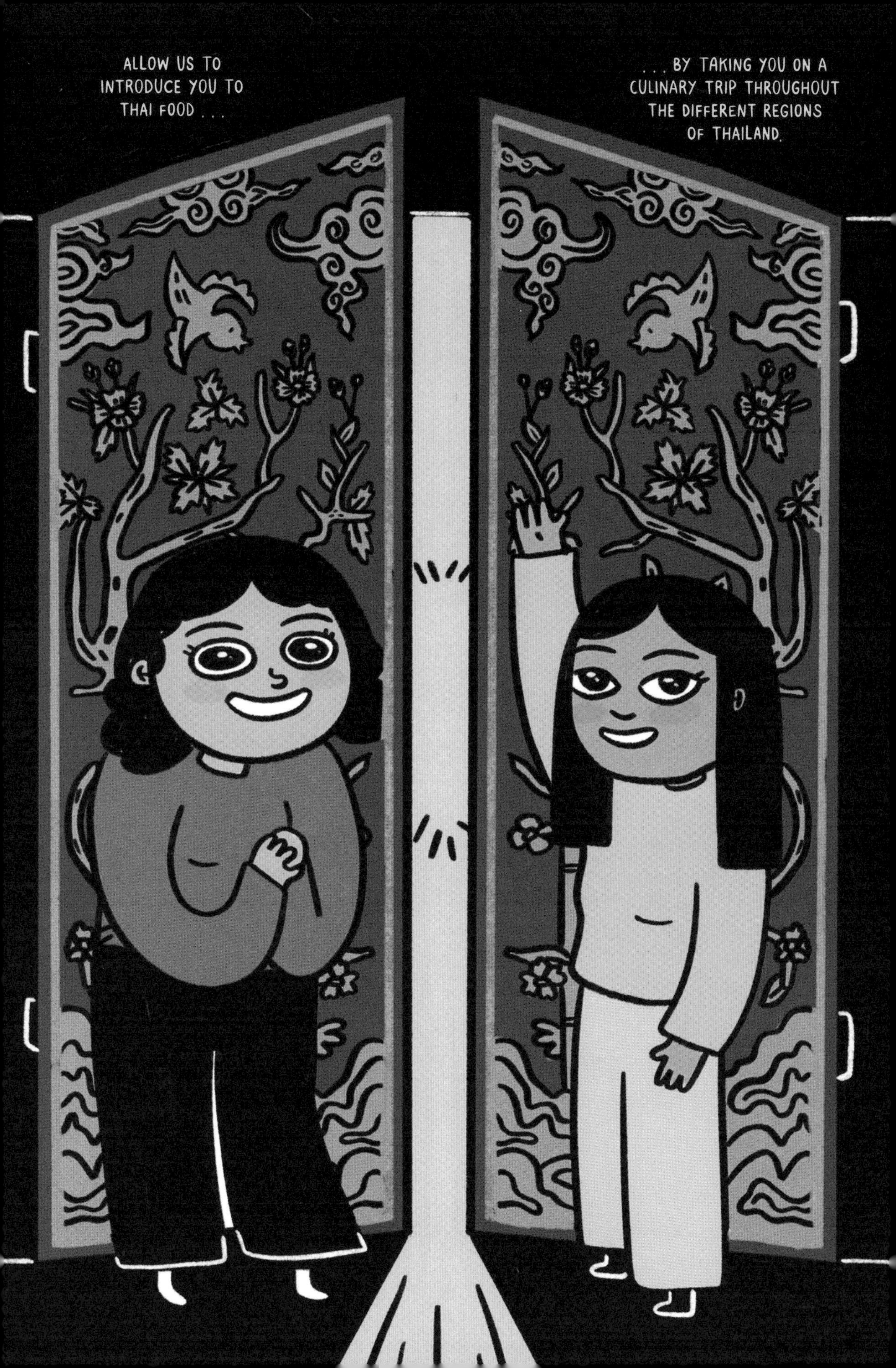
ALLOW US TO INTRODUCE YOU TO THAI FOOD . . .
. . . BY TAKING YOU ON A CULINARY TRIP THROUGHOUT THE DIFFERENT REGIONS OF THAILAND.

INTRODUCTION TO THAI FOOD

THE LAND OF SMILES OFFERS BREATHTAKING JUNGLES, TROPICAL BEACHES, AND A THRILLING CITY CENTER, BUT THE THAI KITCHEN IS REALLY THE BEST PLACE OF ALL.

WHY IS THAI FOOD SO POPULAR? LONG STORY SHORT—IT IS JUST SO FRIGGIN' DELICIOUS. SHORT STORY LONG—IT HAS A VERY RICH HISTORY, INFLUENCED BY EVERY VISITOR WHO HAS EVER SET FOOT ON THIS LAND.

THAILAND IS GEOGRAPHICALLY DIVIDED INTO SIX REGIONS. HOWEVER, IN TERMS OF CULTURE, ONE MIGHT SAY THERE ARE FOUR KEY AREAS: NORTH, NORTHEAST, CENTRAL, AND SOUTH.

EACH CULTURAL REGION HAS ITS OWN UNIQUE FOOD HABITS AND FLAVORS.

LET'S TAKE A TOUR THROUGH ALL FOUR CULINARY REGIONS OF THAILAND, SHALL WE?

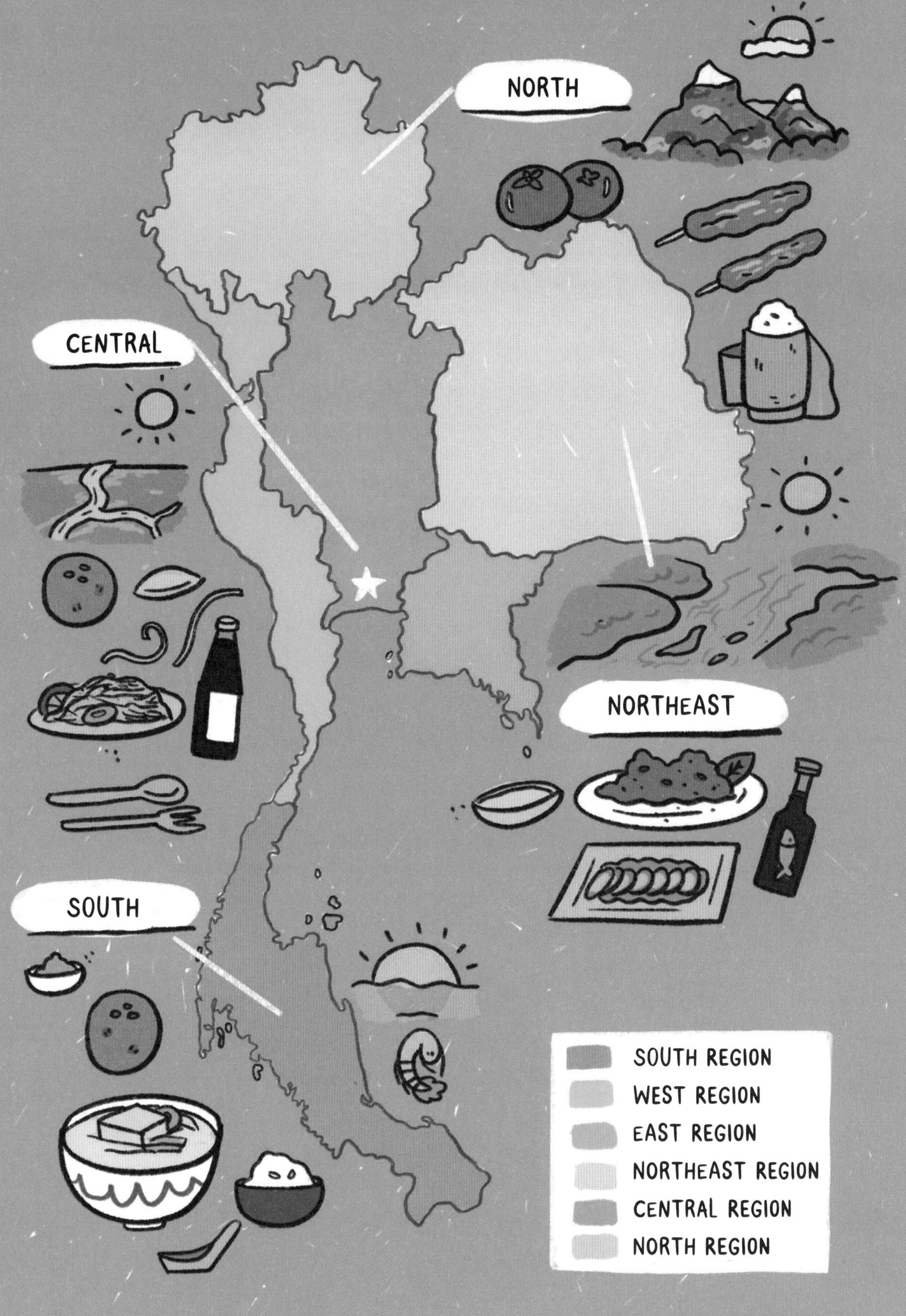
NORTH
CENTRAL
NORTHEAST
SOUTH
SOUTH REGION
WEST REGION
EAST REGION
NORTHEAST REGION
CENTRAL REGION
NORTH REGION

ALONG WITH BEAUTIFUL COASTLINES AND ISLAND BEACHES, THE SOUTH IS FAMOUS FOR SUPER-SPICY FOOD. TURMERIC, BITTER BEAN, COCONUT, FISH ENTRAILS, SHRIMP PASTE, AND SEAFOOD ARE PROMINENT, AND THE DISHES SHOW STRONG MALAYSIAN AND INDONESIAN INFLUENCES.

NEXT STOP: BANGKOK!

BANGKOK IS LOCATED IN THE CENTRAL PART OF THAILAND. HEAVILY POPULATED BY FOLKS FROM ALL OVER THE COUNTRY, IT IS A BIG METROPOLITAN BLEND OF ALL REGIONS. WHEN PEOPLE MOVE TO BANGKOK, THEIR LOCAL DISHES SIMPLY MOVE WITH THEM! HOW COOL IS IT THAT YOU DON'T NEED TO GO HOME TO HAVE A NOSTALGIC MEAL IN BANGKOK?

BANGKOK CUISINE IS KNOWN FOR CURRIES, WOK-FRIED DISHES, STREET FOOD, AND SWEET DESSERTS.

THE DISHES ALWAYS HAVE THE MOST BEAUTIFUL PRESENTATION, MADE WITH THE MOST REFINED AND VARIED COOKING METHODS FROM THE CROSS-CULTURAL IMPACT OF THE AYUTTHAYA PERIOD (1350–1767), WHEN AYUTTHAYA WAS THE CAPITAL CITY OF THAILAND.

A TRUE BANGKOK LOCAL WOULD CONSIDER THESE FOODS AS TOURISTY, THOUGH. SO, IF YOU WANT TO FLEX IN KRUNG THEP (ANOTHER NAME FOR BANGKOK), JUST SAY YOU'RE *TOTALLY* OVER CURRIES AND ORDER A SIMPLE PLATE OF KHAO MAN GAI INSTEAD!

NEXT, WE MOVE RIGHT UP FROM THE CENTRAL REGION TO THE NORTHERN SIDE—THE NORTHEAST TO BE PRECISE. NORTHEASTERN FOOD IS BETTER KNOWN AS ISAAN FOOD.

IN GENERAL, PEOPLE IN THE NORTHEAST HAVE A SIMPLE LIFESTYLE. THEY WORK IN RICE FIELDS, RAISE ANIMALS ON FARMS, AND HUNT OR FISH FOR FOOD NEARBY.

ISAAN FOOD IS ALSO KNOWN FOR ITS SPICINESS. MOST DISHES OFTEN INCLUDE A SPECIAL FERMENTED FISH SAUCE CALLED PLA RA, TOASTED RICE POWDER, AND BEEF—GRILLED, PARTIALLY COOKED, OR EVEN RAW—BUT THE MOST IMPORTANT STAPLE IS STICKY RICE.

AND FINALLY, LET'S GO EVEN FARTHER UP WHERE THE NORTHERN PART OF THAILAND HAS A DEEP HISTORY OF LANNA CULTURE AND TRADITIONS. HERE YOU CAN FIND A MIX OF SMALL REGIONAL TRIBES AND THOSE FROM NEIGHBORING COUNTRIES.

LANNA DIRECTLY TRANSLATES TO "A MILLION RICE FIELDS," WHICH IS AN ACCURATE NAME, CONSIDERING THE AGRICULTURAL LIFESTYLE OF THIS AREA. NORTHERN THAI CUISINE IS MAINLY BASED ON HOMEGROWN OR FOREST VEGETABLES AND ANIMAL FATS. WHILE OTHER REGIONS PREFER MORE INTENSE FLAVORS, NORTHERN THAI PEOPLE ENJOY THE NATURAL SWEETNESS OF THEIR HARVEST AND ARE NOT BIG FANS OF ADDING PROCESSED SUGAR.
A UNIQUE MAIN INGREDIENT USED IN NORTHERN CUISINE IS THUA NAO, WHICH LITERALLY TRANSLATES TO "ROTTEN BEANS" AND GIVES THE DISHES A FAMILIAR LIGHT SALTINESS.

A CUSTOMARY DINING STYLE IN EVERY NORTHERN HOUSEHOLD IS THE USE OF A KHAN TOK, A PEDESTAL TRAY TO HOLD VARIOUS SMALL DISHES AND A SIDE OF FRESH VEGETABLES FOR SHARING AND EATING WITH STICKY RICE.

SOME POPULAR DISHES INCLUDE KHAO SOI (PAGE 78), NAM PHRIK ONG (PAGE 118), AND NAM PHRIK NOOM (PAGE 121).

OKAY, THAT WILL BE 100,000 BAHT, PLEASE.

IN THE SIXTEENTH CENTURY, PORTUGAL WAS THE FIRST EUROPEAN COUNTRY TO VISIT SIAM, THE FORMER NAME OF THAILAND.

A SURPRISING FACT IS THAT THE PORTUGUESE BROUGHT IN SOME OF THE MOST FAMOUS THAI INGREDIENTS, SUCH AS CHILES, PAPAYA, AND PINEAPPLE.

OTHER NON-NATIVE INGREDIENTS INCLUDE TOMATOES, SWEET POTATOES, AND LETTUCE.

WHILE WE'RE STILL IN THE AYUTTHAYA PERIOD, LET'S TALK CURRIES. THAI CURRIES WOULD NOT EXIST WITHOUT THE INFLUENCE AND INCORPORATION OF INDIAN SPICES.

SO, WHAT'S THE DIFFERENCE BETWEEN THE CURRIES? THAI CURRY PASTE IS UNIQUE WITH THE ADDITION OF FRESH LOCAL HERBS, SUCH AS LEMONGRASS, GALANGAL, AND MAKRUT LIME RIND.

ANOTHER GREAT INFLUENCE, AND ARGUABLY THE MOST IMPORTANT, ON THAI CUISINE WAS CHINA.

CHINESE FOOD DID NOT APPEAR ANYWHERE IN THAILAND UNTIL THE PAST TWO HUNDRED YEARS. THE BIGGEST CHANGES? THAI DISHES STARTED INCORPORATING MORE PORK, STIR-FRY, OR WOK-STYLE COOKING, AND *NOODLES!* YEP, THE FOUNDATION FOR EVERY SINGLE THAI NOODLE DISH WAS INSPIRED AND ADAPTED FROM ELSEWHERE. ALWAYS GIVE CREDIT WHERE CREDIT IS DUE!

TOOLS & EQUIPMENT

NOW THAT YOU'VE BEEN PROPERLY SUBMERGED IN A BRIEF HISTORY OF THAI CUISINE, LET US INTRODUCE YOU TO SOME OF THE ESSENTIAL TOOLS AND EQUIPMENT YOU SHOULD HAVE IN YOUR THAI KITCHEN.

LARGE POT

TO MAKE GUAY TIAW, KHAO MAN GAI, OR ANY OTHER DISH THAT INVOLVES MANY STEPS AND INGREDIENTS, MAKE SURE YOU HAVE A LARGE POT THAT HOLDS AT LEAST 5 QUARTS.

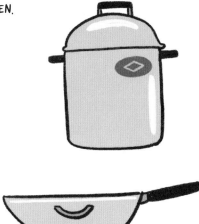

WOK

A LARGE WOK IS THE MOST LOGICAL AND MOST ESSENTIAL PIECE OF EQUIPMENT. THAI CUISINE INVOLVES A LOT OF STIR-FRYING AND DEEP-FRYING, SO INVESTING IN A DECENT WOK IS KEY. WOKS HAVE A DEEP BOTTOM TO PREVENT OIL OR SAUCES FROM SPLASHING WHILE COOKING. YOU CAN FIND A DECENT OPTION IN EVERY PRICE RANGE.

RICE COOKER

BACK IN THE OLD DAYS, THAI PEOPLE COOKED OVER A CLAY STOVE, CONSTANTLY HAVING TO TEND THE FIRE AND CHECK THE RICE. WITH THE INVENTION OF RICE COOKERS, YOUR CONSTANT PRESENCE IS NO LONGER REQUIRED, AND YOU CAN'T EVER REALLY MESS IT UP. IF YOU DON'T ALREADY HAVE A RICE COOKER, YOU MIGHT CONSIDER INVESTING IN ONE SO YOU CAN MAKE ALL THESE DELICIOUS RICE DISHES. (DON'T FORGET TO TURN IT ON BEFORE YOU WALK AWAY, THOUGH!)

STEAMER

THERE ARE MANY DIFFERENT STEAMER OPTIONS: STEAMER POTS WITH MULTIPLE LAYERS, REMOVABLE METAL BASKETS, OR EVEN THE TRADITIONAL THAI BAMBOO STEAMING BASKET. WHICHEVER YOU CHOOSE, THIS IS A MUST-HAVE KITCHEN ITEM FOR MAKING STICKY RICE, STEAMED EGGS, STEAMED VEGETABLES, DESSERTS, AND MORE.

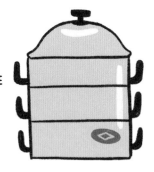

STICKY-RICE BAMBOO BASKET

WHEN YOU MAKE STICKY RICE, IT'S BEST TO KEEP THE RICE WARM AND COVERED AT ALL TIMES, EVEN WHILE EATING. ONCE STICKY RICE HAS BEEN EXPOSED TO AIR, IT QUICKLY BECOMES HARD AND DULL. A SMALL BASKET WITH A COVER MADE OF BAMBOO OR DRIED SUGAR-PALM LEAVES IS WHAT ISAAN AND NORTHERN PEOPLE USE IN THEIR HOMES. AND IT'S SO CUTE TOO!

VEGETABLE PEELER

PEELERS WITH ZIGZAG TEETH FOR JULIENNING AND SHREDDING VEGETABLES ARE USED A LOT IN THE THAI KITCHEN. YOU CANNOT REPLACE THIS PEELER WITH A SMOOTH-BLADED VEGETABLE PEELER BECAUSE IT WILL NOT SHRED VEGETABLES THE SAME WAY. OUR FAVORITE PEELER IS THE POPULAR KIWI BRAND, WHICH YOU CAN FIND IN MANY ASIAN STORES OR ONLINE.

MORTAR AND PESTLE

A MORTAR AND PESTLE IS ESSENTIAL IN THE THAI KITCHEN. THIS TOOL IS USED TO MAKE THE MOST IMPORTANT COMPONENTS OF THAI FOOD: PASTES. WE RECOMMEND THAT YOU GET AT LEAST A SMALL MORTAR AND PESTLE BECAUSE YOU'LL USE IT A LOT IN THE RECIPES OF THIS BOOK. THERE ARE THREE TYPES POPULARLY USED IN THAILAND: WOODEN, CLAY, AND STONE. A WOODEN SET IS THE LIGHTEST OPTION, SUITABLE FOR POUNDING SALADS SUCH AS SOM TUM OR FOR LIGHTLY CRUSHING INDIVIDUAL INGREDIENTS SUCH AS CHILES AND GARLIC. A CLAY SET IS ALSO GREAT FOR MAKING SOM TUM, BUT BEST FOR ACHIEVING A COARSELY POUNDED PASTE. IT IS USUALLY THE CHEAPEST OPTION AND IS VERY EASY TO CLEAN SINCE IT DRIES SO QUICKLY. AND A HEAVIER STONE SET WORKS TO ACHIEVE A SMOOTH, FINE PASTE IN A SHORT AMOUNT OF TIME.

SKIMMER OR TONGS

ANOTHER HELPFUL TOOL IS A SKIMMER OR A SPIDER, WHICH IS VERY HANDY FOR SCOOPING NOODLES OUT OF BOILING WATER OR LOWERING INGREDIENTS INTO HOT OIL FOR DEEP-FRYING. HOWEVER, SOME PEOPLE MIGHT FIND IT EASIER TO USE TONGS. WHATEVER YOU PREFER.

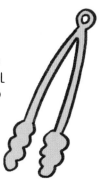

STRAINER

THAI PEOPLE USE A FINE-MESH STRAINER WHEN EXTRACTING LIQUID FROM VEGETABLES OR FRUITS SUCH AS TAMARIND AND COCONUT, RINSING RICE AND NOODLES, AND DRAINING THE OIL AFTER DEEP-FRYING.

CHEESECLOTH

IN THAI COOKING, CHEESECLOTH IS USED WHEN MAKING A BROTH OR STOCK, STEAMING, AND EXTRACTING LIQUID. IN THESE RECIPES, YOU WILL NEED CHEESECLOTH WHEN MAKING GUAY TIAW, DESSERTS, AND, PERHAPS, STICKY RICE ON A STOVE.

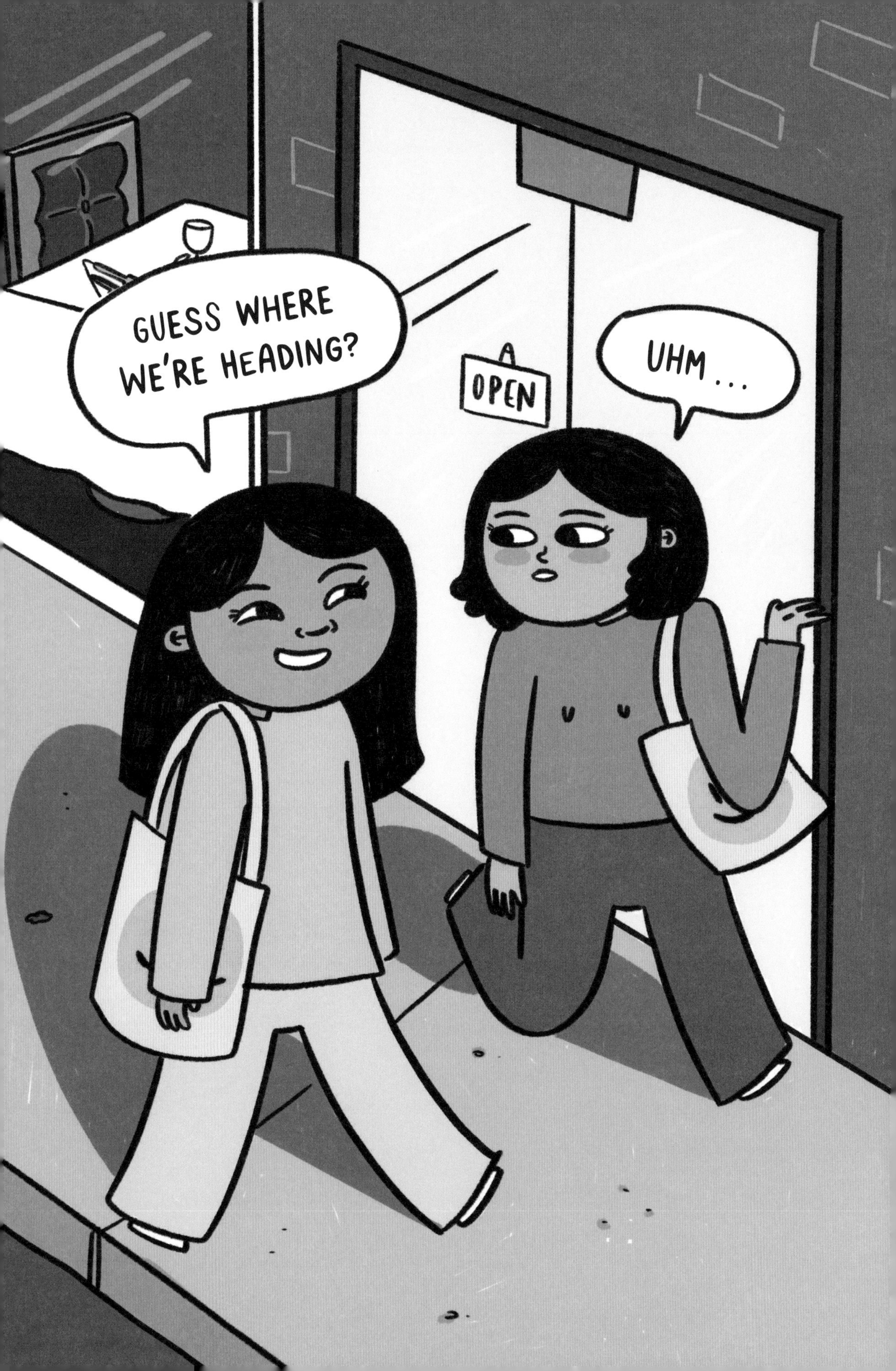
GUESS WHERE WE'RE HEADING?
OPEN
UHM ...

The ASIAN STORE!

THE BEST PLACE TO BUY INGREDIENTS FOR THAI FOOD IS . . . YOU GUESSED IT: YOUR LOCAL THAI OR ASIAN SUPERMARKET! THERE YOU'LL FIND THE RIGHT VEGGIES, SAUCES, EQUIPMENT, AND MORE. THAI RECIPES OFTEN HAVE A LONG LIST OF INGREDIENTS, ESPECIALLY FOR THE CURRIES.

IF YOU LIVE OUTSIDE OF THAILAND, FINDING SOME OF THESE ITEMS MIGHT REQUIRE A BIT OF TIME AND EFFORT—OR MIGHT BE IMPOSSIBLE! THEREFORE, READY-MADE PASTES OR SAUCES ARE A GREAT ALTERNATIVE AND CAN BE PURCHASED ONLINE.

IN EACH RECIPE, WE'VE INDICATED WHICH INGREDIENTS ARE OPTIONAL, ESPECIALLY IF THEY'RE DIFFICULT TO FIND, AND SUBSTITUTIONS WILL BE PROVIDED WHEN POSSIBLE.

IN THIS CHAPTER, YOU'LL FIND LISTS OF EVERYTHING YOU WILL NEED FROM THE FOLLOWING AISLES:

FRUITS AND VEGGIES

DRIED AND PACKAGED GOODS

SAUCES, SEASONINGS, AND SPICES

FIRST STOP: THE FRUITS AND VEGGIES AISLE. INGREDIENTS WITH AN ASTERISK (*) MEAN YOU SHOULD CHECK FOR THEM IN THE FREEZER SECTION IF NOT AVAILABLE FRESH. WHEN BUYING FRESH THAI VEGETABLES AND HERBS THAT ARE OFTEN DIFFICULT TO FIND, YOU CAN PRESERVE THEM IN THE FREEZER BY CUTTING OFF THE ROOTS (IF CILANTRO ROOTS, RESERVE FOR FUTURE USE), WASHING AND DRYING WELL, AND WRAPPING WITH NEWSPAPER BEFORE STORING IN A RESEALABLE BAG.

FRUITS AND VEGGIES

 THAI HOLY BASIL

 THAI ROUND GREEN EGGPLANT

 GALANGAL ROOTS*

 THAI SWEET BASIL

 LEMONGRASS*

 BEAN SPROUTS

 LIMES AND MAKRUT LIMES (RINDS AND LEAVES)

 FRESH THAI CHILES* (PHRIK JINDA) AND BIRD'S EYE CHILES (PHRIK KHEE NOO)

 PANDAN LEAVES*

 CHINESE CELERY

 SAWTOOTH CORIANDER (ALSO KNOWN AS CILANTRO)

 GREEN ONION

 SHALLOTS, RED AND SMALL

 CILANTRO AND CILANTRO ROOTS*

 FINGERROOT* (ALSO CALLED CHINESE GINGER OR LESSER GALANGAL)

 TURMERIC ROOTS*

 WATER SPINACH (ALSO KNOWN AS SWAMP MORNING GLORY)

 THAI PEA EGGPLANT

29

WITH HUNDREDS OF BRANDS FOR SEEMINGLY SIMILAR PRODUCTS, IT'S SMART TO HAVE A GUIDE FOR BUYING CONDIMENTS, DRY GOODS, AND CANNED ITEMS. WE SHOW PERSONAL RECOMMENDATIONS OF BRANDS THAT WE LIKE TO USE, BUT ANYTHING ACCESSIBLE IN YOUR AREA WILL WORK! SOME OF THESE ITEMS CAN BE MADE AT HOME, BUT CANNED AND BOTTLED OPTIONS ARE AVAILABLE WHEN YOU'RE SHORT ON TIME. LET'S HAVE A LOOK.

DRIED AND PACKAGED GOODS

BAMBOO SHOOTS, CANNED

DRIED GROUND CHILES
(SEE PHRIK PON, PAGE 192)

CHILE JAM
(SEE NAM PHRIK
PHAO, PAGE 196)

DRIED WHOLE
RED CHILES

COCONUT MILK

CORNSTARCH

NOODLES/NOODLE
STICKS, DRIED
(SEE PAGE 68)

PALM SEEDS,
CANNED IN HEAVY
SYRUP

JASMINE RICE AND
STICKY RICE
(ALSO KNOWN AS
GLUTINOUS RICE)

RICE PAPER

PALM SUGAR AND
ROCK SUGAR

SHIITAKE MUSHROOMS,
DRIED

SHRIMP PASTE

SPRING ROLL WRAPPERS

TAMARIND PULP
(ALSO KNOWN AS
WET TAMARIND) AND
TAMARIND PASTE

TOASTED RICE POWDER
(SEE KHAO KHUA,
PAGE 190)

SAUCES, SEASONINGS, AND SPICES

 KHAO MAN GAI SEASONING AND OTHER PRE-MADE SEASONINGS

 FISH SAUCE

 DRIED CARDAMOM SEEDS AND LEAVES

 NUTMEG

 THAI SWEET CHILE SAUCE (SEE NAM JIM GAI, PAGE 115)

 OYSTER SAUCE

 STAR ANISE

 PEPPERCORNS: BLACK AND WHITE

 CINNAMON STICKS

 PICKLED GARLIC

 CLOVES

 ROTTEN BEAN: DRIED ROUNDED SHEET

 CORIANDER SEEDS

 SEASONING POWDER AND BOUILLON CUBES

 CUMIN SEEDS

 SOYBEAN PASTE

 CURRY PASTES: GREEN, MASSAMAN, PANANG, AND RED

 SOY SAUCES: THIN, BLACK, BLACK SWEET, AND SEASONING

PSST! CANNED AND BOTTLED PASTES, CURRIES, MARINADES, STIR-FRY SAUCES, AND DIPPING SAUCES WILL BE YOUR BESTIES WHEN YOU'RE IN A HURRY. YOU CAN FIND KHAO MAN GAI SAUCE, GAI SATAY DIPPING SAUCE, KHAO SOI POWDERED SOUP BASE, AND MORE. IT WON'T BE AS GOOD AS THE REAL DEAL, OF COURSE, BUT IT WILL BE TWICE AS FAST!

A QUICK NOTE ABOUT . . .

PALM SUGAR

PALM SUGAR IS CALLED FOR IN MANY OF THE RECIPES IN THIS BOOK. IT IS AVAILABLE IN VARIOUS FORMS BUT THE MOST COMMON IS INDIVIDUAL BLOCKS OR ROUNDS. WHEN GRATED, ONE WHOLE BLOCK OF SUGAR EQUALS APPROXIMATELY 4 TABLESPOONS. SINCE THE SUGAR CAN BECOME VERY HARD OVER TIME, POUND WITH A PESTLE OR MICROWAVE ON FULL POWER FOR UP TO 15 SECONDS TO SOFTEN. IF MICROWAVED, USE THE PALM SUGAR IMMEDIATELY OR IT WILL BECOME EVEN HARDER! STORE THE REMAINING PALM SUGAR PIECES IN AN AIRTIGHT CONTAINER SO THAT THE TEXTURE STAYS SOFT LONGER.

CANNED COCONUT CREAM AND MILK

COCONUT MILK IS ONE OF THE MOST BELOVED INGREDIENTS IN THAI CUISINE. THAI PEOPLE TRADITIONALLY GRATED COCONUT MEAT IN THEIR OWN KITCHENS, SEATED AT A LOW WOODEN STOOL WITH A SPECIAL GRATER CALLED GRATAI KHOOD MAPRAO (WHICH DIRECTLY TRANSLATES TO "RABBIT GRATES COCONUT," SINCE THE ROUND-TOOTHED BLADE LOOKS LIKE LITTLE RABBIT TEETH). THIS WAS THE ONLY KITCHEN DUTY THAT THAI KIDS WOULD FIGHT OVER!

AFTER ALL THE COCONUT MEAT WAS GRATED, IT WAS KNEADED BY HAND TO SQUEEZE OUT AS MUCH LIQUID AS POSSIBLE. A SMALL AMOUNT OF WARM WATER WAS ADDED TO HELP SQUEEZE OUT MORE LIQUID. THIS PRODUCES THE PUREST EXTRACTION CALLED HUA GATHI, OR "HEAD OF COCONUT MILK," WHICH REFERS TO COCONUT *CREAM*. THE SECOND (AND PERHAPS THIRD) ROUND OF WARM WATER THAT IS THEN ADDED RESULTS IN LESS CONCENTRATED COCONUT MILK CALLED HANG GATHI, OR "TAIL OF COCONUT MILK," WHICH REFERS TO COCONUT *MILK*.

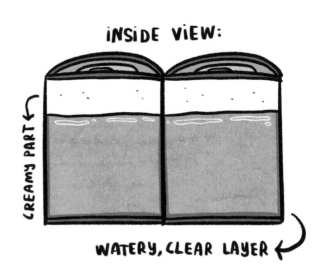

INSIDE VIEW:

CREAMY PART

WATERY, CLEAR LAYER

COCONUT MILK IS GENERALLY USED IN THAI DESSERTS, CURRIES, AND SOUPS. OVERALL, BOTH COCONUT CREAM AND MILK ARE USED IN COOKING, BUT HUA GATHI IS OFTEN RESERVED TO DECORATE FINISHED DISHES, ESPECIALLY DESSERTS.

TODAY, THAI PEOPLE USE BOTH FRESH COCONUT MILK AND CANNED COCONUT MILK--WHICH WILL WORK JUST FINE FOR OUR RECIPES. FEEL FREE TO USE ANY BRAND, BUT FOR DESSERT WE PREFER AROY-D BECAUSE IT HAS A VERY SIMILAR TEXTURE TO FRESH COCONUT MILK AND PROVIDES THE AMAZINGLY RICH, SWEET COCONUT FLAVOR THAT YOU'RE LOOKING FOR IN A THAI TREAT.

THE THREE BUDDIES & SEASONING BOOSTS

SAAM KLER, OR *SAAM SAHAI*, WHICH DIRECTLY TRANSLATES TO "THE THREE BUDDIES," IS THE ICONIC THAI TRIO OF CILANTRO ROOT, GARLIC, AND (WHITE OR BLACK) PEPPERCORN. CILANTRO IS A FUNDAMENTAL INGREDIENT IN THAI COOKING, ESPECIALLY WHEN POUNDED TOGETHER WITH THAI GARLIC (WHICH HAS A BOLDER AND MORE ROBUST AROMA THAN MOST GARLICS) AND BRIGHT, FLAVORFUL PEPPERCORNS TO CREATE THE SPECIAL SEASONING PASTE USED TO FLAVOR MANY POPULAR DISHES. IF CILANTRO ROOT IS NOT AVAILABLE, CILANTRO STEMS CAN BE A GOOD ALTERNATIVE. ONE CILANTRO ROOT IS APPROXIMATELY EQUIVALENT TO FIVE 2-INCH STEMS.

AS LIFE HAS GROWN BUSIER AND BUSIER, IT'S NOW COMMON FOR THAI PEOPLE TO SUPPLEMENT A RECIPE WITH INSTANT SEASONING POWDER OR BOUILLON CUBES TO PROVIDE AN EXTRA PUNCH OF FLAVOR. ROSDEE AND KNORR ARE OUR PREFERRED BRANDS, WHICH ARE AVAILABLE IN DIFFERENT FLAVORS SUCH AS PORK, CHICKEN, AND VEGETARIAN. YOU CAN CHOOSE YOUR FLAVOR ACCORDING TO THE PROTEIN USED IN THE RECIPE, BUT EVEN THAIS DON'T REALLY STICK TO THAT RULE--EXCEPT WHEN IT COMES TO THE BEEF FLAVOR.

CHILES

AS YOU KNOW, THAI FOOD CAN BE *SPICY*. TO MAKE SURE THAT YOU'RE USING THE RIGHT TYPE OF CHILES FOR YOUR PREFERENCE, LET'S LEARN ABOUT SOME OF THE DIFFERENT VARIETIES. ARE YOU READY TO WALK WITH US THROUGH THE ROWS OF A THAI CHILE FIELD? DON'T FORGET YOUR BOOTS, IN CASE YOU STEP ON A SNAKE!

THERE ARE FOUR MAIN CHILES USED IN OUR RECIPES: SPUR CHILE (PHRIK CHEE FA, "CHILE POINTING AT THE SKY"), LONG LIGHT GREEN CHILE (PHRIK NOOM, "YOUNG CHILE"), THAI CHILE (PHRIK JINDA), AND BIRD'S EYE CHILE (PHRIK KHEE NOO, "MOUSE POOP CHILE").

THESE CHILES HAVE VARYING SPICE LEVELS: MILD, MILD-SPICY, SPICY, VERY SPICY, SUPER-SPICY. LET'S SEE WHAT THEY ARE USED FOR.

SPUR CHILE

SPUR CHILE

MILD (FRESH), MILD-SPICY (DRIED)
USED FOR DISH DECORATION, DIPPING SAUCES, AND PASTES.

LONG LIGHT GREEN CHILE

MILD-SPICY
USED FOR NAM PHRIK NOOM (PAGE 121).

LONG LIGHT GREEN CHILE →

THAI CHILE →

THAI CHILE

SPICY (FRESH), VERY SPICY (DRIED)
USED FOR STIR-FRIED DISHES, DIPS, DIPPING SAUCES, PASTES, SOUPS, GARNISH, AND SEASONING.

BIRD'S EYE CHILE

VERY SPICY (FRESH), SUPER-SPICY (DRIED)
USED FOR STIR-FRIED DISHES, DIPS, DIPPING SAUCES,
PASTES, SOUPS, GARNISH, AND SEASONING.

PLEASE NOTE THAT THAI CHILES AND BIRD'S
EYE CHILES CAN BE USED INTERCHANGEABLY,
BUT BECAUSE THAI CHILES ARE MOST COMMON
IN ASIAN STORES, WE USE THEM IN MOST OF
THE RECIPES. FEEL FREE TO USE BIRD'S EYE
CHILES IF THEY ARE AVAILABLE TO YOU, BUT
REMEMBER TO ALWAYS ADJUST THE SPICE
LEVEL ACCORDING TO YOUR TASTE!

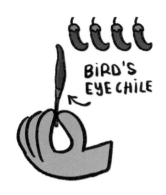

BIRD'S
EYE CHILE

SPICE LEVEL

THIS BOOK'S RECIPES HAVE BEEN CREATED, TESTED, AND ENJOYED BY A THAI NATIVE.
THAT MEANS THEY ARE VERY AUTHENTIC, ESPECIALLY IN TERMS OF THE SPICINESS LEVEL.
IF YOU ARE COMPLETELY NEW TO THAI CUISINE OR NOT A BIG FAN OF HEAT, WE RECOMMEND
THAT YOU INCLUDE ONLY ONE CHILE WHEN A RECIPE CALLS FOR MORE. DEPENDING ON THE
YIELD, OF COURSE, CUTTING DOWN TO THREE CHILES RESULTS IN WHAT WOULD TYPICALLY
BE CONSIDERED MILD IN THAILAND, AND FOLLOWING MOST OF THIS BOOK'S RECIPES AS IS
WOULD PRODUCE RESULTS CONSIDERED MILDLY SPICY TO SPICY.

HOWEVER, ANY RECIPE THAT CALLS FOR MORE THAN FIVE THAI CHILES
CAN BE INTIMIDATING, SO YOU SHOULD CONSIDER THE NUMBER OF
CHILES AS A SUGGESTION AND ADJUST TO YOUR TASTE.

NO MATTER HOW MANY CHILES YOU CHOOSE TO
USE, THE RULE OF THUMB IS: YOU CAN ALWAYS
ADD MORE, BUT YOU CAN *NEVER* REMOVE THEM.

FLAVOR HARMONY

THAI FOOD MAINLY CONSISTS OF A BALANCE OF FOUR FLAVOR PROFILES: SOURNESS, SWEETNESS, SALTINESS, AND SPICINESS. TOM YUM (PAGE 138), SOM TUM (PAGE 46), TOM KHA GAI (PAGE 140), AND MASSAMAN CURRY (PAGE 136) ARE GREAT EXAMPLES OF THESE HARMONIOUS FLAVOR BLENDS.

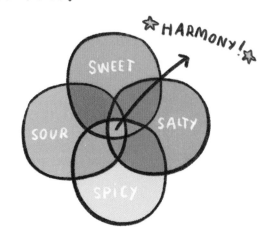

NO, YOU ARE BITTER!

SOME DISHES MIGHT ALSO INCLUDE BITTERNESS, WHICH USUALLY COMES FROM INCORPORATING NATURAL INGREDIENTS, SUCH AS BITTER GOURD OR BITTER BEAN IN PAD SATOR (PAGE 100), RATHER THAN SEASONING.

YOU MIGHT BE THINKING, "SOUR? BUT MY NOODLES AREN'T SOUR AT ALL!" WELL, YOU'RE ABSOLUTELY CORRECT.

HOWEVER, THAI PEOPLE LOVE TO HAVE A SET OF SEASONING INGREDIENTS ON THE SIDE TO ADD TO NOODLE SOUPS.

THESE CONDIMENT RACKS OFTEN INCLUDE PHRIK NAM PLA (PAGE 185), PHRIK NAM SOM (PAGE 186), PHRIK PON (PAGE 192), GRANULATED SUGAR, AND FISH SAUCE.

THESE SEASONING ADDITIONS WILL MAKE SURE YOUR DISH HAS A BALANCED FLAVOR TO YOUR LIKING-- REMEMBER TO START WITH A SMALL QUANTITY AND BUILD FROM THERE!

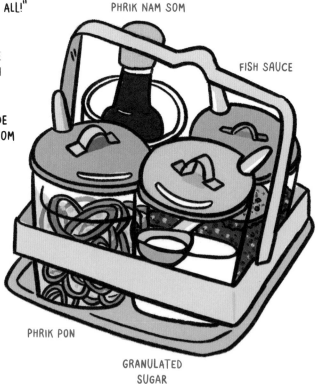

PHRIK NAM SOM

FISH SAUCE

PHRIK PON

GRANULATED SUGAR

THAI EATING STYLE

THAI PEOPLE LOVE TO SIT IN A BIG CIRCLE AND ENJOY FOOD WITH ALL THEIR FRIENDS AND FAMILY. JUST ONE ENTRÉE PER PERSON? NEVER HAPPENS. AT THE THAI TABLE, EVERYONE HAS AN INDIVIDUAL PLATE OF RICE AND THERE ARE GENERALLY TWO TO THREE DIFFERENT LARGE MAIN DISHES FOR SHARING, WITH SPICE LEVELS AND FLAVOR PROFILES THAT PERFECTLY COMPLEMENT ONE ANOTHER.

THEREFORE, THE YIELDS FOR SOME OF THE RECIPES IN THIS BOOK TAKE INTO ACCOUNT THAT YOU WILL BE PAIRING THE DISH WITH A FEW OTHERS. FOR EXAMPLE, OUR GAENG PANANG (PAGE 134) TASTES GREAT WITH SIDE DISHES SUCH AS KHAI TOM (PAGE 180) OR KHAI JIEW (PAGE 176).

ALTHOUGH SERVING AND DINING WITH SPOONS ARE PREVALENT, THE TRADITIONAL THAI PRACTICE OF EATING WITH YOUR HANDS IS STILL COMMON—ESPECIALLY WITH STICKY RICE. IN THE PAST, THAIS USED THEIR HANDS TO EAT RICE WRAPPED IN BANANA LEAVES; SOME FOODS, SUCH AS STEAMED HOR MOK PLA (CURRY FISH CUSTARD) AND SEVERAL DESSERTS, ARE STILL SERVED THIS WAY TODAY.

CHOPSTICKS ARE USED AT STREET NOODLE RESTAURANTS, BUT NOT AS FREQUENTLY IN THAI HOUSEHOLDS AS IS OFTEN ASSUMED OR PORTRAYED. A TRUSTY FORK AND SPOON WILL DO THE TRICK—BUT NO KNIVES! KNIVES ARE CONSIDERED WEAPONS AT THE THAI DINNER TABLE.

SNACKS

AND

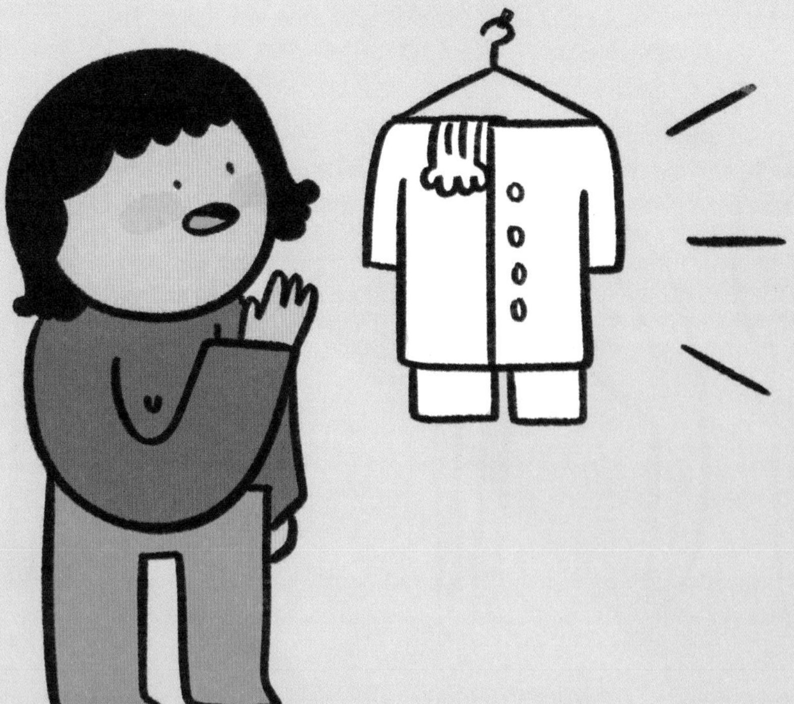

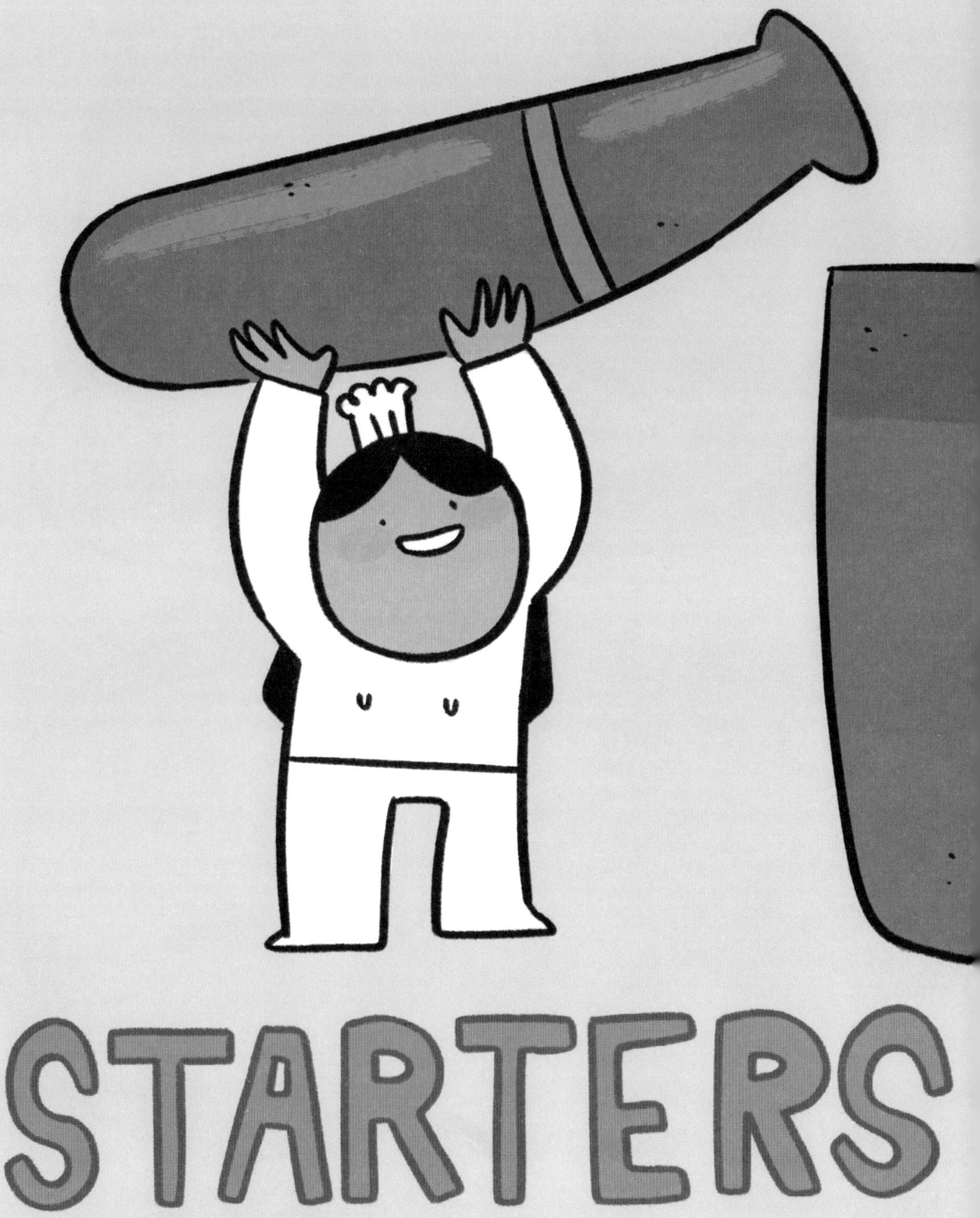

STARTERS

WHEN YOU THINK OF STARTERS, YOU'RE PROBABLY IMAGINING APPETIZERS THAT ARE SERVED BEFORE AN ENTRÉE.

IN THAILAND, HOWEVER, PEOPLE DON'T ALWAYS EAT THESE DISHES *BEFORE* THEIR MAINS.

THE THAI STYLE OF EATING IS TO ENJOY MANY DISHES AT THE SAME TIME AND SNACK ON THEM ALL THROUGHOUT THE DAY! THE STARTERS IN THIS SECTION ARE MORE COMPARABLE TO SMALL NIBBLES IN BETWEEN MEALS. IMAGINE A CUP OF COFFEE DURING AN AFTERNOON BREAK . . .

YOU NEVER HAVE TO WAIT FOR DINNER TO ENJOY A
SAVORY AND DELICIOUS TREAT. THE YIELDS FOR THIS SECTION
ACCOUNT FOR SHARING YOUR SNACKS WITH LOVED ONES . . .
WHICH IS THE BEST PART!

SPICE QUEST: BACKYARD SOM TUM

CHUMPHON, 1998

TO MALLIKA, THE BEST THING ABOUT SOM TUM WAS MAKING IT WITH HER COUSIN AND NEIGHBORHOOD FRIENDS, FETCHING THE INGREDIENTS FROM THEIR OWN GARDEN.

THEY WOULD STOP COUNTING CHILES AFTER TWENTY BECAUSE THEY KNEW IT WAS GONNA HURT ANYWAY AT THIS POINT.

LET'S ADD MORE!

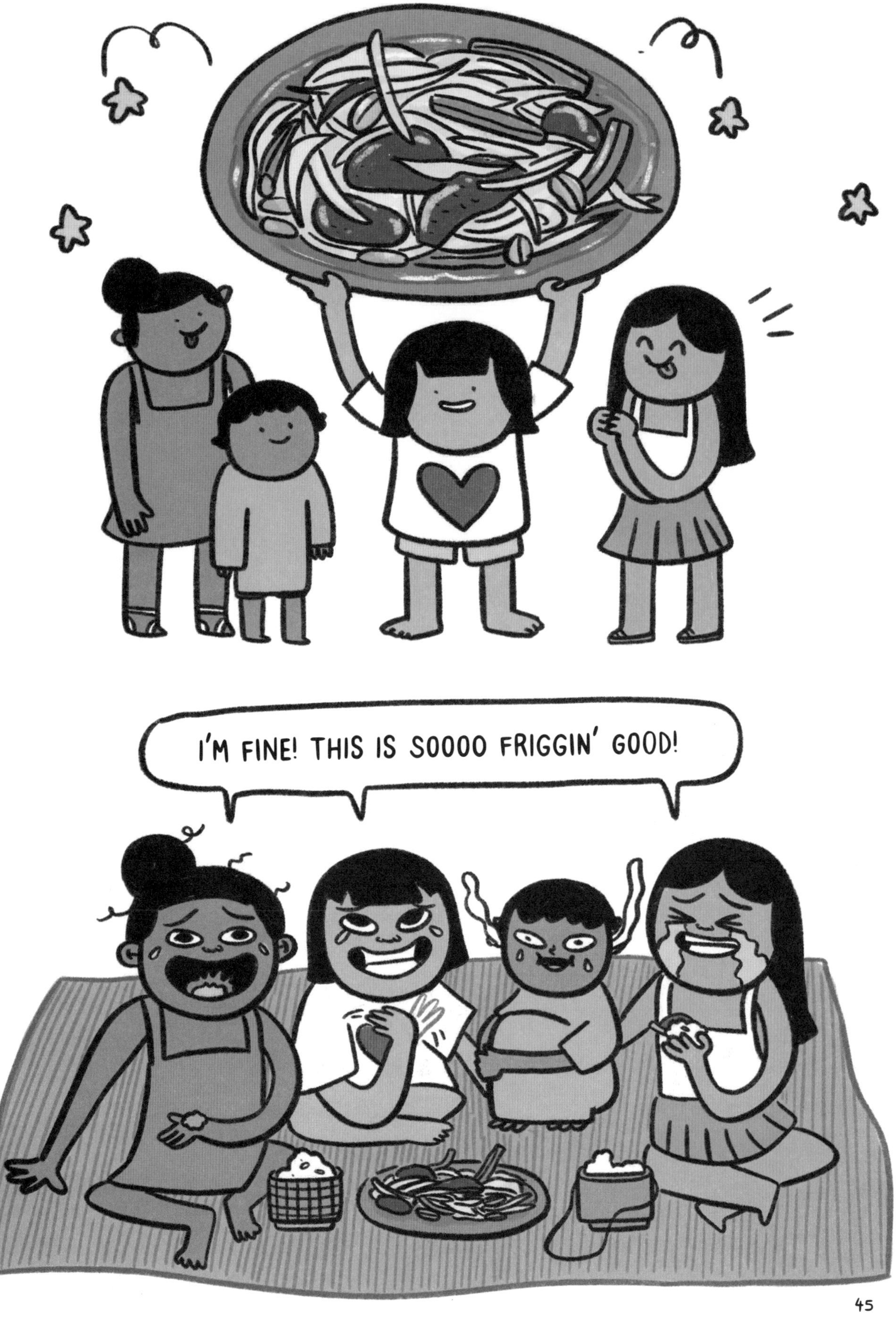
I'M FINE! THIS IS SOOOO FRIGGIN' GOOD!

SOM TUM

SOM TUM, A PAPAYA SALAD, DIRECTLY TRANSLATES TO "POUNDING OF SOUR INGREDIENTS." THE ORIGINAL, ISAAN SOM TUM, FEATURING GREEN PAPAYA AND A SPICY CHILE DRESSING, WAS MADE USING FISH SAUCE FERMENTED WITH TOASTED RICE POWDER, CALLED PLA RA, BUT FOR THIS RECIPE WE'LL USE REGULAR OL' FISH SAUCE. THIS SALAD IS A FLAVOR EXPLOSION IN YOUR MOUTH: THE SWEETNESS, SOURNESS, AND SPICINESS PAIRED WITH A SATISFYING CRUNCHY TEXTURE MAKE SOM TUM THE PERFECT SNACK OR SIDE DISH SERVED WITH KHAO NIAW (PAGE 172) AND GAI YANG (PAGE 112).

MAKES 2 SERVINGS

2 FRESH RED THAI CHILES (OR ADJUST TO TASTE), STEMMED

1 GARLIC CLOVE

1 OR 2 YARDLONG BEANS, CUT INTO 2-INCH PIECES, OR 4 FRESH GREEN BEANS, PLUS MORE FOR SERVING

4 CHERRY TOMATOES, HALVED

1½ TABLESPOONS FISH SAUCE

2 TABLESPOONS GRATED PALM SUGAR (ABOUT ½ PIECE) OR GRANULATED SUGAR

1½ TABLESPOONS FRESH LIME JUICE

3 CUPS LOOSELY PACKED SHREDDED GREEN PAPAYA (SEE PAGE 48)

½ CUP LOOSELY PACKED SHREDDED CARROTS (OPTIONAL)

2 TABLESPOONS ROASTED PEANUTS

GREEN CABBAGE WEDGES FOR GARNISHING (OPTIONAL)

1

IN A LARGE MORTAR AND USING THE PESTLE, COMBINE THE CHILES, GARLIC, AND YARDLONG BEANS AND COARSELY POUND AND CRUSH UNTIL THERE ARE NO MORE BIG CHUNKS. BE CAREFUL NOT TO OVERPOUND.

2

ADD THE TOMATOES, FISH SAUCE, PALM SUGAR, AND LIME JUICE TO THE MORTAR AND POUND GENTLY UNTIL COMBINED.

CHEF MALLIKA SAYS:

CUT YOUR LIMES FROM THE SIDE INSTEAD OF DOWN THE MIDDLE. THAT WAY YOU CAN SQUEEZE LIME JUICE MORE EFFICIENTLY.

3

ADD THE SHREDDED PAPAYA AND CARROTS,
IF USING, TO THE MORTAR AND POUND
GENTLY UNTIL COMBINED.

4

STIR THE ROASTED PEANUTS
INTO THE COMBINED MIXTURE.

5

TRANSFER THE PAPAYA SALAD
TO A PLATE AND GARNISH
WITH CABBAGE WEDGES
AND ADDITIONAL
YARDLONG BEANS.

6

SERVE THE SALAD IMMEDIATELY,
AS A SNACK OR AS PART OF A
FULL MEAL.

HOW TO SHRED A GREEN PAPAYA

IF YOU'VE NEVER SHREDDED A BIG PAPAYA BEFORE, IT CAN BE A BIT INTIMIDATING.
HAVE NO FEAR--GRAB YOUR GRATER AND YOUR GLOVES AND FOLLOW ALONG!
SOAKING THE PAPAYA IN *COLD* WATER HELPS THE PAPAYA BECOME CRUNCHIER,
BUT ROOM-TEMPERATURE WATER ALSO WORKS.

1
CUT OFF THE STEM END OF
THE GREEN PAPAYA.

2
USING A PEELER, REMOVE THE
PEEL FROM THE WHOLE PAPAYA.

3
RINSE THE PEELED PAPAYA WITH
WATER AND RUB THE FLESH UNTIL
IT'S NOT SLIMY ANYMORE.

4
LAY THE CLEAN PAPAYA ON
A CUTTING BOARD AND CUT
IN HALF LENGTHWISE.

5

USING A SPOON, SCRAPE OUT THE SEEDS AND THE INNER WHITE PART FROM BOTH SIDES, AND DISCARD.

PUT THE PAPAYA HALVES IN A LARGE BOWL OF COLD WATER. LET SOAK UNTIL THE PAPAYA IS CHILLED, 5 TO 10 MINUTES, AND THEN DRAIN.

6

HOLD THE PAPAYA AT A 45-DEGREE ANGLE WITH THE *TIP OF THE PAPAYA POINTING TOWARD YOU* AND THE INNER PART FACE DOWN. WORK OVER A LARGE BOWL TO COLLECT THE PAPAYA SHREDS.

7

WORK IN ROUGHLY 3-INCH SECTIONS OF THE PAPAYA AT A TIME, DEPENDING ON THE SIZE OF YOUR PAPAYA. START BY CONSISTENTLY SHREDDING FROM LEFT TO RIGHT AND THEN REPEAT THIS MOTION UNTIL EACH SECTION OF PAPAYA IS COMPLETE.

8

WHEN YOU ARRIVE AT THE STEM END OF THE PAPAYA, IT WILL BE DIFFICULT TO SHRED. USE A FORK TO HOLD THE REMAINING FLESH ON A CUTTING BOARD WHILE YOUR OTHER HAND SHREDS AS MUCH AS POSSIBLE.

9

USE THE SHREDDED PAPAYA IMMEDIATELY OR STORE IN AN AIRTIGHT CONTAINER IN THE FRIDGE FOR UP TO 7 DAYS.

SUEA RONG HAI

SUEA RONG HAI, MEANING "CRYING TIGER," IS A GRILLED BEEF DISH THAT ORIGINATES FROM THE ISAAN REGION. THE TITLE PROBABLY MAKES YOU WONDER HOW IT GOT ITS (RATHER SAD) NAME. THERE ARE A FEW DIFFERENT THEORIES, BUT THE MOST COMMON STORY GOES THAT THE TIGER IS SAD BECAUSE IT COULD NOT HAVE BRISKET, WHICH IS KNOWN TO BE THE BEST CUT OF BEEF. ENJOY THE GRILLED-TO-PERFECTION BEEF WITH NAM JIM JAEW, A SAVORY DIPPING SAUCE WITH TOASTED RICE AND FRESH HERBS, AND YOU'LL CRY ONLY ONCE IT'S ALL GONE.

MAKES 2 SERVINGS

1 TEASPOON WHITE PEPPERCORNS

1 TABLESPOON GRATED PALM SUGAR (ABOUT ¼ PIECE) OR GRANULATED SUGAR

1 TABLESPOON GRATHIAM JIEW (PAGE 188)

1 TABLESPOON SEASONING SOY SAUCE, OR ½ TABLESPOON SEASONING POWDER

1 TABLESPOON OYSTER SAUCE

1 POUND BEEF BRISKET, IN ½-INCH-THICK STEAKS

1 TABLESPOON NEUTRAL OIL

NAM JIM JAEW (PAGE 184) FOR SERVING

KHAO NIAW (PAGE 172) FOR SERVING

1

IN A MORTAR AND USING THE PESTLE, POUND THE PEPPERCORNS UNTIL THEY BECOME A POWDER.

IN A LARGE BOWL, COMBINE THE POUNDED PEPPERCORNS, PALM SUGAR, GRATHIAM JIEW, SEASONING SOY SAUCE, AND OYSTER SAUCE AND STIR TO MIX.

2

ADD THE BRISKET TO THE BOWL AND MIX WITH YOUR HANDS TO EVENLY COAT THE MEAT.

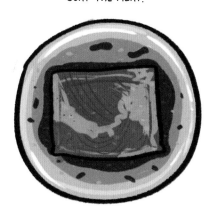

3

COVER THE BOWL WITH PLASTIC WRAP AND LET IT STAND IN THE FRIDGE FOR ABOUT 1 HOUR.

4

REMOVE THE BOWL FROM THE FRIDGE AND LET IT SIT FOR ABOUT 10 MINUTES TO RETURN TO ROOM TEMPERATURE.

5

ADD THE OIL TO A LARGE FRYING PAN AND SET OVER HIGH HEAT.

6

WHEN THE PAN IS VERY HOT OR YOU SEE A LIGHT SMOKE RISING, USE TONGS TO GENTLY PLACE THE BEEF IN THE PAN. TURN THE HEAT TO MEDIUM-HIGH AND COOK UNTIL THE MEAT IS WELL BROWNED WITH CHAR MARKS AT THE BOTTOM, ABOUT 2 MINUTES.

7

USE THE TONGS TO FLIP THE BEEF AND COOK FOR ANOTHER 2 MINUTES. REPEAT THE FLIPPING PROCESS FOR 1 MINUTE ON EACH SIDE. THE BEEF SHOULD BE MEDIUM-WELL DONENESS. IF YOU WANT IT WELL-DONE, COOK FOR ANOTHER 1 MINUTE ON EACH SIDE.

8

TRANSFER THE BEEF TO A CUTTING BOARD AND LET IT REST FOR 2 MINUTES.

9

THINLY SLICE THE BEEF AND TRANSFER TO A SERVING PLATE.

10

SERVE THE BRISKET IMMEDIATELY WITH NAM JIM JAEW AND KHAO NIAW FOR A FULL MEAL.

YUM WOON SEN

THIS GLASS NOODLE SALAD IS DRESSED WITH A REFRESHING MIX OF FISH SAUCE, LIME JUICE, AND CHILES. YUM WOON SEN SHOULD BE SERVED RIGHT AWAY BECAUSE THE NOODLES BECOME MUSHY IF LEFT TO STAND, BUT THIS FAN-FAVORITE WON'T LAST LONG ANYWAY (FOR MORE ON GLASS NOODLES, SEE "WOON SEN" ON PAGE 68). THE FLAVORS IN THIS DISH ARE PRETTY SIMILAR TO LARB (PAGE 116), AND THERE IS EVEN A DISH CALLED LARB WOON SEN THAT IS A COMBINATION OF THE TWO. USING GLASS NOODLES ARE THE CLASSIC WAY TO GO, BUT INSTANT MAMA NOODLES ARE A GREAT ALTERNATIVE. IF YOU CAN'T FIND VIETNAMESE PORK ROLL (MOO YAW IN THAI), YOU CAN SUBSTITUTE AN EQUAL WEIGHT OF HOT DOGS. PAIR THE FINISHED DISH WITH SUEA RONG HAI (PAGE 50) AND KHAO SUAY (PAGE 170) FOR A FULL MEAL.

MAKES 2 SERVINGS

2 CUPS PLUS 3 TABLESPOONS WATER

3 OUNCES GROUND PORK

5 OUNCES CHẢ LỤA (VIETNAMESE PORK ROLL), HALVED LENGTHWISE AND SLICED INTO 1/4-INCH-THICK HALF-MOONS (OPTIONAL)

2 OUNCES GLASS NOODLES, SOAKED IN ROOM TEMPERATURE WATER FOR 15 MINUTES AND DRAINED

1 1/2 TABLESPOONS GRANULATED SUGAR

3 1/2 TABLESPOONS FRESH LIME JUICE

3 TABLESPOONS FISH SAUCE

2 GARLIC CLOVES, CRUSHED (OPTIONAL)

5 FRESH RED THAI CHILES (OR ADJUST TO TASTE), STEMMED AND THINLY SLICED

1/2 MEDIUM YELLOW ONION, THINLY SLICED

1 LARGE TOMATO, CUT INTO WEDGES, OR 8 CHERRY TOMATOES, HALVED LENGTHWISE

1 CUP LOOSELY PACKED CHINESE CELERY LEAVES

1 TABLESPOON ROASTED PEANUTS (OPTIONAL)

CUCUMBER SLICES FOR SERVING

GREEN CABBAGE WEDGES FOR SERVING

1
IN A MEDIUM SAUCEPAN OVER HIGH HEAT, BRING 3 TABLESPOONS OF THE WATER TO A BOIL.

2
ADD THE GROUND PORK TO THE SAUCEPAN AND USE A SPATULA TO QUICKLY BREAK UP THE MEAT. COOK UNTIL BROWNED, ABOUT 1 MINUTE. REMOVE FROM THE HEAT.

3
TRANSFER THE COOKED PORK TO A LARGE BOWL, ALONG WITH ANY REMAINING COOKING LIQUID. SET ASIDE.

CHEF MALLIKA SAYS:

IF YOU'D LIKE TO MAKE THIS DISH VEGETARIAN, REPLACE ALL THE PORK WITH TREMELLA MUSHROOMS AND IMITATION SEAFOOD.

IF YOU WANT TO MAKE YOUR YUM WOON SEN EVEN SPICIER, CRUSH YOUR CHILES INSTEAD OF SLICING THEM TO UNLEASH THE HEAT!

IN A HURRY? YOU CAN FIND YUM WOON SEN POWDER MIX (ROSDEE BRAND IS OUR FAVORITE) ONLINE OR AT YOUR LOCAL ASIAN STORE.

4

IN THE SAME SAUCEPAN OVER HIGH HEAT, BRING THE REMAINING 2 CUPS WATER TO A BOIL. ADD THE CHẢ LỤA, TURN THE HEAT TO MEDIUM-HIGH, AND COOK FOR 2 MINUTES TO WARM THROUGH.

5

USING TONGS OR A SKIMMER, TRANSFER THE COOKED CHẢ LỤA TO THE LARGE BOWL. SET ASIDE.

6

IN THE SAME SAUCEPAN, TURN THE HEAT TO MEDIUM, ADD THE DRAINED GLASS NOODLES TO THE REMAINING LIQUID, AND COOK FOR 5 MINUTES, OR UNTIL FATTENED AND SOFT.

7

WHILE THE GLASS NOODLES ARE COOKING, ADD THE SUGAR, LIME JUICE, FISH SAUCE, GARLIC, AND CHILES TO THE BOWL OF COOKED MEAT. MIX WELL, THEN ADJUST THE SEASONING.

8

DRAIN THE COOKED GLASS NOODLES AND ADD TO THE LARGE BOWL.

9

ADD THE ONION, TOMATO, CHINESE CELERY LEAVES, AND ROASTED PEANUTS (IF USING) TO THE BOWL AND MIX WELL.

10

SERVE THE SALAD IMMEDIATELY WITH CUCUMBER SLICES AND CABBAGE WEDGES.

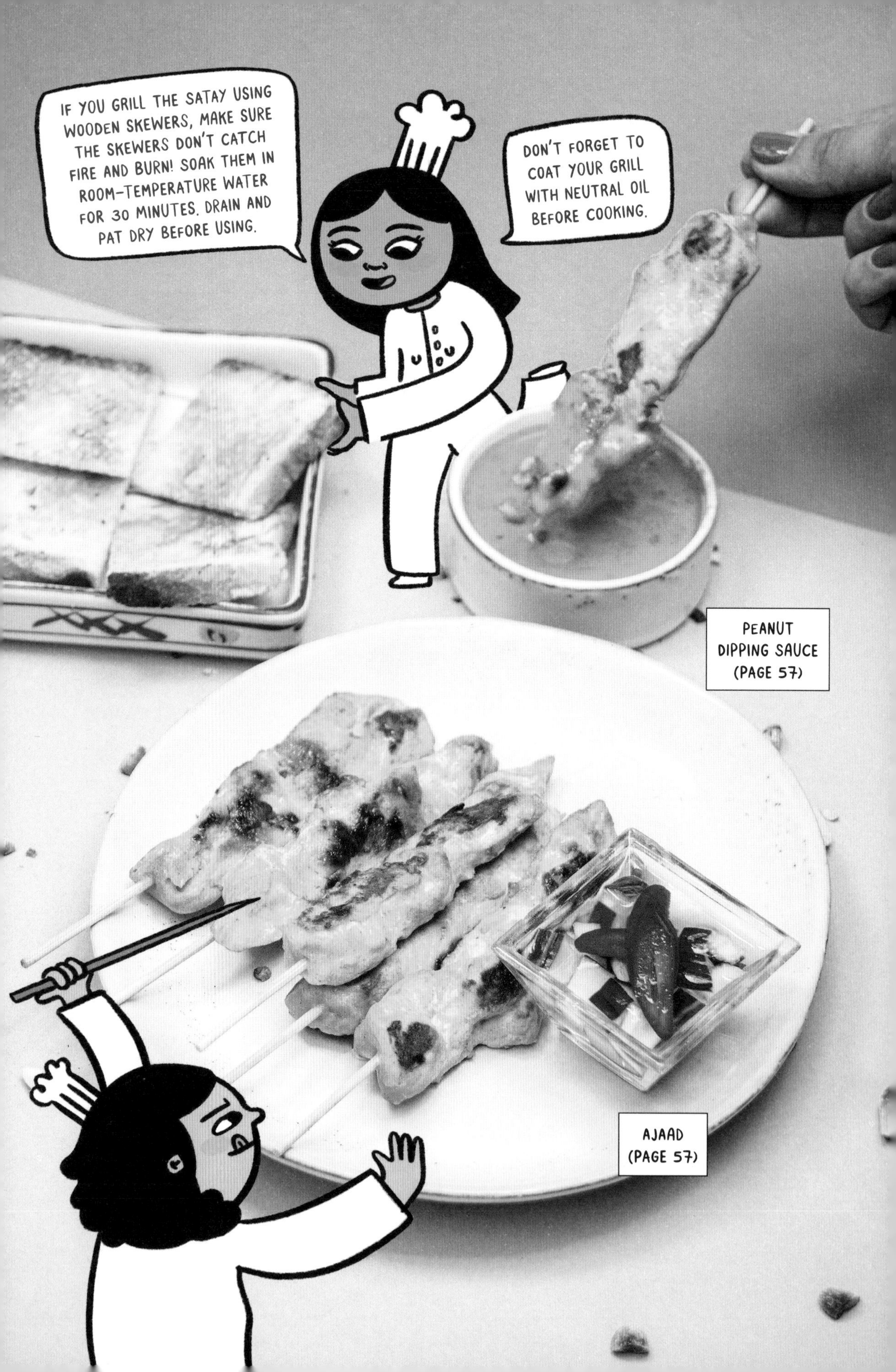
IF YOU GRILL THE SATAY USING WOODEN SKEWERS, MAKE SURE THE SKEWERS DON'T CATCH FIRE AND BURN! SOAK THEM IN ROOM-TEMPERATURE WATER FOR 30 MINUTES. DRAIN AND PAT DRY BEFORE USING.
DON'T FORGET TO COAT YOUR GRILL WITH NEUTRAL OIL BEFORE COOKING.
PEANUT DIPPING SAUCE (PAGE 57)
AJAAD (PAGE 57)

SATAY GAI

GRILLED CHICKEN SKEWERS ARE ONE OF THAILAND'S MOST SUCCESSFUL FUSION DISHES, WITH SO MANY VERSIONS FROM DIFFERENT SURROUNDING COUNTRIES. THE MEAT, OFTEN EITHER CHICKEN OR PORK, IS MARINATED IN SAVORY THAI FLAVORS, CAREFULLY PIERCED ONTO SKEWERS, THEN GRILLED EITHER OVER A LIVE FIRE OR IN THE FRYING PAN. WE PAIR SATAY WITH TRIANGLES OF TOASTED WHITE BREAD, A CREAMY PEANUT DIPPING SAUCE, AND AJAAD (A CRISP, FRESH CUCUMBER RELISH THAT TASTES AMAZING WITH ANYTHING DEEP-FRIED AND GRILLED). THESE FLAVORFUL SKEWERS ARE EASY TO MAKE, FUN TO PREPARE, AND VERY FAMILY FRIENDLY BECAUSE WHO DOESN'T ENJOY EATING FOOD ON A STICK?

MAKES ABOUT 15 SMALL SKEWERS

2 TEASPOONS CORIANDER SEEDS

1/4-INCH PIECE GALANGAL

1 TABLESPOON SLICED LEMONGRASS

1 TABLESPOON GRANULATED SUGAR

1 TABLESPOON CURRY POWDER

1 TABLESPOON GROUND TURMERIC

1 TEASPOON FINE SEA SALT

1/2 CUP COCONUT MILK

1 POUND BONELESS, SKINLESS CHICKEN THIGHS, THINLY SLICED INTO STRIPS

NEUTRAL OIL FOR COATING

PEANUT DIPPING SAUCE (RECIPE FOLLOWS) FOR SERVING

AJAAD (RECIPE FOLLOWS) FOR SERVING

TOASTED WHITE BREAD, CUT IN TRIANGLES, FOR SERVING (OPTIONAL)

1

IN A MORTAR AND USING A PESTLE, COMBINE THE CORIANDER SEEDS, GALANGAL, AND LEMONGRASS AND POUND UNTIL INCORPORATED.

2

IN A LARGE BOWL, COMBINE THE POUNDED MIXTURE, SUGAR, CURRY POWDER, GROUND TURMERIC, SALT, AND COCONUT MILK AND STIR TO MAKE A MARINADE.

3

ADD THE CHICKEN TO THE BOWL AND USE YOUR HANDS TO EVENLY COAT IN THE MARINADE.

4

COVER THE BOWL WITH A PLASTIC WRAP AND LET IT STAND IN THE FRIDGE FOR 1 HOUR.

5

REMOVE THE CHICKEN FROM THE FRIDGE.
THREAD THE PIECES ON SKEWERS AND PLACE
THEM ON A PLATE IN PREPARATION FOR COOKING.
(IF USING SMALL SKEWERS, THREAD TWO
CHICKEN PIECES PER SKEWER.)

6

COAT A LARGE FRYING PAN
WITH OIL AND SET OVER
MEDIUM HEAT.

7

PLACE HALF OF THE CHICKEN SKEWERS
IN THE PAN AND COOK FOR 4 MINUTES.
FLIP THE CHICKEN SKEWERS AND COOK
FOR ANOTHER 4 MINUTES.

8

FLIP THE CHICKEN SKEWERS AGAIN AND
COOK FOR 1 TO 2 MINUTES MORE, OR UNTIL
GOLDEN BROWN WITH CHAR MARKS. REPEAT
FOR THE SECOND SIDE OF THE SKEWERS.
TRANSFER TO A PLATE.

9

USING A PAPER TOWEL, WIPE OUT THE PAN.
ADD ANOTHER COAT OF OIL, SET
OVER MEDIUM HEAT, AND REPEAT WITH
THE REMAINING CHICKEN SKEWERS.

10

SERVE THE SKEWERS WITH PEANUT
SAUCE, AJAAD, AND TOASTED BREAD
(IF DESIRED) ALONGSIDE.

PEANUT DIPPING SAUCE

MAKES 1 CUP

1/4 CUP PACKED GRATED PALM SUGAR
(ABOUT 1 PIECE) OR GRANULATED SUGAR

1 1/2 TABLESPOONS GROUND PEANUTS

1 TABLESPOON NAM MAKHAM PIAK
(PAGE 195)

1/4 TEASPOON FINE SEA SALT

1/2 CUP COCONUT MILK

1/2 TABLESPOON NEUTRAL OIL

1/2 TABLESPOON MASSAMAN CURRY
PASTE (PAGE 32)

1

IN A MEDIUM SAUCEPAN, COMBINE THE
PALM SUGAR, GROUND PEANUTS, NAM MAKHAM
PIAK, SALT, COCONUT MILK, OIL, AND
CURRY PASTE AND STIR TO MIX.

2

SET THE SAUCEPAN OVER MEDIUM HEAT AND
COOK UNTIL THE SAUCE BOILS. REMOVE FROM
THE HEAT AND SET ASIDE TO COOL BEFORE
TRANSFERRING TO A SMALL BOWL FOR SERVING.

3

LEFTOVER PEANUT
SAUCE CAN BE
STORED IN AN
AIRTIGHT CONTAINER
IN THE FRIDGE FOR
UP TO 3 DAYS.

AJAAD

CUCUMBER RELISH

MAKES 1/2 CUP

5 TABLESPOONS GRANULATED SUGAR

3/4 TEASPOON FINE SEA SALT

1/4 CUP DISTILLED WHITE VINEGAR

1 TABLESPOON WATER

3 TABLESPOONS DICED CUCUMBER

2 TABLESPOONS DICED RED ONION

1 TABLESPOON THINLY SLICED RED
SPUR CHILE

1

IN A MEDIUM SAUCEPAN OVER MEDIUM HEAT,
COMBINE THE SUGAR, SALT, VINEGAR, AND
WATER. STIR UNTIL THE SUGAR AND SALT ARE
DISSOLVED. DO NOT BOIL. IF BUBBLES START
TO FORM AT THE BOTTOM OF THE SAUCEPAN,
REMOVE FROM THE HEAT.

DON'T BOIL!

2

LET THE MIXTURE COOL BEFORE
TRANSFERRING TO A SMALL BOWL.

3

WHEN READY TO SERVE,
ADD THE CUCUMBER,
ONION, AND CHILE TO
THE BOWL. MIX WELL.
LEFTOVER AJAAD CAN BE
STORED IN AN AIRTIGHT
CONTAINER IN THE FRIDGE
FOR UP TO 4 DAYS.

POR PIA THORD

POR PIA THORD, OR DEEP-FRIED SPRING ROLLS, ARE THE ABSOLUTE BEST PARTY STARTER--EMPHASIS ON *PARTY*. THIS DISH IS PERFECT FOR SHARING BECAUSE ONE PACK OF SPRING-ROLL WRAPPERS USUALLY COMES WITH FORTY SHEETS AND YOU MIGHT AS WELL MAKE THEM ALL! THIS MIGHT SEEM LIKE A LOT, BUT YOU CAN EASILY FREEZE ANY LEFTOVERS AND REHEAT THEM WHENEVER YOU HAVE A CRAVING. THESE SPRING ROLLS ARE FILLED WITH VEGETABLES AND GLASS NOODLES AND ARE ALREADY DELICIOUS ON THEIR OWN, BUT AS USUAL, OUR SWEET-AND-SOUR NAM JIM POR PIA (SPRING ROLL DIPPING SAUCE) AMPS IT UP TO THE NEXT LEVEL. WE PROMISE YOU WON'T BE ABLE TO EAT JUST ONE!

MAKES ABOUT 40 ROLLS

4 FRESH OR FROZEN (THAWED) CILANTRO ROOTS

7 GARLIC CLOVES

2 TEASPOONS BLACK PEPPERCORNS

2 OUNCES DRIED GLASS NOODLES, SOAKED IN ROOM-TEMPERATURE WATER FOR 15 MINUTES AND DRAINED

3 TABLESPOONS NEUTRAL OIL, PLUS MORE FOR COATING

17 FRESH OR DRIED SHIITAKE MUSHROOMS (SOAKED IN ROOM-TEMPERATURE WATER FOR 1 HOUR AND DRAINED), SLICED 1/8 INCH THICK

1 POUND GROUND PORK

1 TABLESPOON SEASONING POWDER (OPTIONAL)

2 TABLESPOONS GRANULATED SUGAR

1/4 CUP SEASONING SOY SAUCE

2 TABLESPOONS THIN SOY SAUCE

5 TABLESPOONS OYSTER SAUCE

2 POUNDS GREEN CABBAGE, THINLY SLICED

4 CUPS LOOSELY PACKED SHREDDED CARROTS

1 PACKAGE 7-INCH SQUARE SPRING ROLL WRAPPERS (ABOUT 40 WRAPPERS), AT ROOM TEMPERATURE

WATER OR EGG WHITE FOR SEALING

NAM JIM POR PIA (RECIPE FOLLOWS) FOR SERVING

CHEF MALLIKA SAYS:

YOU CAN WRAP THESE BABIES THE NIGHT BEFORE, KEEP THEM IN THE FRIDGE, AND FRY THE NEXT DAY. IF YOU HAVE MADE TOO MANY ROLLS, FREEZE THEM! WHENEVER YOU NEED A POR PIA FIX, JUST THAW AND FRY UNTIL GOLDEN BROWN.

IF YOU WANT TO TRY THE FRESH VERSION OF POR PIA, USE RICE PAPER TO WRAP THE FILLING AND SKIP THE DEEP-FRYING STEP. SUBMERGE A SHEET IN WARM WATER UNTIL SOFT, ABOUT 1 MINUTE. CAREFULLY REMOVE THE SHEET, LAY ONTO A FLAT SURFACE, AND FOLLOW THE SAME WRAPPING INSTRUCTIONS FOR FRIED POR PIA. SINCE THE RICE PAPER IS VERY DELICATE, THIS MIGHT TAKE A FEW TRIES, BUT YOU'LL GET BETTER WITH EACH ONE!

1
IN A MORTAR AND USING THE PESTLE, COMBINE THE CILANTRO ROOTS, GARLIC, AND PEPPERCORNS AND POUND INTO A FINE PASTE. SET ASIDE.

2
CUT THE DRAINED GLASS NOODLES INTO 3-INCH PIECES AND SET ASIDE.

3 INCH

3

IN A LARGE WOK, ADD 3 TABLESPOONS OF OIL AND PLACE OVER MEDIUM-HIGH HEAT. ADD THE SLICED MUSHROOMS AND FRY UNTIL THEY ARE GOLDEN, ABOUT 1 MINUTE.

4

ADD THE RESERVED PASTE TO THE WOK AND STIR-FRY FOR 1 MINUTE.

5

ADD THE GROUND PORK TO THE WOK AND COOK UNTIL BROWNED, ABOUT 2 MINUTES.

6

TURN THE HEAT TO MEDIUM. ADD THE GLASS NOODLES, SEASONING POWDER (IF USING), SUGAR, SEASONING SOY SAUCE, THIN SOY SAUCE, AND OYSTER SAUCE. MIX WELL.

7

ADD THE CABBAGE AND CARROTS TO THE WOK. TURN THE HEAT TO MEDIUM-HIGH AND COOK UNTIL THE CABBAGE AND CARROTS ARE SOFT, UP TO 10 MINUTES.

8

USING A SLOTTED SPOON, TRANSFER THE FILLING TO A LARGE BOWL AND LET COOL FOR 10 MINUTES.

9

PREPARE A SMALL BOWL OF WATER FOR SEALING THE WRAPPERS. PLACE A WRAPPER ON A LARGE CUTTING BOARD WITH ONE OF THE CORNERS POINTING TOWARD YOU.

10

SCOOP 2 TABLESPOONS OF THE FILLING ONTO THE LOWER END OF THE WRAPPER, LEAVING ENOUGH OF THE WRAPPER TO FOLD OVER THE FILLING AND COVER.

11

FOLD THE BOTTOM CORNER OVER THE FILLING AND ROLL TO THE CENTER OF THE WRAPPER. WHILE ROLLING, TIGHTLY FORM THE FILLING INTO A SAUSAGE SHAPE.

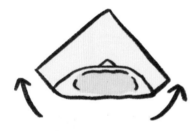

12

ON THE RIGHT SIDE OF THE FILLING, PRESS DOWN ON THE WRAPPER TO SEAL THE EDGE.

13

STILL ON THE RIGHT SIDE, FOLD THE WRAPPER OVER THE FILLING TOWARD THE LEFT SIDE.

14

REPEAT ON THE LEFT SIDE, STARTING WITH MAKING A CORNER AT THE END OF THE FILLING AND THEN FOLDING IN TOWARD THE RIGHT SIDE.

15

DIP YOUR FINGER IN THE WATER AND WET THE EDGES OF THE WRAPPER.

16

FINISH ROLLING THE WRAPPER, TUCKING THE FILLING INWARD WITH EACH ROLL TO TIGHTEN.

17

DIP YOUR FINGER IN THE WATER AGAIN AND WET THE FINAL CORNER OF THE WRAPPER TO PROPERLY SEAL IT.

18

REPEAT THE PROCESS UNTIL ALL THE FILLING MIXTURE HAS BEEN WRAPPED.

19

LINE A PLATE WITH PAPER TOWELS. POUR 1 INCH OF OIL INTO A MEDIUM SAUCEPAN OR WOK AND SET OVER MEDIUM-HIGH HEAT. (TO CHECK FOR THE CORRECT AMOUNT OF THE OIL, DIP THE TIP OF A TEASPOON TO THE BOTTOM OF THE PAN; THE OIL SHOULD COVER HALF OF THE SPOON AT ALL TIMES DURING THE FRYING PROCESS. REPLENISH AS YOU GO.)

20

WHEN THE OIL IS VERY HOT AND BEGINS TO LIGHTLY SMOKE, USE TONGS TO GENTLY ADD THE SPRING ROLLS ONE BY ONE, FOUR TO FIVE ROLLS AT A TIME.

21

USING THE TONGS, ROTATE THE ROLLS BACK AND FORTH IN THE OIL TO MAKE SURE THAT BOTH SIDES ARE EQUALLY GOLDEN. THE PROCESS FOR EACH BATCH TAKES ABOUT 1 MINUTE, OR UNTIL GOLDEN BROWN. REMOVE THE ROLLS TO THE PREPARED PLATE.

22

SERVE THE SPRING ROLLS ALONGSIDE NAM JIM POR PIA.

NAM JIM POR PIA

SWEET-AND-SOUR SPRING ROLL
DIPPING SAUCE

MAKES 1 CUP

1 CUP GRANULATED SUGAR

2 TEASPOONS FINE SEA SALT

3 TABLESPOONS WATER

1/3 CUP DISTILLED WHITE VINEGAR

2 MILD RED CHILES, SEEDED AND MINCED

SHREDDED DAIKON RADISH FOR
GARNISHING

SHREDDED CARROT FOR GARNISHING

3 TABLESPOONS GROUND PEANUTS
(OPTIONAL)

1

IN A MEDIUM SAUCEPAN OVER MEDIUM-LOW
HEAT, COMBINE THE SUGAR, SALT, WATER,
VINEGAR, AND CHILES. STIR AND THEN LET
THIS SAUCE SIMMER FOR 20 MINUTES,
STIRRING OCCASIONALLY.

2

TRANSFER THE DIPPING SAUCE TO
A SMALL BOWL AND GARNISH WITH
THE RADISH, CARROT, AND GROUND
PEANUTS (IF DESIRED).

HOT OR NOT?

NO TIME TO MAKE SAUCE? PICK UP A BOTTLE OF DIPPING SAUCE FROM YOUR LOCAL ASIAN STORE. SERIOUSLY, BASICALLY ANYTHING GOES!

SRIRACHA HOT CHILI SAUCE

NHĂN CON NGỐNG

Net Wt: 730ml.
Poids Net: 860 g.

SWEETENED CHILI SAUCE
FOR SPRING ROLL

NET WT : 32.5 OZ 1730

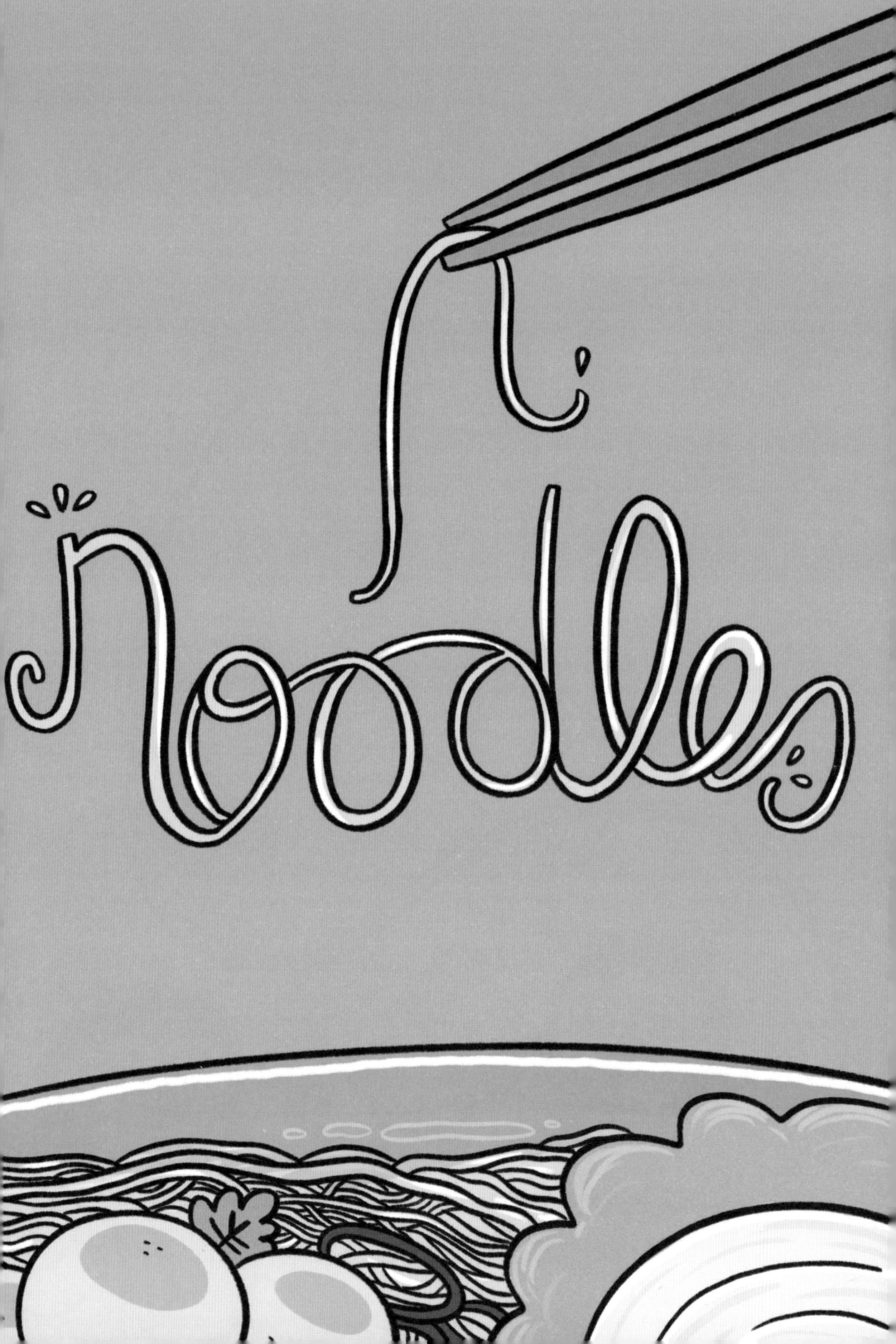
noodles

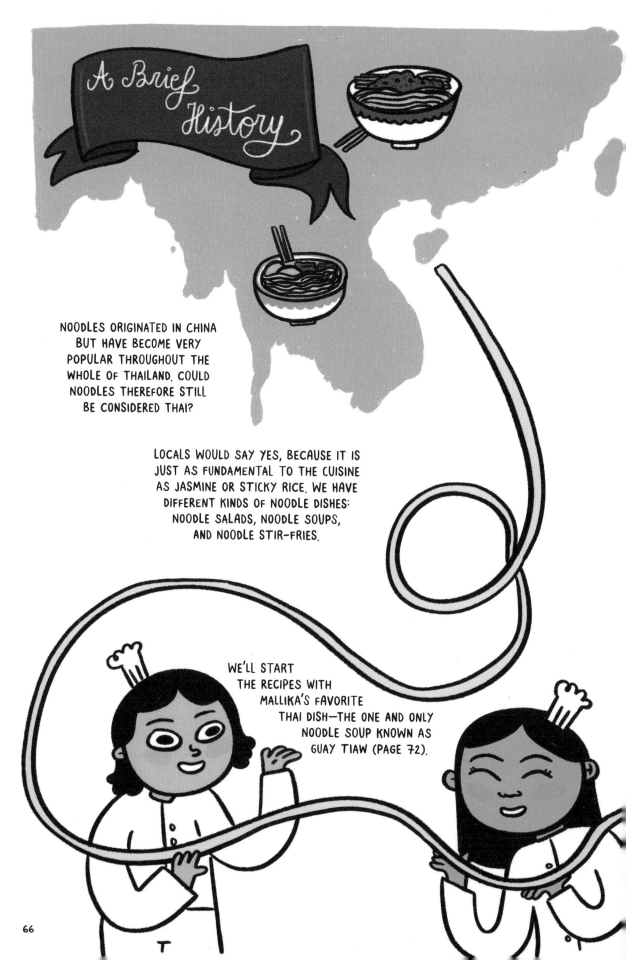

A Brief History

NOODLES ORIGINATED IN CHINA BUT HAVE BECOME VERY POPULAR THROUGHOUT THE WHOLE OF THAILAND. COULD NOODLES THEREFORE STILL BE CONSIDERED THAI?

LOCALS WOULD SAY YES, BECAUSE IT IS JUST AS FUNDAMENTAL TO THE CUISINE AS JASMINE OR STICKY RICE. WE HAVE DIFFERENT KINDS OF NOODLE DISHES: NOODLE SALADS, NOODLE SOUPS, AND NOODLE STIR-FRIES.

WE'LL START THE RECIPES WITH MALLIKA'S FAVORITE THAI DISH—THE ONE AND ONLY NOODLE SOUP KNOWN AS GUAY TIAW (PAGE 72).

YELLOW NOODLES, WHITE NOODLES, CLEAR NOODLES, CURLY NOODLES, STRAIGHT NOODLES . . . THERE ARE PLENTY OF NOODLE TYPES AND EACH ONE IS USED IN A SPECIFIC DISH. SINCE THESE NOODLES ARE OFTEN PURCHASED DRIED, SOME CAN BE BOILED STRAIGHT FROM THE PACKAGE, BUT MOST OF THEM REQUIRE SOAKING IN ROOM-TEMPERATURE WATER UNTIL THEY GET SOFT. TO AVOID RICE NOODLES STICKING TOGETHER IN LUMPS AFTER SOAKING, RINSE WITH COLD WATER BEFORE COOKING.

CAN'T TELL THE DIFFERENCE BETWEEN ALL THE TYPES YET?

NO WORRIES. LET'S SEE WHAT ALL THE NOODLE-Y FUSS IS ABOUT.

TYPES OF NOODLES

SEN YAI

THESE WIDE, FLAT RICE NOODLES, OFTEN LABELED AS "RICE FLAKE NOODLES," ARE 1-INCH-WIDE STRIPS. ANOTHER OPTION IS "EXTRA-LARGE RICE STICK NOODLES" THAT MEASURE 10MM WIDE, AS INDICATED ON THE PACKAGE. IT WILL TAKE UP TO 60 MINUTES TO SOAK THE NOODLES BEFORE USING. IF THEY ARE STILL HARD AFTER SOAKING FOR MORE THAN AN HOUR, DIP THE NOODLES IN BOILING WATER JUST BEFORE COOKING. SEN YAI CAN BE USED IN GUAY TIAW (PAGE 72), PAD SEE EW (PAGE 82), AND PAD KHEE MAO (PAGE 84). WE PREFER COCK BRAND FOR RICE FLAKE NOODLES AND FARMER BRAND FOR RICE STICK NOODLES.

SEN LEK

THIS RICE NOODLE IS THINNER THAN THE WIDE SEN YAI RICE NOODLES, LIKE THE NAME SUGGESTS (*LEK* MEANS "SMALL" AND *YAI* MEANS "BIG"). SEN LEK ARE OFTEN LABELED "RICE STICK NOODLES" WITH THE VARYING SIZES OF 1MM, 3MM, AND 5MM AS INDICATED ON THE PACKAGES. DEPENDING ON THE EXACT SIZE, IT USUALLY TAKES 30 TO 60 MINUTES OF SOAKING. SEN LEK CAN BE USED IN GUAY TIAW (PAGE 72), PAD THAI (PAGE 80), AND PAD KHEE MAO (PAGE 84). WE PREFER FARMER BRAND.

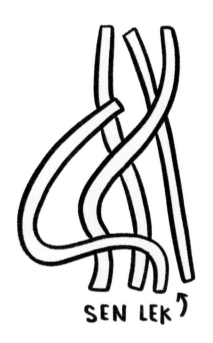

WOON SEN

WOON SEN IS A GLASS NOODLE MADE FROM MUNG BEANS. YOU CAN RECOGNIZE THESE AS THEY ARE SEEMINGLY TRANSPARENT, LIKE GLASS. THEY REQUIRE 15 TO 30 MINUTES OF SOAKING. WOON SEN CAN BE USED IN YUM WOON SEN (PAGE 52) AND GUAY TIAW (PAGE 72). WE PREFER TWIN DRAGON AND TONSON BRANDS.

MAMA INSTANT NOODLES

ARGUABLY THE WORLD'S MOST FAMOUS INSTANT NOODLES, THE MAMA BRAND CAN'T BE EXCLUDED FROM THIS LIST. MAMA NOODLES ARE MADE FROM WHEAT FLOUR, BUT THAI PEOPLE GENERALLY JUST CALL IT BY ITS BRAND NAME. THE NOODLES ALWAYS COME DRIED IN A PACKAGE AND CAN BE BOILED FOR INSTANT USE. MAMA CAN BE USED IN YUM WOON SEN (PAGE 52), GUAY TIAW (PAGE 72), AND PAD KHEE MAO (PAGE 84). IF YOU CAN'T FIND MAMA, THE WAI WAI BRAND WORKS JUST AS WELL.

SEN MEE

ALSO KNOWN AS VERMICELLI, SEN MEE IS A SUPER-THIN RICE NOODLE. THIS ONE SOAKS FOR 15 MINUTES. SEN MEE CAN BE USED IN GUAY TIAW (PAGE 72), PAD SEE EW (PAGE 82), AND PAD KHEE MAO (PAGE 84). WE PREFER MAMA AND WAI WAI BRANDS.

BA MEE SEN BAEN

THIS IS A FLAT EGG NOODLE THAT CAN BE BOILED WITHOUT PRESOAKING. BA MEE SEN BAEN CAN BE USED IN GUAY TIAW (PAGE 72), KHAO SOI (PAGE 78), AND PAD KHEE MAO (PAGE 84).

BA MEE

THIS YELLOW EGG NOODLE IS CHEWIER THAN RICE NOODLES AND CAN BE BOILED WITHOUT PRESOAKING. BA MEE CAN BE USED IN GUAY TIAW (PAGE 72), KHAO SOI (PAGE 78), AND PAD KHEE MAO (PAGE 84).

KHANOM JEEN

FERMENTED RICE FLOUR NOODLES CAN BE BOILED ACCORDING TO THE PACKAGE DIRECTIONS WITHOUT PRESOAKING. SINCE THEY CAN GET MUSHY VERY EASILY, THE NOODLES NEED TO BE RINSED AND SOAKED IN COLD WATER RIGHT AFTER BOILING. THEN, EACH SERVING OF NOODLES IS PULLED UP BY HAND AND COILED INTO INDIVIDUAL NESTS TO PREVENT THEM FROM STICKING TOGETHER. BUN TUOI (VIETNAMESE RICE VERMICELLI NOODLES) ARE A GREAT SUBSTITUTION HERE. KHANOM JEEN CAN BE SERVED WITH GAENG KEOW WAN (PAGE 130).

NOODLES, THE ORIGIN STORY

BANGKOK, 1942

THE CITY WAS DEVASTATED BY THE GREAT FLOOD.

IT BECAME INCONVENIENT FOR GOVERNMENT OFFICERS TO HAVE LUNCH OUTSIDE, BUT THERE WAS STILL ONE OPTION LEFT: A BOAT.

HISTORICALLY, THAI PEOPLE HAVE ALWAYS USED BOATS FOR TRANSPORTATION AND COMMERCE, ESPECIALLY IN BANGKOK SINCE THE CITY IS LINED WITH CANALS. YOU COULD FIND ANYTHING ON THE CANALS, RANGING FROM FRUITS AND VEGGIES TO FULLY PREPARED MEALS.

GUAY TIAW REUA, OR *GUAY TIAW* FOR SHORT, LITERALLY TRANSLATES TO "BOAT NOODLES" BECAUSE IT WAS ONE OF THE DISHES THAT WAS EASY TO MAKE ON A BOAT DURING THE FLOOD.

THERE WERE COURSES TEACHING PEOPLE HOW TO MAKE GUAY TIAW. THE OFFICERS EVEN HAD TO MAKE AND SELL THIS DISH THEMSELVES IN ORDER TO SET AN EXAMPLE TO THE LOCALS.

THEY EVEN HAD A PROMOTION SONG FOR THE NOODLES:

* GUAY TIAW . . . GUAY TIAW IS HERE . . . GUAY TIAW IS HERE . . . GUAY TIAW . . . GUAY TIAW . . . IS THAI. WE USE LOCAL INGREDIENTS . . . ASSETS FROM THE GROUND ARE GENERALLY AVAILABLE. . . . WE HELP EACH OTHER TO SELL AND BUY TO BECOME PROSPEROUS BECAUSE WE, THE THAIS, HELP EACH OTHER ALWAYS. . . .

GUAY TIAW WAS INEXPENSIVE AND NUTRITIOUS. SINCE EVERYBODY COULD AFFORD TO EAT GUAY TIAW, IT ALSO BOOSTED THE THAI ECONOMY DURING THIS ROUGH TIME. TO SOME, THE DISH EVEN BECAME A SYMBOL FOR DEMOCRACY: MADE WITH FRESH, LOCAL INGREDIENTS AND CONSUMED BY EVERYONE, REGARDLESS OF SOCIAL STATUS.

GUAY TIAW, AT THE SAME TIME, WAS ALSO A DISH THAT COULD BE EASILY PERSONALIZED, SINCE YOU COULD ADJUST IT TO YOUR OWN TASTE.

SO, THE NOODLE DISH THAT ORIGINATED WITH THE CHINESE LABOR CLASS BECAME A THAI CUISINE CENTERPIECE, ADAPTED TO THE DELICIOUS LOCAL INGREDIENTS FOUND THROUGHOUT THE COUNTRY.

GUAY TIAW

THERE ARE MANY RECIPES FOR THIS NOODLE SOUP DISH, WITH SO MANY DIFFERENT NOODLES AND BROTH TYPES. FOR THE CLASSIC, WELL-LOVED BOAT NOODLE (GUAY TIAW RUEA), THE BROTH HAS A BASE OF PORK BLOOD. HERE, WE'RE MAKING GUAY TIAW NAM SAI, WHICH MEANS "NOODLES IN CLEAR SOUP"--A RECIPE THAT IS APPROACHABLE FOR EVERYONE. THE MOST FUN PART OF THIS DISH IS THAT THE SIMPLE BROTH MEANS IT IS FULLY CUSTOMIZABLE TO YOUR OWN TASTE, AND YOU CAN PICK YOUR PREFERRED NOODLES (SEE PAGE 68), MEATS, AND VEGGIES. AND DID YOU KNOW GUAY TIAW CAN BE SERVED WITH THE BROTH OR WITHOUT? BOTH VERSIONS OF THE DISH ARE VERY POPULAR!

MAKES 8 SERVINGS

2 POUNDS PORK BACKBONE OR RIBS

5 TABLESPOONS FINE SEA SALT

5 QUARTS WATER

8 GARLIC CLOVES, LIGHTLY CRUSHED

1½ TABLESPOONS WHITE PEPPERCORNS, LIGHTLY CRUSHED

THREE 3-INCH-LONG CELERY STICKS

4 FRESH OR FROZEN (THAWED) CILANTRO ROOTS, LIGHTLY CRUSHED

2 PICKLED WHOLE GARLIC HEADS (OPTIONAL)

MEATBALLS

1 POUND GROUND PORK

3 GARLIC CLOVES, FINELY CRUSHED

1 TABLESPOON TAPIOCA FLOUR OR CORNSTARCH

1 TABLESPOON BAKING POWDER

1 TEASPOON FINE SEA SALT

1 TEASPOON GRANULATED SUGAR

½ TEASPOON FRESHLY GROUND BLACK PEPPER

1 TABLESPOON OYSTER SAUCE

1 OUNCE WHITE ROCK SUGAR (ABOUT 3 PIECES), OR 1 TABLESPOON GRANULATED SUGAR

5 TABLESPOONS THIN SOY SAUCE

ONE 5-INCH-LONG FRESH DAIKON RADISH, SLICED

1 LARGE YELLOW ONION, PEELED

1 POUND RICE STICK NOODLES (PREFERABLY SIZE 3MM), SOAKED FOR 1 HOUR AND DRAINED

3 TABLESPOONS GRATHIAM JIEW (PAGE 188)

8 OUNCES BEAN SPROUTS

1 CUP LOOSELY PACKED CHOPPED CELERY LEAVES OR CILANTRO LEAVES

1 CUP LOOSELY PACKED CHOPPED CHIVES

PHRIK NAM SOM (PAGE 186), TO TASTE

PHRIK PON (PAGE 192), TO TASTE

FISH SAUCE, TO TASTE

GRANULATED SUGAR, TO TASTE

CHEF MALLIKA SAYS:

THIS RECIPE REQUIRES CHEESECLOTH FOR STEEPING THE AROMATICS AND GLOVES FOR KNEADING THE MEATBALLS, SO MAKE SURE YOU HAVE THESE BEFORE YOU START THE PROCESS.

IF YOU CAN, PREPARE THE MEATBALLS AND THE SOUP ONE DAY IN ADVANCE TO SAVE TIME (YOU'LL THANK US LATER!). READY-MADE GUAY TIAW CLEAR SOUP-BASE POWDER (WE RECOMMEND FATHAI BRAND) AND MEATBALLS ARE AVAILABLE IN MOST ASIAN STORES.

ADDING OTHER KINDS OF MEAT, SUCH AS FISH BALLS OR THIN-SLICED CHICKEN OR BEEF, IS ENCOURAGED.

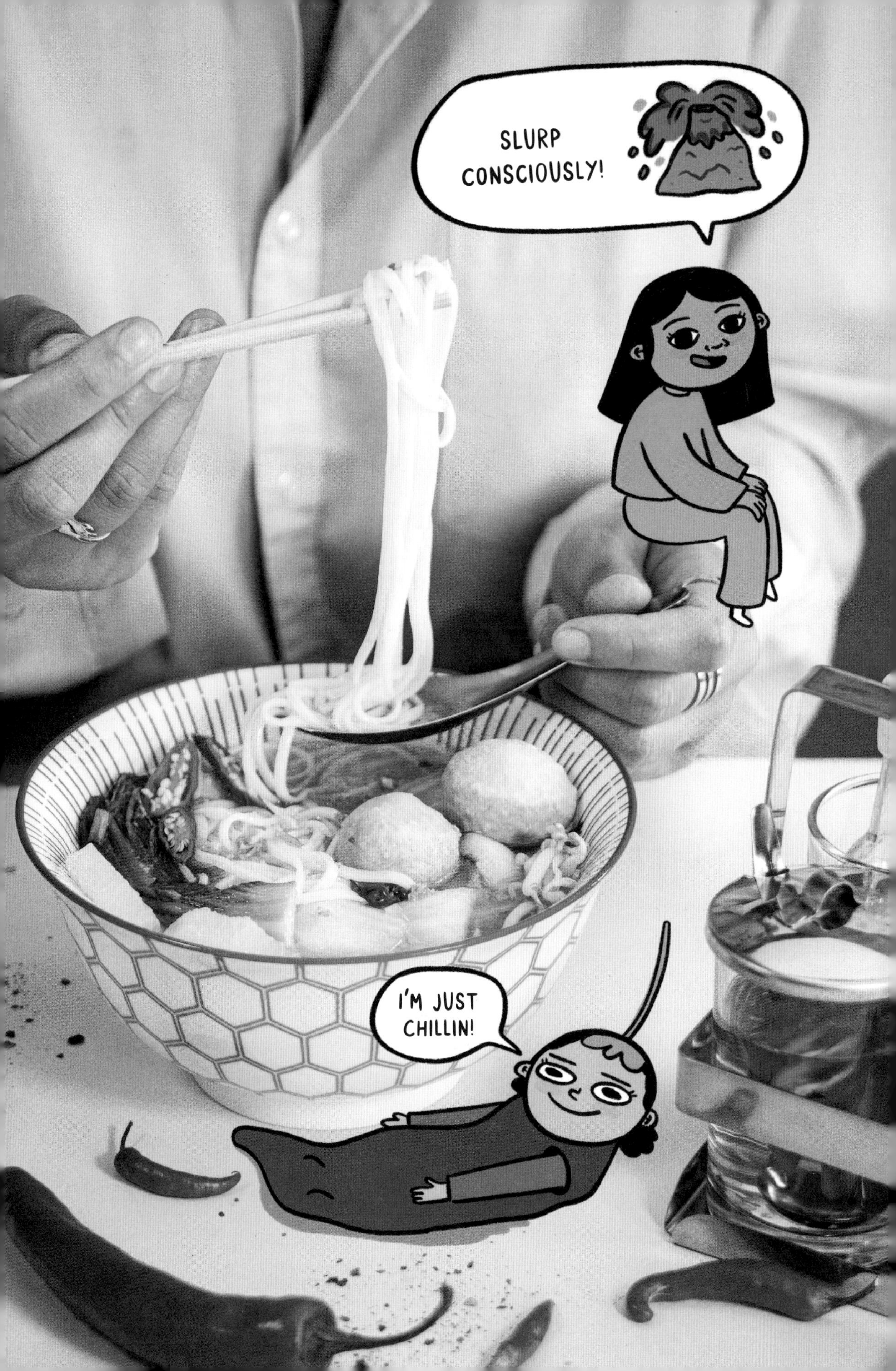
SLURP CONSCIOUSLY!
I'M JUST CHILLIN!

1

IN A LARGE BOWL, PLACE THE PORK BACKBONE AND FILL WITH ENOUGH WATER TO COVER. ADD 2 TABLESPOONS OF THE SALT AND RUB THE BONE WITH SALT TO REMOVE AS MUCH BLOOD, FAT, OR BONE MARROW AS POSSIBLE.

2

DRAIN THE WATER FROM THE BOWL. RINSE THE PORK BACKBONE AND SET ASIDE.

3

IN A LARGE STOCKPOT OR WOK OVER HIGH HEAT, BRING 4 QUARTS OF THE WATER TO A BOIL.

4

IN THE CENTER OF A 15-INCH SQUARE PIECE OF CHEESECLOTH, COMBINE THE GARLIC CLOVES, PEPPERCORNS, CELERY STICKS, CILANTRO ROOTS, AND PICKLED GARLIC HEADS (IF USING). TIE THE CLOTH SECURELY.

5

WHEN THE WATER IS BOILING, ADD THE PORK BACKBONE. IMMEDIATELY TURN THE HEAT TO MEDIUM-HIGH AND LET BOIL GENTLY, UNCOVERED, SO THIS SOUP STAYS CLEAR, FOR ABOUT 12 MINUTES.

6

USE A SPOON OR A SKIMMER TO REMOVE AS MUCH FAT FROM THE SURFACE OF THE SOUP AS POSSIBLE.

7

ADD THE CHEESECLOTH BUNDLE TO THE SOUP, TURN THE HEAT TO MEDIUM, AND LET SIMMER FOR 2 HOURS. CONTINUE TO SKIM THE FAT FROM THE SURFACE AS IT RISES.

8

TO PREPARE THE MEATBALLS:
IN A LARGE BOWL, COMBINE THE GROUND PORK,
CRUSHED GARLIC, TAPIOCA FLOUR, BAKING
POWDER, SALT, SUGAR, GROUND BLACK PEPPER,
AND OYSTER SAUCE.

9

WITH GLOVED HANDS, KNEAD THE PORK MIXTURE
FOR ABOUT 15 MINUTES, OR MIX IN A
FOOD PROCESSOR FOR 5 MINUTES, UNTIL THE
TEXTURE IS COMPLETELY SMOOTH AND SOFT.

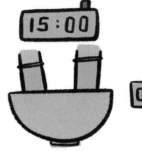

10

COVER THE BOWL WITH
PLASTIC WRAP AND CHILL IN
THE FREEZER FOR 1 HOUR.

11

AFTER THE SOUP HAS SIMMERED FOR 2 HOURS,
ADD THE REMAINING 1 QUART WATER,
REMAINING 3 TABLESPOONS SALT, ROCK SUGAR,
THIN SOY SAUCE, RADISH, AND ONION AND
LET SIMMER FOR 1 HOUR MORE.

12

IN A LARGE SAUCEPAN OR WOK
OVER HIGH HEAT, BRING 2 QUARTS
OF WATER TO A BOIL. LET IT BOIL
FOR 15 MINUTES.

13

REMOVE THE GROUND PORK
MIXTURE FROM THE FREEZER
AND, USING A SPATULA,
BREAK IT UP TO LOOSEN
THE TEXTURE. WITH GLOVED
HANDS, KNEAD THE MEAT FOR
15 MINUTES, OR MIX IN THE
FOOD PROCESSOR FOR
5 MINUTES.

14

TURN THE HEAT TO MEDIUM TO CALM THE BOIL. (THE MEATBALLS WILL BREAK IF THE BOIL IS TOO HIGH, SO MAKE SURE THE WATER IS STILL WITH NO BUBBLES OR MOVEMENT!)

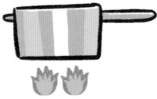

15

GRAB A HANDFUL OF GROUND PORK AND SQUEEZE YOUR HAND INTO A TIGHT FIST, FORCING THE MEAT OUT INTO A BALL. USING A SPOON, SCOOP UP THE MEATBALL AND DROP IT GENTLY IN THE HOT WATER. REPEAT THE PROCESS UNTIL ALL THE GROUND PORK HAS BEEN FORMED INTO MEATBALLS. (OCCASIONALLY DIP YOUR HAND IN WATER OR COAT WITH NEUTRAL OIL WHEN TOO MUCH MEAT STICKS TO YOUR FINGERS.)

16

ONCE THE MEATBALLS ARE FLOATING, LET THEM COOK FOR ABOUT 10 MINUTES MORE.

17

FILL A LARGE BOWL WITH VERY COLD WATER. ONCE THE MEATBALLS ARE READY, USING A SKIMMER, TRANSFER THEM TO THE BOWL. LEAVE SUBMERGED IN THE COLD WATER FOR 2 MINUTES, THEN DRAIN AND SET ASIDE.

18

ONCE THE SOUP IS READY, REMOVE THE HERB BUNDLE AND THE WHOLE ONION. TURN THE HEAT TO MEDIUM-HIGH, ADD THE MEATBALLS, AND COOK FOR 5 MINUTES MORE.

19

IN A MEDIUM SAUCEPAN OR WOK OVER HIGH HEAT, BRING 8 CUPS OF WATER TO A BOIL. YOU WILL BE MAKING ONE SERVING AT A TIME, SO HAVE INDIVIDUAL SERVING BOWLS NEXT TO THE PAN.

20

PLACE ABOUT 2 CUPS LOOSELY PACKED SOAKED AND DRAINED NOODLES ON A FINE-MESH SKIMMER AND DIP IT IN THE BOILING WATER FOR ABOUT 10 SECONDS, USING TONGS OR CHOPSTICKS TO KEEP THE NOODLES FROM FLOATING OFF. RAISE THE SKIMMER OVER THE POT TO DRAIN FOR A FEW SECONDS, THEN QUICKLY TRANSFER THE COOKED NOODLES TO ONE OF THE SERVING BOWLS. REPEAT THE PROCESS UNTIL ALL THE BOWLS ARE FILLED.

21

POUR THE SOUP OVER THE NOODLES IN EACH BOWL AND ADD THE MEATBALLS, PORK BONES (IF DESIRED), AND RADISH. SPRINKLE THE GRATHIAM JIEW, BEAN SPROUTS, CELERY LEAVES, AND CHIVES ON TOP. ADJUST THE FLAVORS OF YOUR NOODLE SOUP WITH THE SEASONING SET. MIX WELL AND ENJOY! SLURPING IS ALLOWED AND ENCOURAGED.

AROY!

*DELICIOUS!

KHAO SOI

ORIGINATING FROM THE NORTHERN PART OF THAILAND, THIS DISH CONSISTS OF EGG NOODLES IN A RICH CURRY BROTH AND THE FLAVORS ARE HEAVILY INFLUENCED BY THE CHINESE MUSLIM COMMUNITY. LATER, THAI LOCALS ADJUSTED SOME OF THE INGREDIENTS TO INCLUDE FAMILIAR ELEMENTS, SUCH AS CILANTRO ROOTS, SHALLOTS, AND COCONUT MILK. IF YOU'RE VISITING NORTHERN THAILAND, KHAO SOI IS A MUST-TRY, BUT THIS RECIPE WILL GET YOU AS CLOSE AS YOU CAN WITHOUT LEAVING YOUR HOME.

MAKES 2 TO 4 SERVINGS

KHAO SOI PASTE

10 LARGE DRIED THAI CHILES (OR ADJUST TO TASTE), SOAKED IN BOILING WATER FOR 20 MINUTES, DRAINED, STEMMED, AND SEEDED

8 SMALL DRIED THAI CHILES (OR ADJUST TO TASTE), SOAKED IN BOILING WATER FOR 20 MINUTES, DRAINED, AND STEMMED

1 TABLESPOON SLICED LEMONGRASS

1/2 TEASPOON FINE SEA SALT

3 PIECES FINGERROOT, UNPEELED AND CHOPPED

1-INCH PIECE GINGER, PEELED AND THINLY SLICED

2-INCH PIECE TURMERIC ROOT, CHOPPED

5 GARLIC CLOVES, HALVED

5 SMALL RED SHALLOTS, OR 1 MEDIUM RED ONION, COARSELY CHOPPED

1 TEASPOON CURRY POWDER

1 TABLESPOON SHRIMP PASTE

TWO 14-OUNCE CANS COCONUT MILK

2 POUNDS CHICKEN DRUMSTICKS

2 CUPS WATER

3 TABLESPOONS PACKED GRATED PALM SUGAR (ABOUT 3/4 PIECE) OR GRANULATED SUGAR

1 TABLESPOON FINE SEA SALT

1 TABLESPOON FISH SAUCE

1/2 POUND DRIED FLAT EGG NOODLES

1 CUP LOOSELY PACKED CHOPPED CHIVES

1 CUP LOOSELY PACKED CHOPPED CILANTRO LEAVES AND STEMS

1 MEDIUM RED ONION, DICED

1 CUP CHOPPED PICKLED CHINESE MUSTARD GREENS (OPTIONAL)

PHRIK PON THORD (PAGE 194), TO TASTE

LIME WEDGES

1
TO MAKE THE PASTE: IN A MORTAR AND USING A PESTLE, COMBINE THE LARGE AND SMALL SOAKED AND DRAINED CHILES, LEMONGRASS, AND SALT AND POUND UNTIL INCORPORATED.

CHEF MALLIKA SAYS:

IN A PINCH, YOU CAN USE A PREMADE KHAO SOI CURRY PASTE, WHICH IS OFTEN AVAILABLE AT ASIAN STORES. ALTERNATIVELY, YOU CAN COMBINE TWO PARTS RED CURRY PASTE WITH ONE PART YELLOW CURRY PASTE.

2

ADD THE FINGERROOT, GINGER, TURMERIC, GARLIC, SHALLOTS, CURRY POWDER, AND SHRIMP PASTE TO THE MORTAR AND POUND UNTIL INCORPORATED INTO A FINE PASTE. SET ASIDE.

3

IN A LARGE SAUCEPAN OVER MEDIUM-HIGH HEAT, COMBINE ONE CAN OF COCONUT MILK AND THE KHAO SOI PASTE. STIR FREQUENTLY UNTIL INCORPORATED AND THE MIXTURE BOILS, ABOUT 3 MINUTES.

4

ADD THE CHICKEN TO THE PAN AND STIR-FRY UNTIL BROWNED ON ALL SIDES, ABOUT 7 MINUTES MORE.

5

ADD THE WATER TO THE CHICKEN, FOLLOWED BY THE PALM SUGAR, SALT, AND FISH SAUCE. MIX WELL, TURN THE HEAT TO MEDIUM, COVER, AND LET COOK, STIRRING OCCASIONALLY, UNTIL THE CHICKEN IS COOKED THROUGH, ABOUT 20 MINUTES.

6

ADD THE REMAINING CAN OF COCONUT MILK TO THE PAN. COVER AND LET COOK UNTIL INCORPORATED, ABOUT 5 MINUTES MORE. REMOVE FROM THE HEAT AND SET ASIDE.

7

IN A MEDIUM SAUCEPAN OR WOK OVER HIGH HEAT, BRING 8 CUPS OF WATER TO A BOIL. ADD THE NOODLES, TURN THE HEAT TO MEDIUM-HIGH, AND COOK UNTIL SOFT, ABOUT 5 MINUTES. YOU WILL BE MAKING ONE SERVING AT A TIME, SO HAVE INDIVIDUAL SERVING BOWLS NEXT TO THE PAN.

USING A SKIMMER, TRANSFER A PORTION OF NOODLES TO ONE OF THE SERVING BOWLS. REPEAT THE PROCESS UNTIL ALL THE BOWLS ARE FILLED.

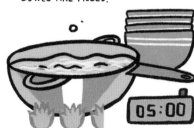

8

POUR THE CURRY OVER THE NOODLES IN EACH BOWL AND TOP WITH THE CHICKEN, CHIVES, CILANTRO, ONION, AND PICKLED MUSTARD GREENS (IF DESIRED). ADJUST THE FLAVORS OF YOUR NOODLE SOUP WITH THE SEASONING SET. MIX WELL AND ENJOY!

PAD THAI

PAD THAI MIGHT BE THE MOST WELL-KNOWN THAI DISH IN THE WHOLE WIDE WORLD--HENCE THE SIMPLE AND ICONIC NAME. MAKING THESE NOODLES FOR YOURSELF IS ACTUALLY VERY EASY SINCE IT'S JUST A STIR-FRY! THE TRADITIONAL RECIPE REQUIRES A BUNCH OF INGREDIENTS, SUCH AS TAMARIND PULP OR PALM SUGAR, THAT CAN BE DIFFICULT TO FIND, SO THERE'S A CHANCE YOU'VE NEVER TRIED *THE REAL DEAL*. ONCE YOU'VE MADE IT, DON'T WAIT TO EAT IT OR THE NOODLES WILL START TO CLUMP TOGETHER!

PAD THAI SAUCE

1/2 CUP PACKED GRATED PALM SUGAR (ABOUT 2 PIECES)

1/4 CUP GRANULATED SUGAR

2 1/2 CUPS WATER

1/4 CUP FISH SAUCE

1/4 CUP NAM MAKHAM PIAK (PAGE 195)

1/4 CUP HOM JIEW (PAGE 188)

3 TABLESPOONS NEUTRAL OIL

8 OUNCES COLOSSAL (U15) SHRIMP WITH TAILS, PEELED AND DEVEINED

3 OUNCES FIRM TOFU, CUT INTO 1 1/2-INCH-THICK STRIPS

3 TABLESPOONS PRESERVED SWEET RADISH, CHOPPED (OPTIONAL)

1 TABLESPOON DRIED SHRIMP (OPTIONAL)

8 OUNCES RICE STICK NOODLES (PREFERABLY 3 OR 5MM SIZE), SOAKED IN ROOM-TEMPERATURE WATER FOR 1 HOUR AND DRAINED

2 EGGS

1 CUP LOOSELY PACKED BEAN SPROUTS

1 CUP LOOSELY PACKED 1 1/2-INCH-LONG CUT GARLIC CHIVES OR GREEN ONIONS (WHITE AND GREEN PARTS)

CHOPPED ROASTED PEANUTS FOR GARNISHING

LIME WEDGES FOR GARNISHING

PHRIK PON (PAGE 192) FOR GARNISHING

1

TO MAKE THE SAUCE: IN A MEDIUM SAUCEPAN OR WOK OVER MEDIUM-HIGH HEAT, COMBINE THE PALM SUGAR, GRANULATED SUGAR, WATER, FISH SAUCE, AND NAM MAKHAM PIAK AND COOK, STIRRING OCCASIONALLY, UNTIL THE SUGARS HAVE DISSOLVED, ABOUT 10 MINUTES.

2

TURN THE HEAT TO MEDIUM AND ADD THE HOM JIEW. STIR OCCASIONALLY UNTIL THE SAUCE HAS THICKENED, ABOUT 15 MINUTES MORE. REMOVE FROM THE HEAT AND SET ASIDE.

CHEF MALLIKA SAYS:

THIS RECIPE MAKES ENOUGH PAD THAI SAUCE FOR FOUR SERVINGS. LEFTOVER SAUCE CAN BE STORED IN AN AIRTIGHT CONTAINER IN THE FRIDGE FOR UP TO 2 WEEKS.

3

IN A LARGE WOK OVER MEDIUM-HIGH HEAT, WARM THE NEUTRAL OIL. ADD THE COLOSSAL SHRIMP TO THE WOK AND COOK UNTIL BROWNED, 1 TO 2 MINUTES. REMOVE THE SHRIMP FROM THE PAN AND SET ASIDE.

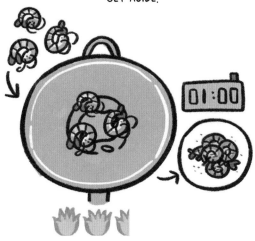

4

IN THE SAME WOK, COMBINE THE TOFU, PRESERVED SWEET RADISH (IF USING), AND DRIED SHRIMP (IF USING).

COOK OVER MEDIUM-HIGH HEAT UNTIL GOLDEN, 1 TO 2 MINUTES.

5

ADD THE DRAINED RICE NOODLES AND ½ CUP OF THE SAUCE TO THE WOK. MIX UNTIL WELL INCORPORATED AND THE NOODLES BECOME SOFT, ABOUT 3 MINUTES. PUSH THE NOODLES TO ONE SIDE OF THE PAN TO MAKE ROOM FOR THE EGGS.

6

CRACK THE EGGS STRAIGHT ONTO THE EMPTY SIDE OF THE WOK. LIGHTLY STIR TO BREAK THE YOLKS AND COMBINE WITH THE WHITES, BUT AVOID SCRAMBLING.

WHEN THE WHITES FIRM UP, ABOUT 1 MINUTE, FLIP THE EGGS TO COOK THE OTHER SIDE, ABOUT 30 SECONDS MORE.

7

PUSH THE NOODLES OVER THE EGGS AND WAIT A FEW SECONDS BEFORE GENTLY MIXING TOGETHER.

ADD THE BEAN SPROUTS, GARLIC CHIVES, AND COOKED SHRIMP TO THE WOK. MIX WELL TO INCORPORATE ALL THE COMPONENTS AND THEN REMOVE FROM THE HEAT.

8

GARNISH THE PAD THAI WITH PEANUTS, LIME WEDGES, AND PHRIK PON AND SERVE IMMEDIATELY.

PAD SEE EW

PAD SEE EW TRANSLATES AS "STIR-FRIED NOODLES WITH SOY SAUCE." COLLARD GREENS ARE A KEY PLAYER IN PAD SEE EW, BUT EVERYONE KNOWS THAT THE REAL SUPERSTARS OF THIS DISH ARE THE WIDE, SILKY-SMOOTH NOODLES! THIS IS THE BIGGEST DIFFERENCE BETWEEN PAD SEE EW AND PAD THAI, ITS STIR-FRIED SIBLING WITH THE THINNER RICE NOODLES. THANKS TO THE SOY SAUCE AND OYSTER SAUCE, PAD SEE EW HAS A DEEPER FLAVOR--AND COLOR! THE CRUNCHY COLLARD GREENS AND EGG ARE A MUST TO ROUND OUT THE OVERALL FLAVOR. IF YOU ARE NOT A BIG FAN OF SPICINESS, THIS DISH IS IDEAL FOR YOU. BUT IF YOU *DO* LOVE CHILES, YOU CAN ALWAYS UP THE ANTE WITH OUR GOOD OL' SEASONING SET.

MAKES 2 SERVINGS

1 TABLESPOON PLUS 1/2 TEASPOON GRANULATED SUGAR

2 TABLESPOONS SEASONING SOY SAUCE

8 OUNCES PORK COLLAR OR PORK TENDERLOIN, THINLY SLICED

8 OUNCES RICE FLAKE NOODLES (PREFERABLY 1-INCH SIZE) OR RICE STICK NOODLES (PREFERABLY 10MM SIZE), SOAKED IN ROOM-TEMPERATURE WATER FOR 1 HOUR AND DRAINED

1 1/2 TEASPOONS BLACK SOY SAUCE

3 TABLESPOONS NEUTRAL OIL

4 GARLIC CLOVES, COARSELY CRUSHED

2 EGGS

1 TABLESPOON BLACK SWEET SOY SAUCE

1 TABLESPOON OYSTER SAUCE

3 CUPS LOOSELY PACKED COLLARD GREENS OR KALE, CUT INTO 2-INCH RIBBONS, STEMS DISCARDED

PHRIK NAM SOM (PAGE 186), TO TASTE

FISH SAUCE, TO TASTE

GRANULATED SUGAR, TO TASTE

PHRIK PON (PAGE 192), TO TASTE

1

IN A LARGE BOWL, COMBINE 1/2 TEASPOON OF THE SUGAR AND 1 TABLESPOON OF THE SEASONING SOY SAUCE AND STIR TO FORM A MARINADE. ADD THE PORK AND, USING YOUR HANDS, EVENLY COAT WITH THE MARINADE. LET MARINATE AT ROOM TEMPERATURE FOR 30 MINUTES.

2

IN A SMALL SAUCEPAN OVER HIGH HEAT, BRING 4 CUPS OF WATER TO A BOIL. WHEN THE WATER IS BOILING, PLACE THE SOAKED NOODLES ON A SKIMMER AND DIP IT IN THE BOILING WATER FOR ABOUT 10 SECONDS, USING TONGS OR CHOPSTICKS TO KEEP THE NOODLES FROM FLOATING OFF.

3

RAISE THE SKIMMER OVER THE POT TO DRAIN, THEN QUICKLY RINSE THE NOODLES WITH ROOM-TEMPERATURE WATER AND TRANSFER TO A LARGE BOWL.

4

EVENLY COAT THE HALF-COOKED NOODLES WITH THE BLACK SOY SAUCE AND SET ASIDE.

5

IN A LARGE WOK OVER MEDIUM-HIGH HEAT, WARM THE OIL.

6

ADD THE GARLIC TO THE WOK AND COOK FOR SEVERAL SECONDS, OR UNTIL THE GARLIC TURNS GOLDEN.

7

ADD THE MARINATED PORK TO THE WOK AND COOK UNTIL BROWNED, ABOUT 1 MINUTE. PUSH THE PORK TO ONE SIDE OF THE PAN.

8

CRACK THE EGGS STRAIGHT ONTO THE EMPTY SIDE OF THE WOK. LIGHTLY STIR TO BREAK THE YOLKS AND COMBINE WITH THE WHITES, BUT AVOID SCRAMBLING.

9

WHEN THE WHITES FIRM UP, ABOUT 1 MINUTE, PUSH THE PORK ON TOP OF THE EGGS AND WAIT FOR A FEW SECONDS BEFORE GENTLY MIXING TOGETHER.

10

ADD THE MARINATED NOODLES, REMAINING 1 TABLESPOON SUGAR, REMAINING 1 TABLESPOON SEASONING SOY SAUCE, THE BLACK SWEET SOY SAUCE, AND OYSTER SAUCE TO THE WOK. MIX WELL UNTIL INCORPORATED AND THE NOODLES BECOME SOFT, ABOUT 2 MINUTES.

11

TURN THE HEAT TO HIGH. ADD THE COLLARD GREENS TO THE WOK, MIX WELL TO INCORPORATE, AND THEN REMOVE FROM THE HEAT AT ONCE.

12

SERVE THE NOODLES WITH THE SEASONING SET.

YUM!

PAD KHEE MAO

MAKES 2 SERVINGS

THIS DISH WAS INVENTED BY SOME DRUNK GUY (PAD KHEE MAO LITERALLY MEANS "DRUNKARD'S STIR-FRY") WHO CAME HOME HUNGRY LATE ONE NIGHT, THREW TOGETHER WHATEVER INGREDIENTS HE HAD LEFT IN THE FRIDGE, AND ACCIDENTALLY CREATED THE PERFECT RECIPE. PAD KHEE MAO IS KNOWN AS A (VERY!) FIERY STIR-FRIED NOODLE DISH BECAUSE OF THE COMBINATION OF A WHOLE BUNCH OF THAI CHILES AND SPICY BASIL LEAVES. YOU MIGHT EVEN GET DRUNK FROM ALL THE HEAT CIRCULATING INSIDE--NO JOKE! BUT HAVE NO FEAR: TO PERFECTLY BALANCE THE HEAT, YOU'LL ALSO GET A NICE HINT OF FINGERROOT AND MAKRUT LIME LEAVES. NEXT TIME YOU GET THE MUNCHIES, PAD KHEE MAO IS THE PERFECT DISH TO MAKE FOR YOURSELF-- IF YOU'RE BRAVE ENOUGH!

- 1 TABLESPOON PLUS ½ TEASPOON GRANULATED SUGAR
- 3 TABLESPOONS SEASONING SOY SAUCE
- 8 OUNCES BEEF SIRLOIN OR FLANK STEAK, THINLY SLICED
- 8 OUNCES THIN RICE STICK NOODLES (PREFERABLY 3MM SIZE), SOAKED IN ROOM-TEMPERATURE WATER FOR 1 HOUR AND DRAINED, OR INSTANT NOODLES
- 1½ TEASPOONS BLACK SOY SAUCE
- 6 FRESH RED THAI CHILES (OR ADJUST TO TASTE), STEMMED
- 4 GARLIC CLOVES
- 1 TEASPOON SHRIMP PASTE
- 3 TABLESPOONS NEUTRAL OIL
- 2 TABLESPOONS OYSTER SAUCE
- 2 CUPS LOOSELY PACKED 2-INCH-RIBBONS COLLARD GREENS OR KALE, STEMS DISCARDED
- 1 CUP LOOSELY PACKED JULIENNED CARROTS
- 4 BUNCHES FRESH GREEN PEPPERCORNS
- 8 MAKRUT LIME LEAVES, STEMMED
- 2 CUPS LOOSELY PACKED HOLY BASIL OR SWEET BASIL LEAVES

1

IN A LARGE BOWL, COMBINE ½ TEASPOON OF THE SUGAR AND 1 TABLESPOON OF THE SEASONING SOY SAUCE AND STIR TO FORM A MARINADE. ADD THE BEEF AND, USING YOUR HANDS, EVENLY COAT IN THE MARINADE. FOR BEST RESULTS, LET THE BEEF MARINATE AT ROOM TEMPERATURE FOR 30 MINUTES.

2

IN ANOTHER LARGE BOWL, COMBINE THE NOODLES AND BLACK SOY SAUCE AND STIR TO EVENLY COAT. SET ASIDE AT ROOM TEMPERATURE.

3

IN A MORTAR AND USING A PESTLE, COMBINE THE CHILES, GARLIC, AND SHRIMP PASTE AND POUND INTO A FINE PASTE. SET ASIDE.

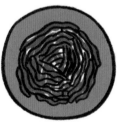

CHEF MALLIKA SAYS:

IF YOU'RE USING INSTANT NOODLES, BOIL THE NOODLES FOR 1 MINUTE ONLY. DO NOT OVERCOOK, OTHERWISE THE NOODLES BECOME MUSHY WHEN STIR-FRYING.

4

IN A LARGE WOK OVER MEDIUM-HIGH HEAT, WARM THE OIL. ADD THE PASTE TO THE WOK AND COOK UNTIL IT TURNS GOLDEN, SEVERAL SECONDS.

5

ADD THE MARINATED BEEF TO THE WOK AND STIR-FRY UNTIL BROWNED, ABOUT 1 MINUTE.

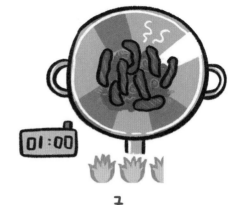

6

ADD THE MARINATED NOODLES, REMAINING 1 TABLESPOON SUGAR, REMAINING 1 TABLESPOON SEASONING SOY SAUCE, AND OYSTER SAUCE TO THE WOK AND MIX WELL.

7

TURN THE HEAT TO HIGH. IMMEDIATELY ADD THE COLLARD GREENS, CARROTS, AND GREEN PEPPERCORNS TO THE WOK. MIX WELL UNTIL INCORPORATED AND THE NOODLES BECOME SOFT, 2 TO 3 MINUTES.

8

IMMEDIATELY ADD THE MAKRUT AND HOLY BASIL TO THE WOK, MIX UNTIL INCORPORATED, AND THEN REMOVE FROM THE HEAT AT ONCE.

9

SERVE THE NOODLES IMMEDIATELY.

PHET!

*SPICY!

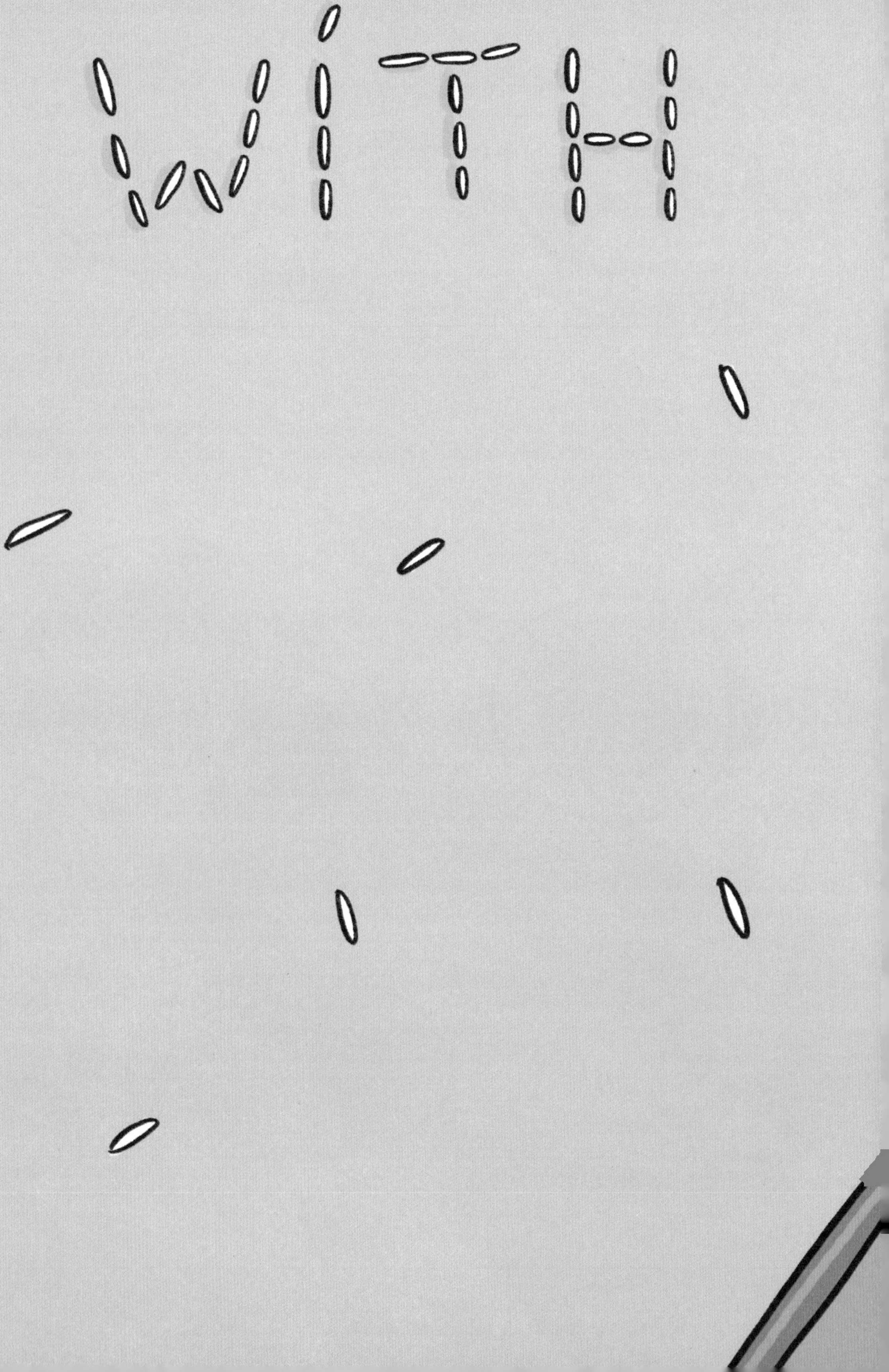
WITH

RICE

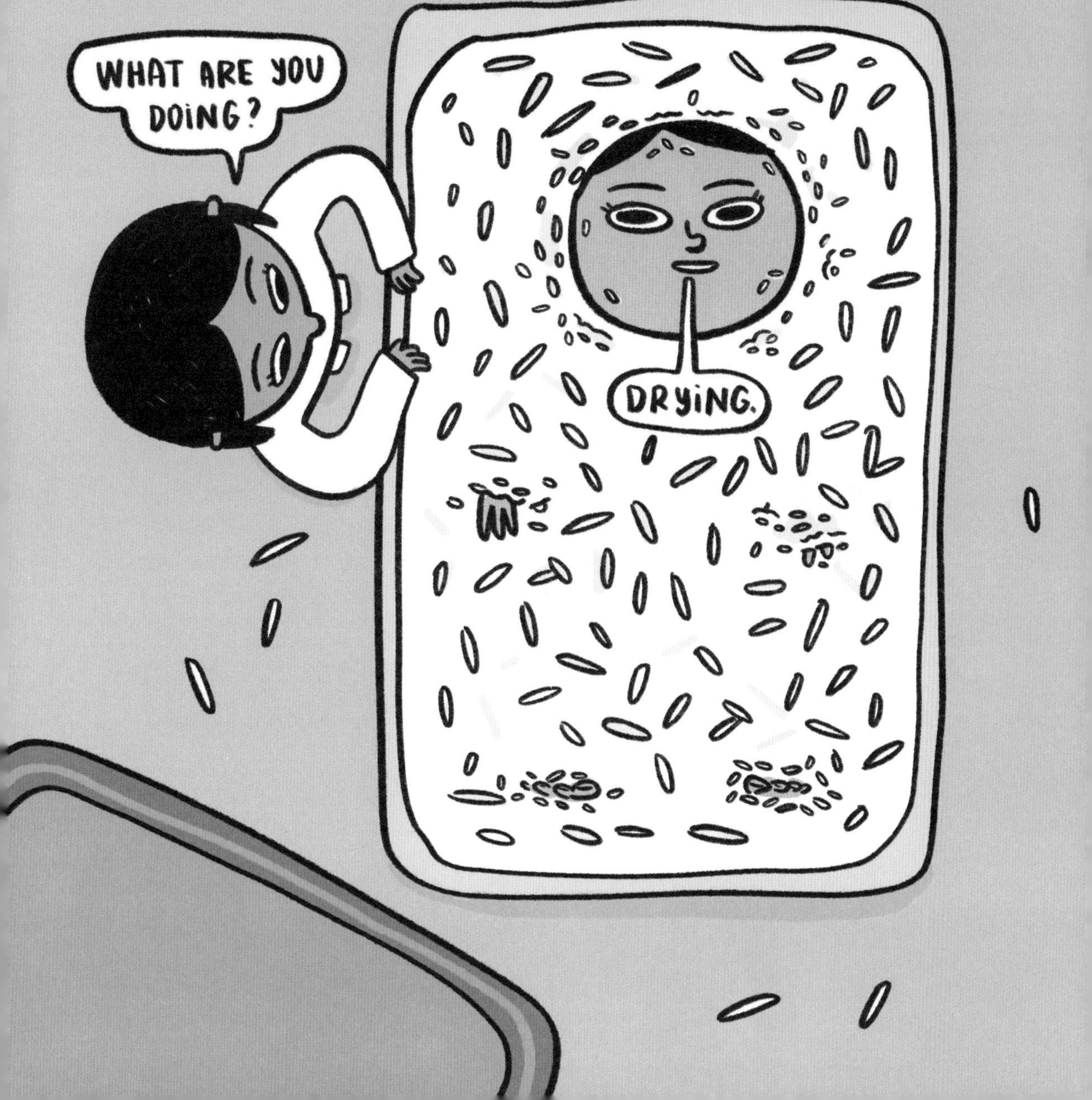

TO THAI PEOPLE, RICE REPRESENTS MORE THAN A LITTLE WHITE GRAIN;
IT'S DEEPLY INTERTWINED WITH THE CULTURE, LANGUAGE, TRADITION, AND DAILY LIFE.
AS THAILAND'S NUMBER-ONE EXPORT PRODUCT (THERE ARE THOUSANDS OF
RICE VARIETIES!), RICE MIGHT HAVE MORE SOCIOECONOMIC VALUE THAN GOLD.

A MEAL IS NEVER REALLY COMPLETE
WITHOUT RICE--EVEN THE VERB
KIN KHAO USED FOR "TO EAT"
DIRECTLY TRANSLATES TO
"EAT RICE."

THAI KIDS ARE TAUGHT IN SCHOOL TO FINISH EVERY
SINGLE GRAIN ON THEIR PLATES, SO THEY DON'T WASTE
ANY RICE. EACH GRAIN IS EVEN BELIEVED TO HAVE
ITS OWN LIFE AND SOUL, SO IT'S FAIR TO SAY IT'S
CONSIDERED MORE THAN JUST A STAPLE FOOD.

IN THIS CHAPTER, WE SHARE SOME ALL-TIME FAVORITE RICE DISHES, GATHERED FROM ALL FOUR REGIONS OF THAILAND. FIRE UP THAT RICE COOKER BECAUSE YOU'RE ABOUT TO DISCOVER SOME EXCITING NEW DISHES TO PAIR WITH RICE!

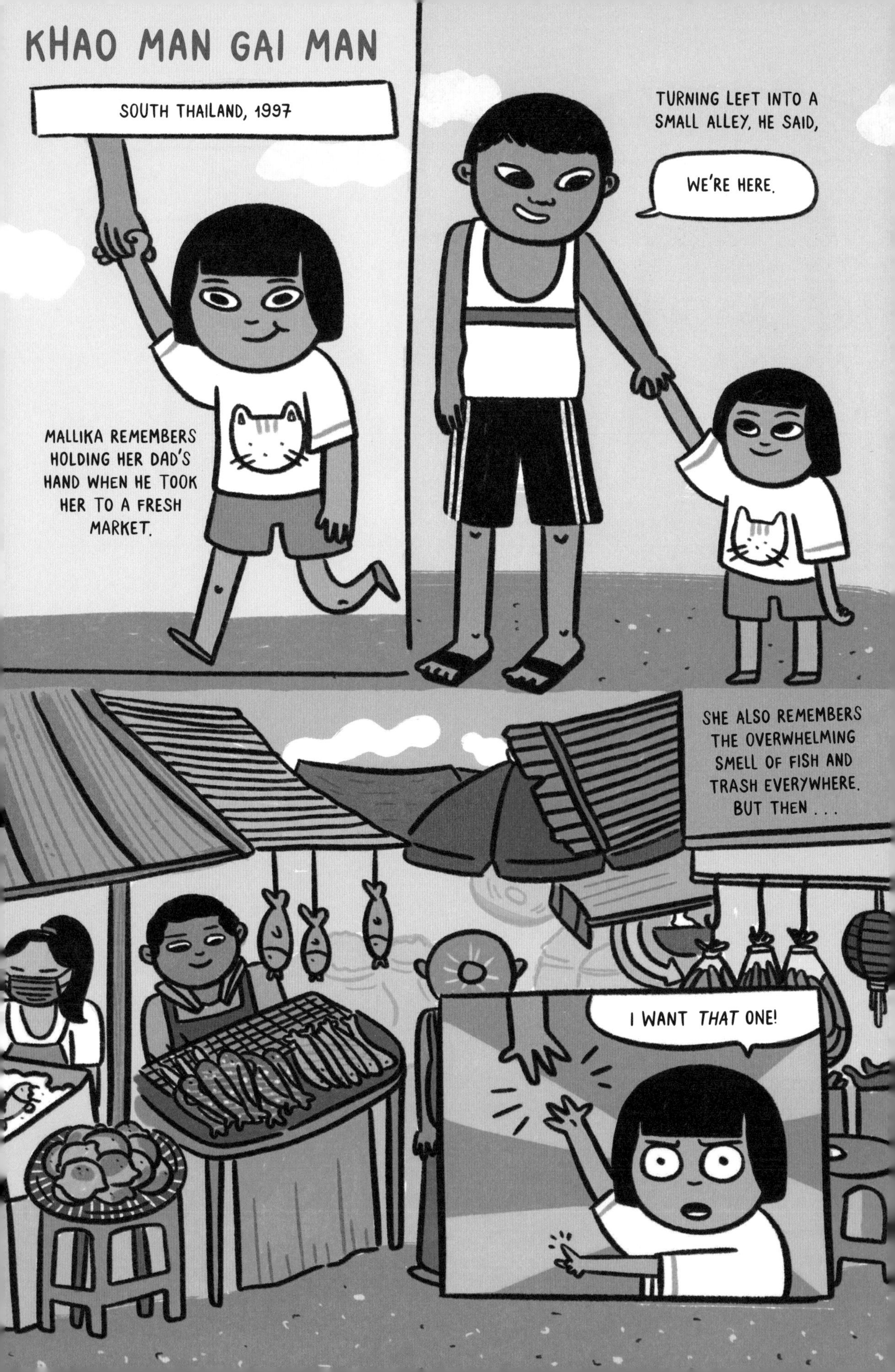
KHAO MAN GAI MAN
SOUTH THAILAND, 1997
MALLIKA REMEMBERS HOLDING HER DAD'S HAND WHEN HE TOOK HER TO A FRESH MARKET.
TURNING LEFT INTO A SMALL ALLEY, HE SAID,
WE'RE HERE.
SHE ALSO REMEMBERS THE OVERWHELMING SMELL OF FISH AND TRASH EVERYWHERE. BUT THEN . . .
I WANT THAT ONE!

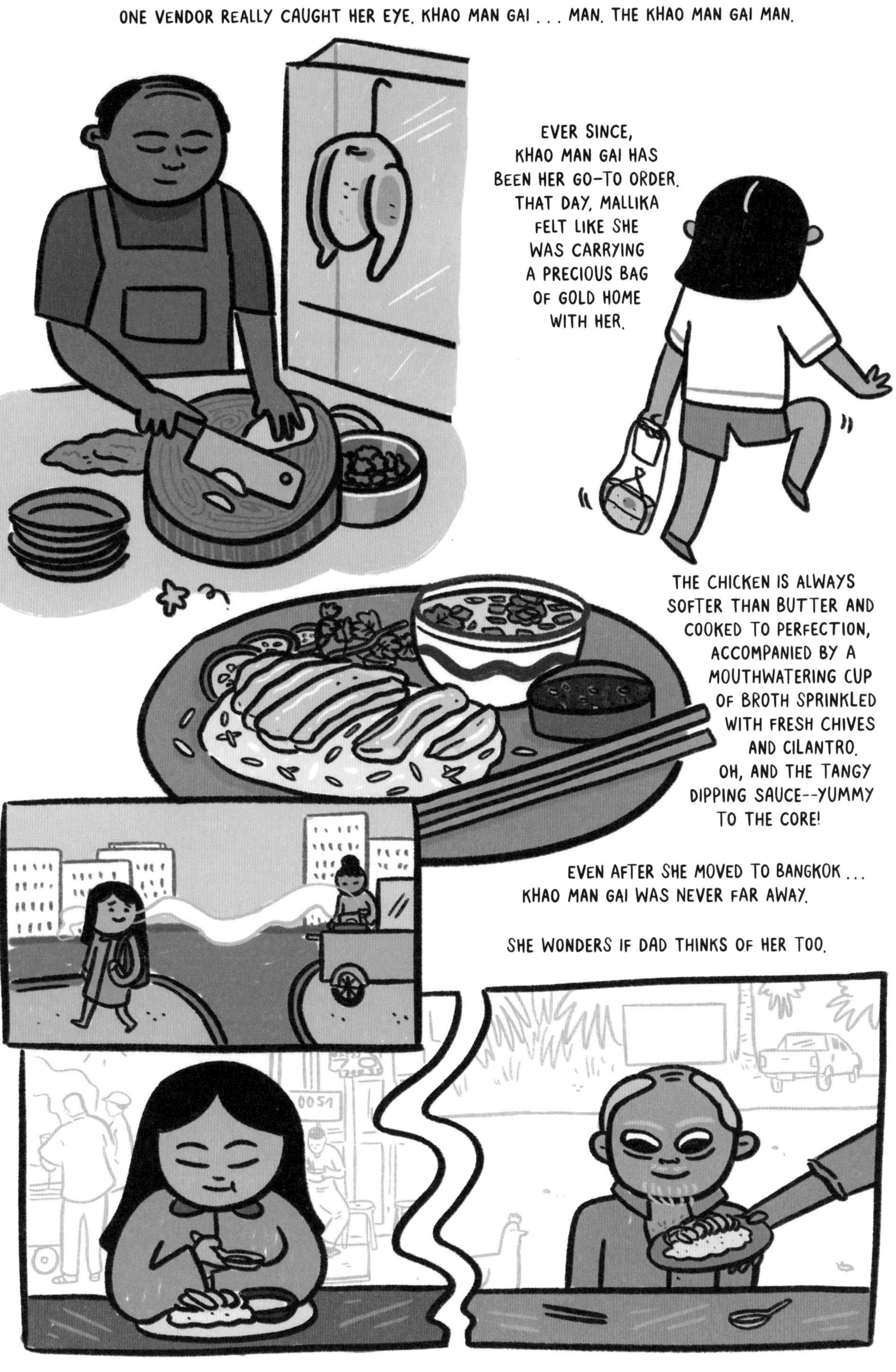
ONE VENDOR REALLY CAUGHT HER EYE. KHAO MAN GAI . . . MAN. THE KHAO MAN GAI MAN.
EVER SINCE, KHAO MAN GAI HAS BEEN HER GO-TO ORDER. THAT DAY, MALLIKA FELT LIKE SHE WAS CARRYING A PRECIOUS BAG OF GOLD HOME WITH HER.
THE CHICKEN IS ALWAYS SOFTER THAN BUTTER AND COOKED TO PERFECTION, ACCOMPANIED BY A MOUTHWATERING CUP OF BROTH SPRINKLED WITH FRESH CHIVES AND CILANTRO. OH, AND THE TANGY DIPPING SAUCE--YUMMY TO THE CORE!
EVEN AFTER SHE MOVED TO BANGKOK . . . KHAO MAN GAI WAS NEVER FAR AWAY.
SHE WONDERS IF DAD THINKS OF HER TOO.
0051

KHAO MAN GAI

KHAO MAN GAI, MOIST BOILED CHICKEN WITH OILY RICE, IS A DISH SERVED WITH
A SPECIAL TANGY SAUCE AND CLEAR BROTH ON THE SIDE. IT IS ONE OF THE MOST
POPULAR STREET-VENDOR FOODS. HEAVILY INFLUENCED BY HAINANESE CHICKEN,
THIS THAI VERSION IS ABSOLUTELY MICHELIN-STAR WORTHY. YOU CAN'T REALLY
WALK AROUND BANGKOK WITHOUT SMELLING THE AROMATIC BROTH BREWING
EVERYWHERE. THE SPECIAL DIPPING SAUCE CONSISTS OF SWEET AND SALTY SOY
MIXED WITH CHILE SLICES AND GINGER, WHICH MAKES OR BREAKS YOUR KHAO MAN
GAI. ALTHOUGH THIS DISH REQUIRES SEVERAL STEPS, IT'S VERY EASY OVERALL.
CAN'T DECIDE WHAT TO HAVE FOR DINNER, BUT YOU DO HAVE PLENTY OF TIME?
KHAO MAN GAI WILL NEVER--AND YOU HAVE OUR WORD FOR IT--DISAPPOINT.

MAKES 4 SERVINGS

KHAO MAN GAI SAUCE

3 TABLESPOONS SOYBEAN PASTE

3 TABLESPOONS BLACK SWEET SOY SAUCE

1 1/2 TABLESPOONS DISTILLED WHITE VINEGAR

1 TABLESPOON PACKED GRATED PALM SUGAR
(ABOUT 1/4 PIECE) OR GRANULATED SUGAR

1 TEASPOON FRESH LIME JUICE

4-INCH PIECE FRESH GINGER, PEELED
AND MINCED

3 GARLIC CLOVES, MINCED

5 FRESH RED THAI CHILES (OR ADJUST
TO TASTE), STEMMED AND THINLY SLICED

10 CUPS WATER

1 FRESH OR FROZEN (THAWED) PANDAN LEAF,
TIED IN A KNOT (OPTIONAL)

3 CILANTRO ROOTS, LIGHTLY CRUSHED

2-INCH PIECE FRESH GINGER, PEELED AND
THINLY SLICED ON THE DIAGONAL

2 POUNDS BONE-IN, SKIN-ON CHICKEN THIGHS

OILY RICE

5 TABLESPOONS NEUTRAL OIL

4-INCH PIECE FRESH GINGER, PEELED AND SLICED

5 GARLIC CLOVES, CRUSHED

2 CUPS JASMINE RICE, RINSED WITH WATER
AND DRAINED

1 TEASPOON GRANULATED SUGAR

3 TABLESPOONS THIN SOY SAUCE

PANDAN LEAF (RESERVED FROM COOKING
THE CHICKEN; OPTIONAL)

2 CUPS CHICKEN STOCK (RESERVED FROM
COOKING THE CHICKEN)

SIDE SOUP

CHICKEN STOCK (RESERVED FROM
COOKING THE CHICKEN)

1 CUP PEELED, SEEDED, AND CUBED
THAI WINTER MELON OR DAIKON RADISH
(OPTIONAL)

1 TEASPOON FINE SEA SALT

1 TEASPOON GRANULATED SUGAR

3 TABLESPOONS THIN SOY SAUCE

CUCUMBER SLICES FOR GARNISHING

CILANTRO LEAVES FOR GARNISHING

CHOPPED CHIVES OR GREEN ONIONS
(GREEN PARTS ONLY) FOR GARNISHING

FRESHLY GROUND WHITE PEPPER (OPTIONAL)

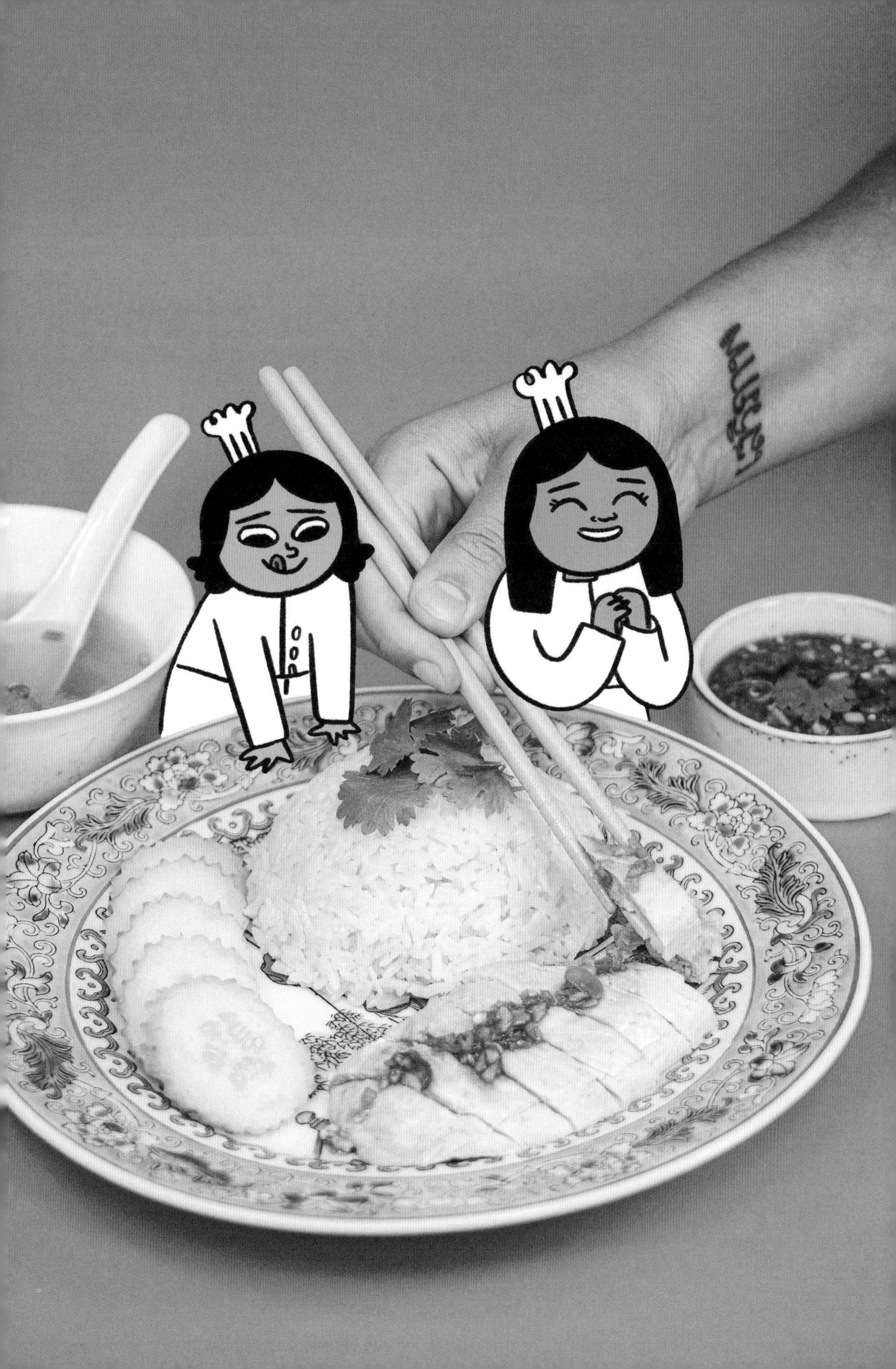

1

TO MAKE THE KHAO MAN GAI SAUCE:
IN A SMALL BOWL, COMBINE THE SOYBEAN
PASTE, BLACK SWEET SOY SAUCE, VINEGAR,
SUGAR, LIME JUICE, GINGER, GARLIC, AND
THAI CHILES. MIX WELL AND SET ASIDE.

2

IN A MEDIUM SAUCEPAN OR WOK OVER
HIGH HEAT, COMBINE THE WATER,
PANDAN LEAF (IF USING), CILANTRO ROOTS,
AND GINGER AND BRING TO A BOIL.

3

ADD THE CHICKEN THIGHS TO THE SAUCEPAN, BUT DO NOT
STIR. IMMEDIATELY TURN THE HEAT TO MEDIUM AND LET
SIMMER FOR 30 TO 40 MINUTES. LEAVING IT TO COOK GENTLY,
UNDISTURBED AND UNCOVERED, HELPS KEEP THE SOUP CLEAR.

4

USING A SPOON OR A SKIMMER,
OCCASIONALLY REMOVE THE FAT FROM
THE SURFACE OF THE SOUP.

5

WHEN THE CHICKEN THIGHS ARE COOKED THROUGH
(THE MEAT SHOULD BE WHITE WHEN CUT WITH A PARING
KNIFE), TRANSFER TO A LARGE BOWL OF COLD WATER
AND LEAVE FOR 2 MINUTES. (THIS IS AN IMPORTANT STEP
BECAUSE IT PREVENTS THE CHICKEN FROM CONTINUING
TO COOK AND BECOMING CRUMBLY OR DRY.)

THE CHICKEN WILL REMAIN FIRM
AND MOIST AFTER SOAKING. STRAIN
THE CHICKEN STOCK, RESERVING
THE PANDAN LEAF (IF DESIRED), AND
SET ASIDE.

CHEF MALLIKA SAYS:

YOU CAN BUY DELICIOUS PREMADE VERSIONS FOR MOST OF THE KHAO MAN GAI COMPONENTS,
ESPECIALLY THE DIPPING SAUCE (WE RECOMMEND LOBO BRAND).

TO ACHIEVE THE RESTAURANT-STYLE, STAR-SHAPE CUCUMBER SLICES, USE THE ZIG-ZAG
VEGETABLE PEELER ON THE OUTSIDE OF THE CUCUMBER AND SLICE ON THE DIAGONAL INTO
1/8-INCH PIECES.

TO MAKE SURE YOUR CHICKEN IS LOOKING JUICY, BRUSH WITH OIL BEFORE SERVING.

6

TO MAKE THE OILY RICE: IN A LARGE WOK OVER MEDIUM-HIGH HEAT, WARM THE OIL. ADD THE GINGER AND GARLIC AND COOK UNTIL THEY TURN YELLOW, 1 TO 2 MINUTES.

7

ADD THE RICE TO THE WOK, THEN ADD THE SUGAR AND THIN SOY SAUCE AND COOK, STIRRING FREQUENTLY, FOR 5 MINUTES.

8

POUR THE 2 CUPS CHICKEN STOCK OVER THE RICE, AND ADD THE PANDAN LEAF (IF USING). TURN THE HEAT TO HIGH, BRING TO A BOIL, AND THEN TURN THE HEAT TO MEDIUM. COVER WITH A LID AND COOK FOR 10 MINUTES.

9

LIFT THE LID, FLUFF THE RICE WITH A SPOON, AND THEN RE-COVER FOR 5 MINUTES MORE. REMOVE THE POT FROM THE HEAT AND LET THE RICE REST, COVERED, FOR 10 MINUTES.

10

IF USING A REGULAR RICE COOKER, UNPLUG AS SOON AS THE COOKING IS FINISHED, FLUFF THE RICE, AND LET IT REST FOR 10 MINUTES.

11

TO MAKE THE SIDE SOUP: PLACE THE REMAINING CHICKEN STOCK OVER MEDIUM HEAT. ADD THE WINTER MELON (IF USING), SALT, SUGAR, AND THIN SOY SAUCE TO THE STOCK AND COOK FOR 20 MINUTES. (IF OMITTING THE WINTER MELON, THE SOUP NEEDS ONLY 5 MINUTES.)

12

ONCE THE WINTER MELON IS COOKED (IT WILL BE TRANSPARENT), TURN THE HEAT TO THE LOWEST SETTING TO KEEP THE SOUP WARM UNTIL THE REST OF THE MEAL IS READY.

13

PLACE THE CHICKEN THIGHS ON A CUTTING BOARD AND, USING YOUR HANDS AND A KNIFE, SEPARATE THE MEAT FROM THE BONES. YOU CAN EITHER KEEP OR REMOVE THE SKIN.

14

WITH THE SKIN SIDE UP, PRESS THE CHICKEN WITH THE KNIFE TO FLATTEN IT AND CUT INTO 1/2-INCH-THICK STRIPS. SET ASIDE.

15

SCOOP SOME OF THE RICE INTO A SMALL BOWL AND INVERT A SERVING PLATE ON TOP OF IT. FLIP EVERYTHING UPSIDE DOWN AND REMOVE THE BOWL. REPEAT UNTIL EACH SERVING PLATE HAS A PORTION OF RICE.

16

ADD THE CHICKEN TO THE RICE AND GARNISH WITH CUCUMBER SLICES AND CILANTRO. DIVIDE THE SAUCE AMONG DIPPING-SAUCE BOWLS.

17

DIVIDE THE SOUP AMONG SMALL BOWLS AND GARNISH WITH CILANTRO, CHIVES, AND GROUND WHITE PEPPER (IF DESIRED). SERVE THE KHAO MAN GAI PAIRED WITH THE SOUP AND SAUCE.

PAD PHAK BUNG

PAD PHAK BUNG IS A POPULAR STIR-FRY DISH USING WATER SPINACH (ALSO KNOWN AS SWAMP MORNING GLORY). IT'S COOKED QUICKLY OVER VERY HIGH HEAT, OFTEN RESULTING IN A BIG, SUDDEN OPEN FLAME LIKE THE ONES YOU SEE IN MOVIES, RESTAURANTS, AND MOVIES ABOUT RESTAURANTS. BECAUSE OF THIS, THAI PEOPLE CALL IT *PAD PHAK BUNG FAI DAENG*, WHICH LITERALLY TRANSLATES TO "STIR-FRIED WATER SPINACH RED FLAME"! THE HEAT SOFTENS THE WATER SPINACH AND RELEASES MOISTURE TO BLEND WITH THE SALTY SOYBEAN PASTE AND SWEET OYSTER SAUCE. THIS VIBRANTLY COLORED, HEALTHFUL VEGETABLE DISH CAN BE MADE AND SERVED IN MINUTES AS THE PERFECT COMPANION TO JASMINE RICE.

MAKES 2 SERVINGS

5 CUPS LOOSELY PACKED WATER SPINACH, CUT INTO 2-INCH PIECES

6 FRESH RED THAI CHILES (OR ADJUST TO TASTE), STEMMED AND CRUSHED

6 GARLIC CLOVES, CRUSHED

2¼ TEASPOONS GRANULATED SUGAR

1 TABLESPOON SOYBEAN PASTE

1 TABLESPOON SEASONING SOY SAUCE

1 TABLESPOON OYSTER SAUCE

3 TABLESPOONS NEUTRAL OIL

GRATHIAM JIEW (PAGE 188) FOR TOPPING (OPTIONAL)

KHAO SUAY (PAGE 170) FOR SERVING

1

PUT THE WATER SPINACH IN A LARGE BOWL AND TOP WITH THE CHILES, GARLIC, SUGAR, SOYBEAN PASTE, SEASONING SOY SAUCE, AND OYSTER SAUCE.

2

IN A LARGE WOK OVER HIGH HEAT, WARM THE NEUTRAL OIL UNTIL LIGHTLY SMOKING.

THEN POUR THE CONTENTS OF THE BOWL INTO THE WOK AND STIR QUICKLY AND CONSTANTLY FOR ABOUT 1 MINUTE.

3

THE DISH IS READY WHEN THE WATER SPINACH HAS SOFTENED AND THERE IS MORE SAUCE FROM THE MOISTURE RELEASED. REMOVE FROM THE HEAT AT ONCE AND TRANSFER TO A PLATE.

4

TOP THE WATER SPINACH WITH GRATHIAM JIEW (IF DESIRED), AND SERVE IMMEDIATELY WITH KHAO SUAY.

PAD GAPRAO

OFTEN MADE WITH GROUND PORK OR CHICKEN, BUT LOVED EQUALLY WITH OTHER PROTEINS SUCH AS BEEF, FISH, TOFU, AND SHRIMP, STIR-FRIED HOLY BASIL HAS BECOME ONE OF THE MOST COMMON DAY-TO-DAY DISHES IN THAILAND. THIS SIMPLE DISH ORIGINATES FROM CENTRAL THAILAND, BUT IT HAS BEEN ELEVATED TO A NATIONAL TREASURE. BRINGING BOTH THE HEAT AND HERBY FRESHNESS, PAD GAPRAO IS THE PERFECT ADDITION TO YOUR WEEKNIGHT DINNER ROTATION. DON'T FORGET THE SIGNATURE TOUCH: A PERFECTLY FRIED EGG ON TOP!

MAKES 2 SERVINGS

6 FRESH RED THAI CHILES (OR ADJUST TO TASTE), STEMMED

5 SMALL DRIED THAI CHILES (OR ADJUST TO TASTE), STEMMED (OPTIONAL)

6 GARLIC CLOVES

3 TABLESPOONS NEUTRAL OIL

1 POUND GROUND PORK OR THINLY SLICED CHICKEN BREAST

1 TABLESPOON GRANULATED SUGAR

2 TABLESPOONS OYSTER SAUCE

2 TABLESPOONS SEASONING SOY SAUCE

1½ TEASPOONS BLACK SOY SAUCE

1½ TEASPOONS FISH SAUCE

2 CUPS LOOSELY PACKED HOLY BASIL LEAVES OR SWEET BASIL LEAVES

KHAI DAO (PAGE 178) FOR GARNISHING

KHAO SUAY (PAGE 170) FOR SERVING

CUCUMBER SLICES FOR SERVING

PHRIK NAM PLA (PAGE 185) FOR SERVING

1

IN A MORTAR AND USING THE PESTLE, COMBINE THE FRESH CHILES, DRIED CHILES (IF USING), AND GARLIC AND POUND INTO A PASTE. SET ASIDE.

2

IN A LARGE WOK OVER MEDIUM-HIGH HEAT, WARM THE OIL.

3

ADD THE PASTE TO THE WOK AND
COOK FOR SEVERAL SECONDS,
UNTIL THE PASTE TURNS GOLDEN.

4

ADD THE GROUND PORK TO THE WOK AND IMMEDIATELY
USE A SPATULA TO BREAK UP THE MEAT INTO
SMALLER PIECES. COOK UNTIL BROWNED, ABOUT
1 MINUTE, BEING CAREFUL NOT TO OVERCOOK.

5

TURN THE HEAT TO MEDIUM. ADD THE SUGAR,
OYSTER SAUCE, SEASONING SOY SAUCE,
BLACK SOY SAUCE, AND FISH SAUCE TO
THE WOK AND MIX UNTIL INCORPORATED.

6

TURN THE HEAT TO HIGH. ADD THE
HOLY BASIL LEAVES TO THE WOK AND
MIX IN. REMOVE FROM THE HEAT.

7

GARNISH THE PORK WITH KHAI DAO
AND SERVE WITH KHAO SUAY, CUCUMBER
SLICES, AND PHRIK NAM PLA ALONGSIDE.

ICONIC!

PAD SATOR

SATOR, OFTEN CALLED "BITTER BEANS" OR "STINK BEANS," HAVE A VERY STRONG TASTE AND AROMA THAT IS SWEET, BITTER, AND LIGHTLY NUTTY. ORIGINATING FROM THE SOUTH, IT'S ALMOST AS IF IT'S ONLY *REALLY* GOOD WHEN A SOUTHERN THAI PERSON PREPARES IT . . . BUT LUCKY FOR YOU, THIS RECIPE IS A FIRST-HAND SOURCE. SPICE LOVERS, TAKE NOTE OF THE HIGH COUNT OF CHILES--THIS ONE CAN BE CHALLENGING! THE HEAT IS BALANCED WITH SWEET, SALTY, AND SMOKY FLAVORS FOR A FULL-BODIED PUNCH. DON'T BE DISCOURAGED BY THE UNSAVORY NAME. STIR-FRIED STINK BEANS ARE A PROUD REGIONAL FAVORITE FOR A REASON!

MAKES 2 SERVINGS

4 OUNCES PEELED BITTER BEANS, HALVED, SOAKED IN COLD WATER FOR 15 MINUTES, AND DRAINED

8 FRESH RED THAI CHILES (OR ADJUST TO TASTE), STEMMED

4 GARLIC CLOVES

1 SMALL RED SHALLOT, OR 1/4 MEDIUM RED ONION, COARSELY CHOPPED

1 1/2 TEASPOONS SHRIMP PASTE

3 TABLESPOONS NEUTRAL OIL

8 OUNCES GROUND PORK

1 TABLESPOON GRANULATED SUGAR

2 TABLESPOONS OYSTER SAUCE

1 TABLESPOON SEASONING SOY SAUCE

1 1/2 TEASPOONS FISH SAUCE

8 OUNCES JUMBO (21/25) WHITE SHRIMP WITH TAILS, PEELED AND DEVEINED

KHAO SUAY (PAGE 172) FOR SERVING

CUCUMBER SLICES FOR SERVING

1

IF YOU BUY BITTER BEANS IN THE PODS, USE A KNIFE TO MAKE A SLIT AROUND THE IMPRINT OF EACH BEAN, FOLD OVER THE SKIN, AND REMOVE THE BEAN.

2

IN A MEDIUM BOWL, SOAK THE PEELED BITTER BEANS IN COLD WATER FOR 15 MINUTES. ROOM TEMPERATURE WATER ALSO WORKS.

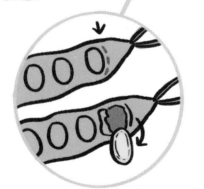

3

IN A MORTAR AND USING THE PESTLE, COMBINE THE CHILES, GARLIC, SHALLOT, AND SHRIMP PASTE AND POUND UNTIL YOU HAVE A FINE PASTE. SET ASIDE.

4

IN A LARGE WOK OVER
MEDIUM-HIGH HEAT,
WARM THE OIL.

5

ADD THE PASTE TO THE WOK AND COOK
FOR SEVERAL SECONDS, UNTIL THE PASTE
IS GOLDEN BROWN AND FRAGRANT.

6

ADD THE GROUND PORK TO THE WOK AND USE A
SPATULA TO QUICKLY BREAK UP THE MEAT INTO
SMALLER PIECES. COOK UNTIL BROWNED, ABOUT
1 MINUTE, BEING CAREFUL TO AVOID OVERCOOKING.

7

TURN THE HEAT TO MEDIUM AND MIX THE BITTER
BEANS, SUGAR, OYSTER SAUCE, SEASONING SOY
SAUCE, AND FISH SAUCE INTO THE PORK. STIR-FRY
UNTIL THE BEANS ARE SOFTENED, ABOUT 2 MINUTES.

8

TURN THE HEAT TO HIGH AND ADD
THE SHRIMP TO THE WOK. STIR-FRY
UNTIL BROWNED, UP TO 1 MINUTE,
BEING CAREFUL NOT TO OVERCOOK.
REMOVE FROM THE HEAT.

9

SERVE THE PORK AND BEANS WITH
KHAO SUAY AND CUCUMBER SLICES.

KHAO PAD KHAI

FRIED RICE WITH EGGS IS VERY POPULAR--
ESPECIALLY AMONG YOUNG CHILDREN--BECAUSE
IT'S ONE OF THE FEW THAI DISHES THAT DOESN'T
CONTAIN CHILES AND IS VERY EASY TO MAKE!
KHAO PAD KHAI JUST USES STAPLE INGREDIENTS
THAT ARE OFTEN ALREADY FOUND AROUND THE
HOUSE, MAKING IT THE PERFECT QUICK FIX.
IF YOU'RE A BACON OR HAM LOVER, TRY KICKING
IT UP A NOTCH BY CHOPPING A FEW PIECES
AND FRYING BEFORE THE GARLIC!

MAKES 2 SERVINGS

3 TABLESPOONS NEUTRAL OIL

4 GARLIC CLOVES, MINCED

2 EGGS

4 CUPS KHAO SUAY (PAGE 170)

1½ TABLESPOONS GRANULATED SUGAR

½ TEASPOON FRESHLY GROUND BLACK PEPPER
(OPTIONAL)

2 TABLESPOONS SEASONING SOY SAUCE

2 TABLESPOONS DICED CARROT (OPTIONAL)

2 TABLESPOONS CHOPPED CHIVES OR
GREEN ONIONS (GREEN PARTS ONLY)

CUCUMBER SLICES FOR GARNISHING

PHRIK NAM PLA (PAGE 185; OPTIONAL)

1
IN A LARGE WOK OVER MEDIUM HEAT,
WARM THE OIL. ADD THE GARLIC
TO THE WOK AND STIR-FRY FOR
SEVERAL SECONDS, UNTIL IT
TURNS GOLDEN.

2
CRACK THE EGGS STRAIGHT INTO
THE WOK AND TURN THE HEAT
TO MEDIUM-HIGH.

CHEF MALLIKA SAYS:

TO PREVENT THE FRIED RICE TEXTURE FROM BECOMING MUSHY,
LET YOUR COOKED RICE SIT IN THE FRIDGE FOR AT LEAST 1 HOUR
BEFORE COOKING OR MAKE IT A DAY IN ADVANCE.

3

IMMEDIATELY STIR THE EGGS TO COMBINE
THE YOLKS AND WHITES WELL UNTIL THE EGGS
ARE SLIGHTLY FIRMED, ABOUT 30 SECONDS.

4

ADD THE KHAO SUAY TO THE
WOK AND, USING A SPATULA TO
FLATTEN THE LUMPS, MIX WELL.
STIR UNTIL COMBINED.

5

ADD THE SUGAR, GROUND BLACK PEPPER
(IF USING), SEASONING SOY SAUCE,
AND CARROT (IF USING) TO THE WOK.
MIX WELL.

6

TURN THE HEAT TO HIGH.
ADD THE CHIVES TO
THE WOK AND MIX WELL.
REMOVE FROM
THE HEAT.

7

SERVE THE FRIED RICE AND EGGS
WITH CUCUMBER SLICES AND TOP
WITH PHRIK NAM PLA (IF DESIRED).

MM!

KHAI PALO

KHAI PALO IS A SWEET AND SAVORY EGG STEW THAT IS A VERY FRAGRANT FUSION OF CHINESE FIVE-SPICE POWDER AND THE THAI "THREE BUDDIES" PASTE (SEE PAGE 35). IT'S A HEARTY HOME-COOKED DISH FEATURING HARD-BOILED EGGS AND SLOW-COOKED MEAT, SERVED OVER RICE. IN THE STEWING PROCESS, THE EGGS ARE DYED AN ICONIC DEEP BROWN COLOR AND BECOME INFUSED WITH THE FLAVORS OF THE DELICIOUS BROTH--SO TRY NOT TO EAT ALL THE EGGS RIGHT OUT OF THE POT!

MAKES 2 SERVINGS

3 FRESH OR FROZEN (THAWED) CILANTRO ROOTS

7 GARLIC CLOVES

1 TEASPOON WHITE PEPPERCORNS

4 TO 6 KHAI TOM, PEELED (PAGE 180)

1 TABLESPOON BLACK SOY SAUCE

2 TABLESPOONS NEUTRAL OIL

1/3 CUP PACKED GRATED PALM SUGAR (ABOUT 1 1/2 PIECES) OR GRANULATED SUGAR

2 1/4 CUPS PLUS 1/3 CUP WATER

1 POUND PORK BELLY OR PORK COLLAR, CUBED, OR CHICKEN WINGS

3 TABLESPOONS FISH SAUCE

1 1/2 TABLESPOONS THIN SOY SAUCE

3 PIECES STAR ANISE

1 CINNAMON STICK (OPTIONAL)

3 OUNCES FRIED OR FIRM TOFU, CUBED

1 CUP LOOSELY PACKED 1-INCH-LONG CUT CILANTRO STEMS AND LEAVES (OPTIONAL)

KHAO SUAY (PAGE 170) FOR SERVING

PHRIK NAM PLA (PAGE 185) FOR SERVING (OPTIONAL)

1

IN A MORTAR AND USING THE PESTLE, COMBINE THE CILANTRO ROOTS, GARLIC, AND WHITE PEPPERCORNS AND POUND INTO A FINE PASTE. SET ASIDE.

2

IN A MEDIUM BOWL, COMBINE THE KHAI TOM AND BLACK SOY SAUCE. USING YOUR HANDS, COAT THE EGGS UNTIL THE SOY SAUCE TURNS THEM AN EVEN BROWN COLOR. SET ASIDE TO MARINATE.

3

IN A MEDIUM SAUCEPAN OVER MEDIUM HEAT, WARM THE OIL. ADD THE PASTE AND COOK FOR SEVERAL SECONDS, UNTIL IT TURNS FRAGRANT AND GOLDEN.

4

ADD THE PALM SUGAR AND 1/3 CUP OF THE WATER TO THE PAN AND STIR GENTLY UNTIL THE PALM SUGAR IS DISSOLVED.

5

ADD THE PORK TO THE PAN, TURN THE HEAT TO MEDIUM-HIGH, AND COOK THE PORK UNTIL BROWNED, ABOUT 3 MINUTES.

6

ADD THE FISH SAUCE, THIN SOY SAUCE, STAR ANISE, AND CINNAMON STICK (IF USING) TO THE PAN AND MIX WELL.

7

ADD THE REMAINING 2 1/4 CUPS WATER, THE TOFU, AND SOY SAUCE—MARINATED EGGS TO THE PAN.

8

COVER THE PAN, TURN THE HEAT TO MEDIUM-LOW, AND COOK FOR 30 MINUTES.

9

REMOVE THE LID AND STIR GENTLY. TURN HEAT TO MEDIUM AND COOK, UNCOVERED, FOR ANOTHER 10 MINUTES TO THICKEN.

10

REMOVE THE PAN FROM THE HEAT, ADD THE CILANTRO (IF USING), AND MIX WELL.

11

SERVE THE STEW WITH KHAO SUAY AND PHRIK NAM PLA (IF DESIRED).

SO GOOD!

MOO THORD

DEEP-FRIED PORK AND STICKY RICE MIGHT BE ONE OF THE BEST PAIRINGS OF ALL TIME! AS THE PERFECT TO-GO MEAL FOR BRINGING ALONG ON ADVENTURES AND PICNICS, MANY THAI FAMILIES HAVE FOND MEMORIES OF THIS MEAL. CHRISTINA'S MOM PUTS A PIECE OF FRIED PORK ON TOP OF A MINI STICKY-RICE BALL FOR A COMPLETE BITE-SIZE TREAT, AND MALLIKA ALWAYS BRINGS FRIED PORK AND RICE ON LONG ROAD TRIPS. THE MARINADE IS VERY SIMPLE AND GUARANTEED TO TASTE JUST LIKE MALLIKA'S MOM'S FRIED PORK.

MAKES 2 SERVINGS

3 FRESH OR FROZEN (THAWED) CILANTRO ROOTS

5 GARLIC CLOVES

1 TEASPOON WHITE PEPPERCORNS

1/2 TEASPOON FINE SEA SALT

1 TABLESPOON PACKED GRATED PALM SUGAR (ABOUT 1/4 PIECE) OR GRANULATED SUGAR

1 1/2 TEASPOONS SEASONING POWDER (OPTIONAL)

3 TABLESPOONS SEASONING SOY SAUCE

2 POUNDS PORK COLLAR OR PORK BELLY, THINLY SLICED INTO 2-INCH LENGTHS

1 1/4 CUPS NEUTRAL OIL

GRATHIAM JIEW (PAGE 188) FOR GARNISHING (OPTIONAL)

KHAO NIAW (PAGE 172) FOR SERVING

NAM JIM JAEW (PAGE 184) OR PHRIK NAM PLA (PAGE 185) FOR SERVING

1

IN A MORTAR AND USING THE PESTLE, COMBINE THE CILANTRO ROOTS, GARLIC, AND WHITE PEPPERCORNS AND POUND INTO A FINE PASTE. SET ASIDE.

2

IN A LARGE BOWL, COMBINE THE SALT, PALM SUGAR, SEASONING POWDER (IF USING), AND SEASONING SOY SAUCE TO MAKE A MARINADE.

3

ADD THE PORK AND PASTE TO THE BOWL. USING YOUR HANDS, EVENLY COAT THE PORK WITH THE MARINADE.

4

COVER THE BOWL WITH PLASTIC WRAP AND LET IT STAND IN THE FRIDGE FOR 1 HOUR.

1:00:00

5

LINE A PLATE WITH PAPER TOWELS. IN A LARGE WOK OVER HIGH HEAT, WARM THE OIL.

6

USING TONGS, TRANSFER HALF OF THE MARINATED PORK TO THE HOT OIL. SPREAD OUT THE MEAT EVENLY AND TURN THE HEAT TO MEDIUM-HIGH.

7

COOK THE PORK UNTIL BROWNED, ABOUT 7 MINUTES. IF YOU NOTICE THAT THERE IS LIQUID BUBBLING IN THE PAN, INCREASE THE HEAT. THERE SHOULD NOT BE ANY LIQUID OTHER THAN THE OIL WHEN THE PORK IS COOKED.

KLENG KLENG

(OBLIGATORY TONG TEST WHILE WAITING!)

8

USING TONGS, TRANSFER THE COOKED PORK TO THE PREPARED PLATE. REPEAT THIS PROCESS UNTIL ALL THE MARINATED PORK IS COOKED.

9

GARNISH THE FRIED PORK WITH GRATHIAM JIEW (IF DESIRED), AND SERVE WITH KHAO NIAW AND YOUR PREFERRED SAUCE.

YUMMY!

PLA THORD RAD PHRIK

THIS FRIED FISH COVERED WITH CHILE SAUCE ORIGINATES FROM CENTRAL THAILAND, BUT SOME ITERATION CAN BE FOUND ALL OVER THE COUNTRY. THE BEAUTY OF THIS DISH IS THAT YOU CAN CHOOSE ANY KIND OF FISH: TILAPIA, COD, CATFISH, OR SALMON, TO NAME A FEW. THAI PEOPLE LOVE PLA THORD RAD PHRIK SO MUCH THAT YOU CAN EVEN FIND A CANNED VERSION IN STORES. BUT, OF COURSE, FRESHLY FRIED FISH IS WAY BETTER. FOR THIS RECIPE, YOU CAN CHOOSE TO COVER YOUR FISH WITH NAM PHRIK SAM ROD, A SWEET AND SPICY CHILE SAUCE, OR NAM YAM MAMUANG, A FRESH GREEN MANGO SALAD. HOW WILL YOU EVER DECIDE?!

MAKES 2 SERVINGS

1 WHOLE TILAPIA, CLEANED

1 1/2 TEASPOONS FINE SEA SALT

2 CUPS NEUTRAL OIL

NAM PHRIK SAM ROD OR NAM YAM MAMUANG (RECIPES FOLLOW) FOR SERVING

CILANTRO LEAVES FOR GARNISHING

2 FRESH RED THAI CHILES (OR ADJUST TO TASTE), STEMMED, SEEDED, AND JULIENNED FOR GARNISHING

CASHEWS FOR GARNISHING

KHAO SUAY (PAGE 170) FOR SERVING

1

USING A SHARP KNIFE, MAKE THREE DIAGONAL OR CROSSCUTS ON EACH SIDE OF THE FISH AND COAT IT WITH THE SALT. SET ASIDE.

2

LINE A PLATE WITH PAPER TOWELS. IN A LARGE WOK OVER HIGH HEAT, WARM THE OIL.

3

WHEN THE OIL IS VERY HOT, PLACE THE FISH ON A SPATULA AND SLIDE IT INTO THE HOT OIL VERY GENTLY.

4

IMMEDIATELY TURN THE HEAT TO MEDIUM—HIGH AND COOK UNTIL THE BOTTOM SIDE OF THE FISH BECOMES GOLDEN AND CRISPY, 5 TO 7 MINUTES. (TO PREVENT THE FISH SKIN FROM STICKING TO THE BOTTOM OF THE PAN, LET IT COOK WITHOUT ANY INTERRUPTION FOR THE FIRST 4 MINUTES.)

5

USING TONGS OR A SPATULA, FLIP THE FISH AND CONTINUE COOKING UNTIL THE OTHER SIDE IS EQUALLY GOLDEN AND CRISPY, 5 TO 7 MINUTES MORE. IF THE TIP OF THE FISH'S HEAD AND TAIL WERE NOT SUBMERGED IN THE OIL WHILE COOKING, DIP THEM IN THE HOT OIL FOR ABOUT 30 SECONDS. TRANSFER THE FISH TO THE PREPARED PLATE TO REST FOR A FEW MINUTES.

6

PLACE THE FISH ON A LARGE SERVING PLATE. COVER COMPLETELY WITH EITHER NAM PHRIK SAM ROD OR NAM YUM MAMUANG OR SERVE THE SAUCE IN A SEPARATE BOWL. IF USING NAM PHRIK SAM ROD, GARNISH WITH CILANTRO LEAVES AND CHILES; IF USING NAM YAM MAMUANG, GARNISH WITH CILANTRO LEAVES AND CASHEWS. SERVE IMMEDIATELY WITH KHAO SUAY.

NICE!

NAM PHRIK SAM ROD

THREE-FLAVOR CHILE SAUCE

MAKES 1 CUP

10 FRESH RED THAI CHILES (OR ADJUST TO TASTE), STEMMED

1 WHOLE GARLIC HEAD, PEELED

2 FRESH OR FROZEN (THAWED) CILANTRO ROOTS

3 TABLESPOONS NEUTRAL OIL

1/4 CUP NAM MAKHAM PIAK (PAGE 195)

1/4 CUP FISH SAUCE

6 TABLESPOONS PACKED GRATED PALM SUGAR (ABOUT 1 1/2 PIECES), OR GRANULATED SUGAR

1/4 CUP WATER

1
IN A MORTAR AND USING THE PESTLE, COMBINE THE CHILES, GARLIC, AND CILANTRO ROOTS AND POUND INTO A PASTE.

2
IN A MEDIUM WOK OVER MEDIUM HEAT, WARM THE OIL. WHEN THE OIL IS HOT, ADD THE PASTE AND COOK FOR SEVERAL SECONDS, OR UNTIL IT IS FRAGRANT.

3
ADD THE NAM MAKHAM PIAK, FISH SAUCE, PALM SUGAR, AND WATER TO THE WOK. MIX WELL AND CONTINUE TO COOK UNTIL THICKENED, ABOUT 5 MINUTES.

4
SERVE WARM.

NAM YAM MAMUANG

GREEN MANGO SALAD

MAKES 2 CUPS

2 TABLESPOONS GRANULATED SUGAR

3 TABLESPOONS FISH SAUCE

3 TABLESPOONS FRESH LIME JUICE

3 FRESH RED THAI CHILES (OR ADJUST TO TASTE), STEMMED AND THINLY SLICED

2 TABLESPOONS DICED RED SHALLOT OR RED ONION

2 CUPS LOOSELY PACKED PEELED AND SHREDDED GREEN MANGO, OR 1 PEELED, CORED, AND SHREDDED SOUR-GREEN APPLE

1 CUP LOOSELY PACKED 1-INCH-LONG CUT CHIVES OR GREEN ONION (WHITE AND GREEN PARTS)

1 CUP LOOSELY PACKED CHINESE CELERY LEAVES

2 TABLESPOONS CASHEWS

1

IN A MEDIUM BOWL, COMBINE THE GRANULATED SUGAR, FISH SAUCE, AND LIME JUICE AND MIX WELL UNTIL THE SUGAR IS DISSOLVED.

2

ADD THE CHILES AND SHALLOT TO THE BOWL AND MIX.

3

THEN ADD THE GREEN MANGO, CHIVES, CHINESE CELERY LEAVES, AND CASHEWS AND MIX WELL TO COMBINE.

4

SERVE AT ROOM TEMPERATURE.

MJAM!

GAI YANG

THAI CUISINE HAS COUNTLESS MARINATED MEAT RECIPES, BUT, HEY, THEY'RE ALL JUST SO DELICIOUS! EACH REGION HAS A UNIQUE WAY OF GLAZING MEAT, MAKING DIPPING SAUCES, AND COOKING STICKY RICE. GAI YANG--GRILLED CHICKEN--IS TRADITIONALLY COOKED OVER A LIVE FIRE, BUT HERE'S A VERSION THAT IS JUICY PERFECTION FROM USING THE OVEN IN YOUR VERY OWN HOME KITCHEN. DON'T FORGET TO MAKE NAM JIM GAI (SWEET CHILE DIPPING SAUCE)--YOU'RE GOING TO WANT TO SLATHER IT ON EVERY BITE! IN THAI, SWEET CHILE SAUCE IS JUST REFERRED TO AS "CHICKEN DIPPING SAUCE" BECAUSE THIS PAIRING IS A MATCH MADE IN HEAVEN.

MAKES 2 SERVINGS

2 FRESH OR FROZEN (THAWED) CILANTRO ROOTS

4 GARLIC CLOVES, CRUSHED

1 TEASPOON BLACK PEPPERCORNS

1 TEASPOON FINE SEA SALT

2 TABLESPOONS PACKED GRATED PALM SUGAR (ABOUT 1/2 PIECE) OR GRANULATED SUGAR

3 TABLESPOONS SEASONING SOY SAUCE

1 TABLESPOON BLACK SWEET SOY SAUCE

2 TABLESPOONS OYSTER SAUCE

1 TABLESPOON GROUND TURMERIC (OPTIONAL)

2 POUNDS BONE-IN, SKIN-ON CHICKEN THIGHS AND DRUMSTICKS

NEUTRAL OIL FOR GLAZING

HONEY FOR GLAZING

KHAO NIAW (PAGE 172) FOR SERVING

NAM JIM GAI (RECIPE FOLLOWS) OR NAM JIM JAEW (PAGE 184) FOR SERVING

1
IN A MORTAR AND USING THE PESTLE, COMBINE THE CILANTRO ROOTS, GARLIC, AND PEPPERCORNS AND POUND INTO A FINE PASTE. TRANSFER TO A LARGE BOWL.

2
ADD THE SALT, PALM SUGAR, SEASONING SOY SAUCE, BLACK SWEET SOY SAUCE, OYSTER SAUCE, AND GROUND TURMERIC (IF USING) TO THE BOWL AND STIR TO MAKE A MARINADE.

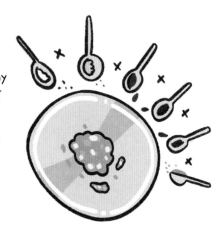

3
ADD THE CHICKEN TO THE BOWL AND, USING YOUR HANDS, EVENLY COAT THE CHICKEN WITH THE MARINADE.

4
COVER THE BOWL WITH A PLASTIC WRAP AND LET IT STAND IN THE FRIDGE FOR 1 HOUR.

5

REMOVE THE CHICKEN FROM THE FRIDGE AND LET IT SIT FOR 20 MINUTES TO REACH ROOM TEMPERATURE.

6

PLACE AN OVEN RACK IN THE SECOND POSITION FROM THE BOTTOM AND PREHEAT THE OVEN TO 475°F.

7

LINE A SHEET PAN WITH PARCHMENT PAPER AND TOP WITH A WIRE RACK. PLACE THE CHICKEN ON THE RACK.

8

PUT THE CHICKEN IN THE OVEN AND IMMEDIATELY TURN THE TEMPERATURE TO 400°F. ROAST FOR 30 MINUTES.

9

USING A PASTRY BRUSH, GLAZE THE CHICKEN WITH OIL AND HONEY. THEN, FLIP THE CHICKEN AND LET IT ROAST FOR 20 MINUTES MORE.

REPEAT THE GLAZING PROCESS AND FLIP THE CHICKEN AGAIN. LET IT ROAST UNTIL GOLDEN BROWN WITH CHAR MARKS, ABOUT 5 MINUTES MORE, BEFORE REMOVING FROM THE OVEN.

10

SERVE THE CHICKEN WITH KHAO NIAW AND NAM JIM GAI OR NAM JIM JAEW.

YUM!

GAI YANG
(PAGE 112)

SOM TUM
(PAGE 46)

KHAO NIAW
(PAGE 172)

LARB MOO
(PAGE 116)

NAM JIM GAI

CHICKEN DIPPING SAUCE

MAKES ½ CUP

8 GARLIC CLOVES, PEELED

8 FRESH RED THAI CHILES (OR ADJUST TO TASTE), STEMMED

½ CUP GRANULATED SUGAR

1½ TEASPOONS FINE SEA SALT

½ CUP DISTILLED WHITE VINEGAR

¼ CUP WATER

CILANTRO LEAVES FOR GARNISHING (OPTIONAL)

1

IN A MORTAR AND USING THE PESTLE, COMBINE THE GARLIC AND CHILES AND POUND INTO A FINE PASTE. SET ASIDE.

2

IN A SMALL SAUCEPAN OVER MEDIUM HEAT, COMBINE THE SUGAR, SALT, VINEGAR, AND WATER. MIX WELL AND LET COOK UNTIL IT STARTS TO BOIL, ABOUT 6 MINUTES.

3

ADD THE PASTE TO THE SAUCEPAN AND MIX WELL. TURN THE HEAT TO MEDIUM-LOW AND LET SIMMER, STIRRING OCCASIONALLY, UNTIL THICKENED, ABOUT 10 MINUTES.

4

REMOVE THE SAUCE FROM THE HEAT, LET REST FOR 3 MINUTES, AND THEN TRANSFER TO DIPPING-SAUCE BOWLS. GARNISH WITH CILANTRO (IF DESIRED) BEFORE SERVING.

SWEET!

LARB MOO

MAKES 2 SERVINGS

THIS SPICY GROUND PORK SALAD ORIGINATES FROM THE ISAAN REGION. IT USES BRIGHT AND AROMATIC HERBS TO ACHIEVE A FRESH AND TANGY FULL-BODIED FLAVOR. IN ADDITION TO BEING SO SINGULARLY TASTY, LARB HAS A CULTURAL IMPORTANCE, AS IT'S OFTEN SERVED DURING CEREMONIES OR SPECIAL GATHERINGS SINCE IT IS SO PERFECT FOR SHARING. MAKE SURE TO SERVE WITH CUCUMBERS, CABBAGE, OR ANY OTHER FRESH VEGETABLE FOR RELIEF IN CASE THINGS GET TOO SPICY!

1 POUND GROUND PORK OR CHICKEN

1/4 CUP WATER

1 TEASPOON SEASONING POWDER (OPTIONAL)

1/2 TEASPOON GRANULATED SUGAR

3 TABLESPOONS FRESH LIME JUICE

2 TABLESPOONS FISH SAUCE

2 TEASPOONS PHRIK PON (PAGE 192)

2 TABLESPOONS KHAO KHUA (PAGE 190)

1/4 CUP THINLY SLICED RED SHALLOT OR RED ONION

1/4 CUP CHOPPED CHIVES OR GREEN ONIONS (WHITE AND GREEN PARTS)

1/4 CUP CHOPPED CILANTRO LEAVES AND STEMS

1 CUP LOOSELY PACKED FRESH MINT LEAVES

KHAO NIAW (PAGE 172) OR KHAO SUAY (PAGE 170) FOR SERVING

RAW VEGETABLES (CUCUMBER SLICES, GREEN CABBAGE WEDGES, YARDLONG BEANS CUT INTO 3-INCH PIECES) FOR SERVING (OPTIONAL)

1

KNEAD THE GROUND PORK AND BREAK IT INTO SMALLER PIECES TO ACHIEVE THE CORRECT FINE CRUMBLE TEXTURE OF LARB. IT WILL COOK QUICKLY IN A HOT PAN.

2

IN A MEDIUM SAUCEPAN OVER HIGH HEAT, BRING THE WATER TO A BOIL. ADD THE GROUND PORK AND USE A SPATULA TO QUICKLY SEPARATE THE MEAT INTO SMALLER CRUMBLES. COOK UNTIL BROWNED, ABOUT 1 MINUTE, BEING CAREFUL NOT TO OVERCOOK. TRANSFER THE COOKED PORK TO A LARGE BOWL.

3

ADD THE SEASONING POWDER (IF USING),
SUGAR, LIME JUICE, FISH SAUCE,
PHRIK PON, AND KHAO KHUA TO
THE BOWL AND MIX WELL.

4

ADD THE SHALLOT, CHIVES,
CILANTRO, AND MINT TO
THE BOWL. MIX WELL.

5

SERVE THE PORK IMMEDIATELY, WITH
KHAO NIAW OR KHAO SUAY AND RAW
VEGETABLES (IF DESIRED) ALONGSIDE.

NAM PHRIK ONG

NAM PHRIK ONG IS A CHILE DIP MADE WITH TOMATOES, GROUND PORK, AND A CORE NORTHERN INGREDIENT: THUA NAO, WHICH TRANSLATES TO "ROTTEN BEAN," BUT IT'S JUST FERMENTED SOYBEAN. THIS DIP IS BEST SERVED WITH STICKY RICE, A MEDLEY OF VEGETABLES, CRISPY FRIED PORK SKIN, BOILED EGGS, AND ANYTHING YOU CAN USE TO SCOOP UP THIS DELICIOUSNESS. IT REPRESENTS TRUE NORTHERN-STYLE THAI CUISINE BECAUSE THEY *LOVE* THEIR CHILE DIPS AND ANY CHANCE TO EAT A BUNCH OF FRESH VEGETABLES WITH THEIR MEAL. WITH TOMATOES AS THE STAR, THIS DIP IS ON THE MILD SIDE AND BALANCES SWEETNESS, SOURNESS, SALTINESS, AND SPICINESS. NAM PHRIK ONG IS USUALLY SERVED IN A SMALL BOWL FOR SHARING, SO THIS RECIPE MAKES TWO SERVINGS. DON'T MISS OUT ON ADDING THIS ON TO YOUR SPREAD!

MAKES 4 CUPS

5 DRIED THAI CHILES (OR ADJUST TO TASTE), STEMMED

1 TEASPOON FINE SEA SALT

2 FRESH OR FROZEN (THAWED) CILANTRO ROOTS

6 GARLIC CLOVES

5 SMALL RED SHALLOTS, OR 1/2 LARGE RED ONION, COARSELY CHOPPED

1/2 TABLESPOON SHRIMP PASTE

1 SHEET DRIED FERMENTED SOYBEAN PASTE, OR 2 TABLESPOONS SOYBEAN PASTE

3 TABLESPOONS NEUTRAL OIL

1 POUND GROUND PORK

1 TABLESPOON PACKED GRATED PALM SUGAR (ABOUT 1/4 PIECE) OR GRANULATED SUGAR

1 TABLESPOON SEASONING SOY SAUCE, OR 1/2 TABLESPOON SEASONING POWDER (OPTIONAL)

1 TABLESPOON FISH SAUCE

3 LARGE TOMATOES, OR 12 CHERRY TOMATOES, DICED

CHOPPED CHIVES OR GREEN ONIONS (GREEN AND WHITE PARTS) FOR GARNISHING

CHOPPED CILANTRO LEAVES AND STEMS FOR GARNISHING

RAW VEGETABLES (CUCUMBER SLICES, YARDLONG BEANS, THAI ROUND GREEN EGGPLANTS, GREEN CABBAGE WEDGES, CARROTS) FOR SERVING

FRIED PORK RINDS FOR SERVING (OPTIONAL)

KHAI TOM (PAGE 180) FOR SERVING (OPTIONAL)

KHAO NIAW (PAGE 172) OR KHAO SUAY (PAGE 170) FOR SERVING

1
IN A MORTAR AND USING THE PESTLE, COMBINE THE CHILES, 1/2 TEASPOON OF THE SALT, AND THE CILANTRO ROOTS AND POUND UNTIL WELL COMBINED.

2
ADD THE GARLIC, SHALLOTS, AND SHRIMP PASTE TO THE MORTAR AND POUND TO MAKE A FINE PASTE. ADD THE FERMENTED SOY BEAN PASTE AND POUND UNTIL INCORPORATED. SET ASIDE. (THESE INGREDIENTS ARE ADDED LATER BECAUSE THEY ARE MOIST AND WOULD MAKE THE PASTE TOO WET IF THEY WERE POUNDED WITH THE INITIAL INGREDIENTS.)

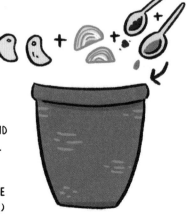

3

IN A LARGE SAUCEPAN OVER MEDIUM HEAT, WARM THE OIL.

ADD THE PASTE TO THE SAUCEPAN AND COOK UNTIL GOLDEN BROWN AND FRAGRANT, ABOUT 1 MINUTE.

4

ADD THE GROUND PORK TO THE SAUCEPAN, TURN THE HEAT TO MEDIUM-HIGH. USE A SPATULA TO QUICKLY BREAK UP THE MEAT AND COOK UNTIL BROWNED, ABOUT 2 MINUTES.

5

TURN THE HEAT TO MEDIUM. ADD THE REMAINING 1/2 TEASPOON SALT AND THE PALM SUGAR, SOY SAUCE, AND FISH SAUCE TO THE PAN. MIX UNTIL THE PORK TURNS BROWN.

6

TURN THE HEAT TO MEDIUM-HIGH, ADD THE TOMATOES TO THE PAN AND MIX WELL. COOK UNTIL THE MIXTURE BOILS, ABOUT 2 MINUTES. REMOVE FROM THE HEAT.

7

TRANSFER THE NAM PHRIK ONG TO A SERVING BOWL AND GARNISH WITH CHIVES AND CILANTRO.

8

SERVE THE DIP WITH ASSORTED RAW VEGETABLES, PORK RINDS (IF DESIRED), KHAI TOM (IF DESIRED), AND KHAO NIAW.

SUPERB!

KHAI TOM
(PAGE 180)

NAM PHRIK NOOM
(OPPOSITE PAGE)

KHAO NIAW
(PAGE 172)

NAM PHRIK ONG
(PAGE 118)

MOO THORD
(PAGE 106)

NAM PHRIK NOOM

THIS SMOKY GREEN CHILE DIP IS MADE USING RELATIVELY MILD GREEN CHILES (CALLED PHRIK NOOM, WHICH MEANS "YOUNG CHILE" IN THAI) SUCH AS SERRANO, ANAHEIM, OR BANANA PEPPERS. WITH BASICALLY JUST TWO COOKING STEPS--ROAST AND POUND! THIS DIP IS RIDICULOUSLY EASY TO MAKE AND SERVES AS A GREAT COMPLEMENTARY SIDE DISH TO OTHER MAIN ATTRACTIONS. THE CHARRED FLAVOR FROM ROASTING THE INGREDIENTS BRINGS OUT THE FRUITINESS AND SPICINESS OF THE CHILES, SO DON'T CUT CORNERS!

10 FRESH GREEN SERRANO OR ANAHEIM CHILES OR BANANA PEPPERS (OR ADJUST TO TASTE)

7 FRESH GREEN THAI CHILES (OR ADJUST TO TASTE)

4 SMALL RED SHALLOTS, UNPEELED, OR ½ MEDIUM RED ONION, PEELED AND COARSELY CHOPPED

10 GARLIC CLOVES, UNPEELED

1 TEASPOON FINE SEA SALT

1 TEASPOON FISH SAUCE

¼ TEASPOON GRANULATED SUGAR (OPTIONAL)

CHOPPED CILANTRO LEAVES AND STEMS FOR GARNISHING

CHOPPED CHIVES OR GREEN ONIONS (WHITE AND GREEN PARTS) FOR GARNISHING

RAW VEGETABLES (CUCUMBER SLICES, YARDLONG BEANS, THAI ROUND GREEN EGGPLANTS, GREEN CABBAGE WEDGES, CARROT STICKS) FOR SERVING

FRIED PORK RINDS FOR SERVING (OPTIONAL)

KHAI TOM (PAGE 180) FOR SERVING (OPTIONAL)

KHAO NIAW (PAGE 172) OR KHAO SUAY (PAGE 170) FOR SERVING

1

IN A LARGE FRYING PAN OVER MEDIUM-HIGH HEAT, COMBINE ALL THE CHILES, THE SHALLOTS, AND GARLIC AND TOAST UNTIL CHARRED AND SOFT, ABOUT 10 MINUTES ON EACH SIDE. TOSS THE PAN OCCASIONALLY TO MAKE SURE THEY ARE CHARRED ALL OVER.

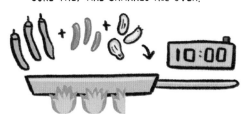

2

REMOVE THE PAN FROM THE HEAT AND ALLOW TO COOL FOR A FEW MINUTES. USING A SMALL KNIFE, REMOVE THE PEELS AND THE STEMS FROM THE CHILES, SHALLOTS, AND GARLIC.

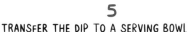

3

IN A MORTAR AND USING THE PESTLE, COMBINE THE TOASTED CHILES, SHALLOTS, GARLIC, AND THE SALT AND GENTLY POUND TO COMBINE. THE RESULTING TEXTURE SHOULD BE CLOSE TO A PASTE, BUT NOT COMPLETELY MASHED.

4

ADD THE FISH SAUCE AND SUGAR (IF USING) TO THE MORTAR AND GENTLY POUND UNTIL MIXED WELL.

5

TRANSFER THE DIP TO A SERVING BOWL AND GARNISH WITH CILANTRO AND CHIVES. SERVE WITH RAW VEGETABLES, FRIED PORK RINDS (IF DESIRED), KHAI TOM (IF DESIRED), AND KHAO NIAW.

Curries &

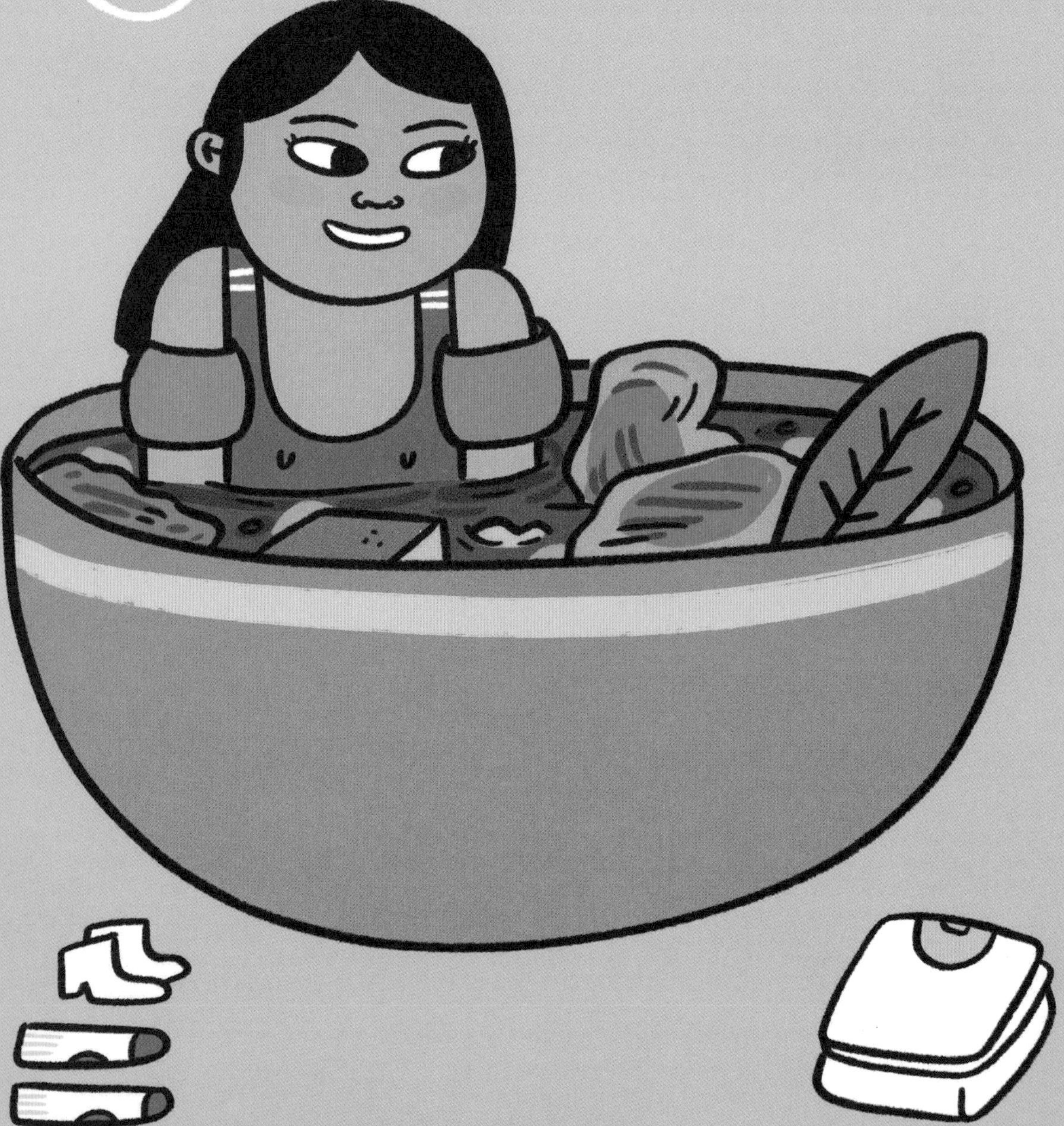

Soups

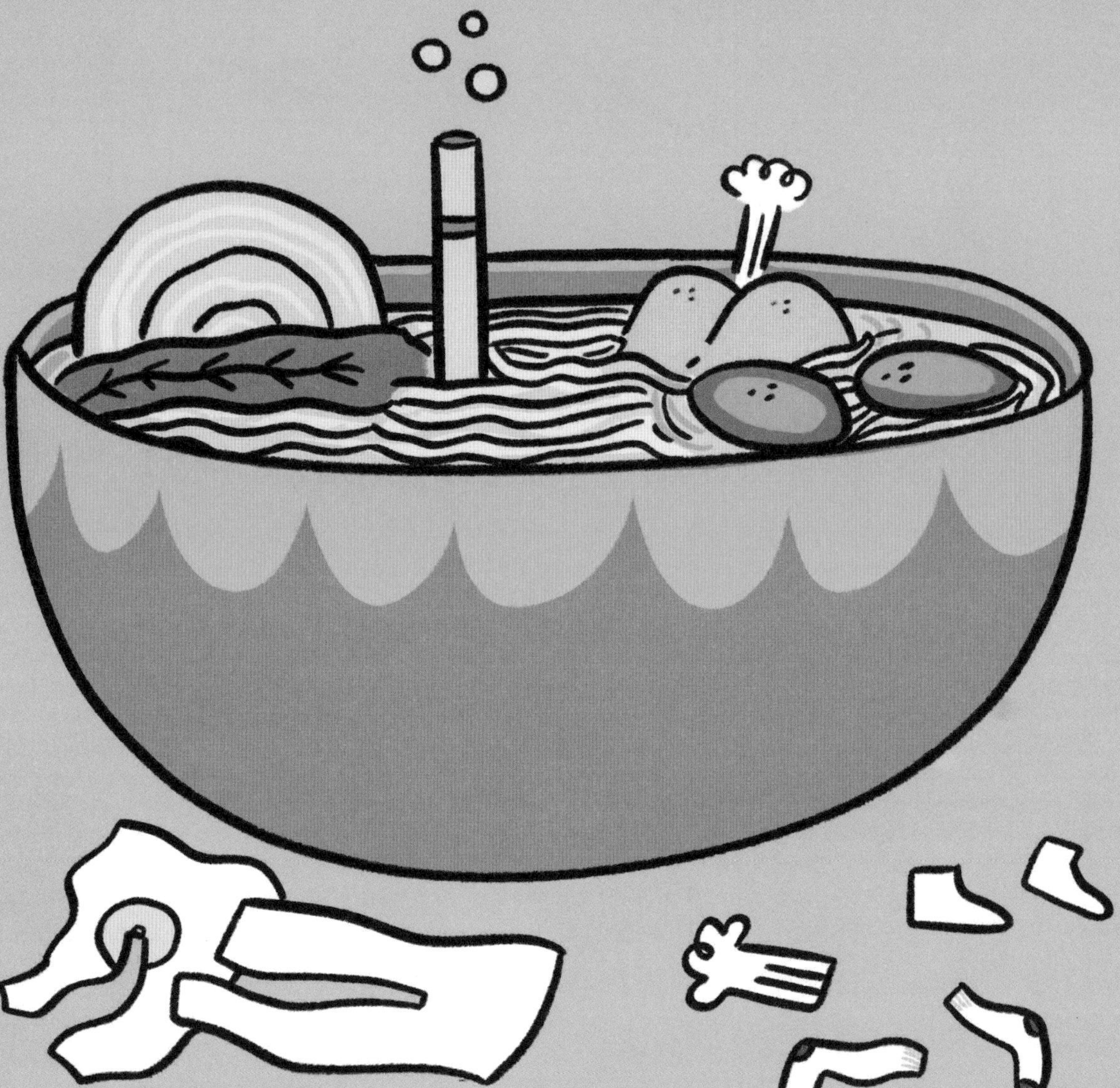

WHAT'S RED, GREEN, AND YELLOW ALL OVER?
THAT'S RIGHT! A SPREAD OF ALL THE
FAMOUS THAI CURRIES.

CURRY IS THE PERFECT
GATEWAY TO
THAI CUISINE.

IT'S AN IMPRESSIVE SKILL TO KNOW HOW TO MAKE YOUR OWN CURRY PASTE, SO WE STRONGLY ENCOURAGE YOU TO TRY CREATING THESE CURRIES FROM SCRATCH FOR A NEW EXPERIENCE.

CURRY TIPS

IN THE FOLLOWING CURRY RECIPES, YOU WILL COMBINE STORE-BOUGHT PASTE WITH YOUR HOMEMADE ONE. YOU'RE RIGHTFULLY QUESTIONING WHY THE HECK YOU WOULD ADD READY-MADE PASTE WHEN YOU'RE ALSO MAKING IT FROM SCRATCH. MAYBE YOU'VE JUST SPENT MINUTES OR EVEN HOURS(!) POUNDING THOSE INGREDIENTS IN YOUR MORTAR AND PESTLE.

WELL . . . IT'S ACTUALLY A BEST-KEPT SECRET. ADDING STORE-BOUGHT PASTE SIMPLY ENSURES YOU'LL ACHIEVE THE BEST PASTE POSSIBLE IN TERMS OF COLOR AND FLAVOR.

HOLD UP!

SINCE THE FRESH INGREDIENTS ARE NOT *ALWAYS* AVAILABLE IN THE STORES NEAR YOU, A PURELY HOMEMADE PASTE MIGHT BE INCOMPLETE. COMBINING THE TWO ENSURES YOU WILL ACHIEVE THE CORRECT COLOR AND FULL-BODIED FLAVOR. IF YOU'RE ONLY MISSING, LET'S SAY, THE LEMONGRASS, YOU'LL BE GOOD. BUT IF YOU'RE MISSING THREE KEY INGREDIENTS (FOR INSTANCE, SHRIMP PASTE, GALANGAL, AND LEMONGRASS), THIS MIGHT BE YOUR SIGN TO OPT FOR A READY-MADE SUPPLEMENT.

AND NO WORRIES, YOU'RE NOT A FRAUD IF YOU END UP COMBINING THE TWO. JUST LIKE PEOPLE WHO ADD CANNED TOMATO SAUCE TO A HOMEMADE PASTA SAUCE, IT MAY NOT FEEL LIKE THE RIGHT THING TO DO, BUT YOU JUST *KNOW* IT WILL BE GOOD. WE CAN CONFIRM THAT THIS IS, IN FACT, HOW THEY DO IT IN THAILAND. SO, TECHNICALLY, THIS IS THE *RIGHT* WAY.

CURRY PASTES REQUIRE A LOT OF INGREDIENTS, SO WHEN POUNDING YOUR PASTES, CHANCES ARE THERE WILL BE A BUNCH OF STUFF CATAPULTING STRAIGHT OUT OF YOUR MORTAR. WEAR SAFETY GLASSES OR SWIMMING GOGGLES BECAUSE, BOY, THESE (SPICY!) THINGS CAN FLY INTO YOUR EYES FASTER THAN YOU'D EXPECT. IF YOU'RE INTIMIDATED BY THE STRENUOUS POUNDING PROCESS, A FOOD PROCESSOR IS A CONVENIENT OPTION FOR MAKING SMOOTH CURRY PASTE IN A SHORT AMOUNT OF TIME!

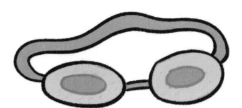

BUT MAKE SURE TO USE A HEAVY-DUTY KITCHEN BLENDER OR FOOD PROCESSOR, THOUGH NOT A SMOOTHIE MAKER! CURRY PASTE HAS A THICK, FIBER-Y TEXTURE, NOT RUNNY. AND TRUST US, A PANANG SMOOTHIE IS *NOT* SOMETHING YOU'D WANT!

WE USE CHICKEN AND PORK IN THESE RECIPES, BUT YOU CAN ALWAYS USE YOUR PREFERRED MEAT OR SUBSTITUTES. IF YOU ARE A BEEF LOVER, SWAP IN SOME CHUCK STEAK. ALSO NOTE THAT OUR CHICKENS ARE BONE-IN AND SKIN-ON BECAUSE IT IS TYPICAL FOR THAIS TO ENJOY EATING MEAT OFF THE BONES!

IF YOU'RE HAVING GUESTS OVER FOR CURRY, WE RECOMMEND PREPARING THE CURRY PASTE THE DAY BEFORE. THIS WILL SAVE YOU A BUNCH OF TIME AND LESSEN THE COOKING STRESS ON THE DAY ITSELF.

USE COCONUT CREAM IN YOUR CURRY IF YOU WANT A RICHER COCONUT FLAVOR, BUT COCONUT MILK DOES THE JOB PERFECTLY. THEY BOTH CAN WORK AS A GARNISH FOR YOUR FINISHED DISH SINCE CANNED COCONUT OPTIONS ALREADY HAVE A THICKER TEXTURE THAN THE FRESH VARIETY.

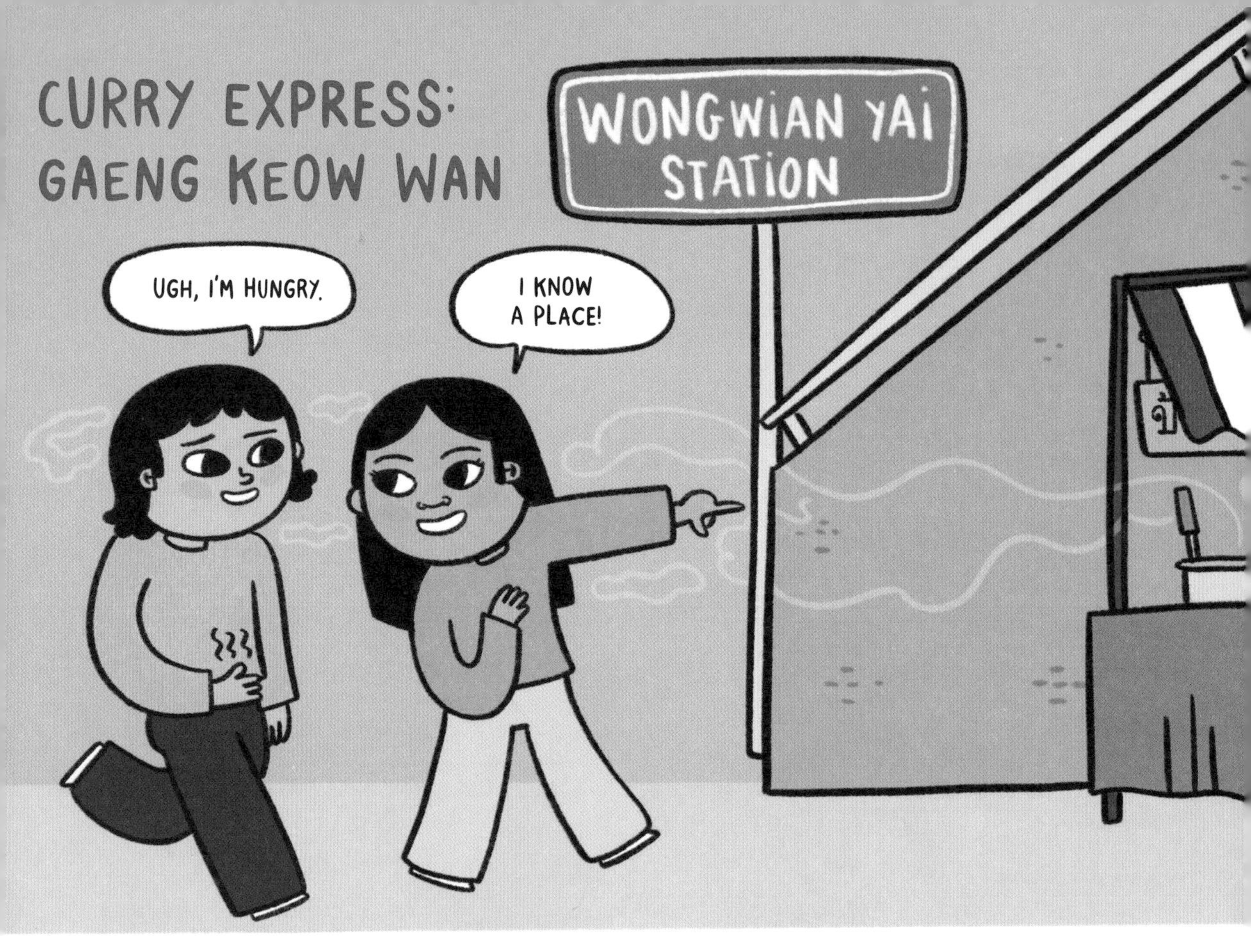
CURRY EXPRESS:
GAENG KEOW WAN
WONGWIAN YAI STATION
UGH, I'M HUNGRY.
I KNOW A PLACE!

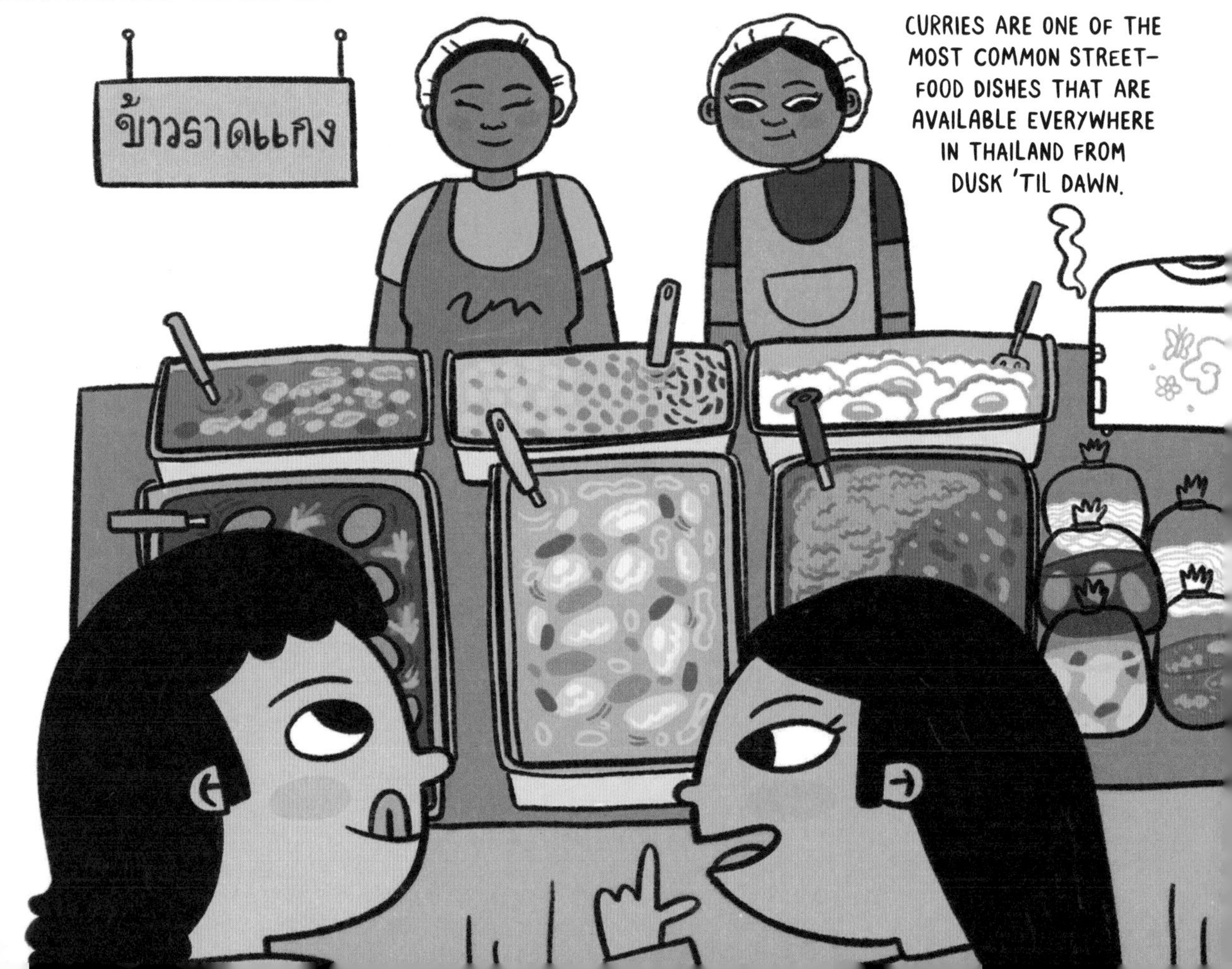
ข้าวราดแกง
CURRIES ARE ONE OF THE MOST COMMON STREET-FOOD DISHES THAT ARE AVAILABLE EVERYWHERE IN THAILAND FROM DUSK 'TIL DAWN.

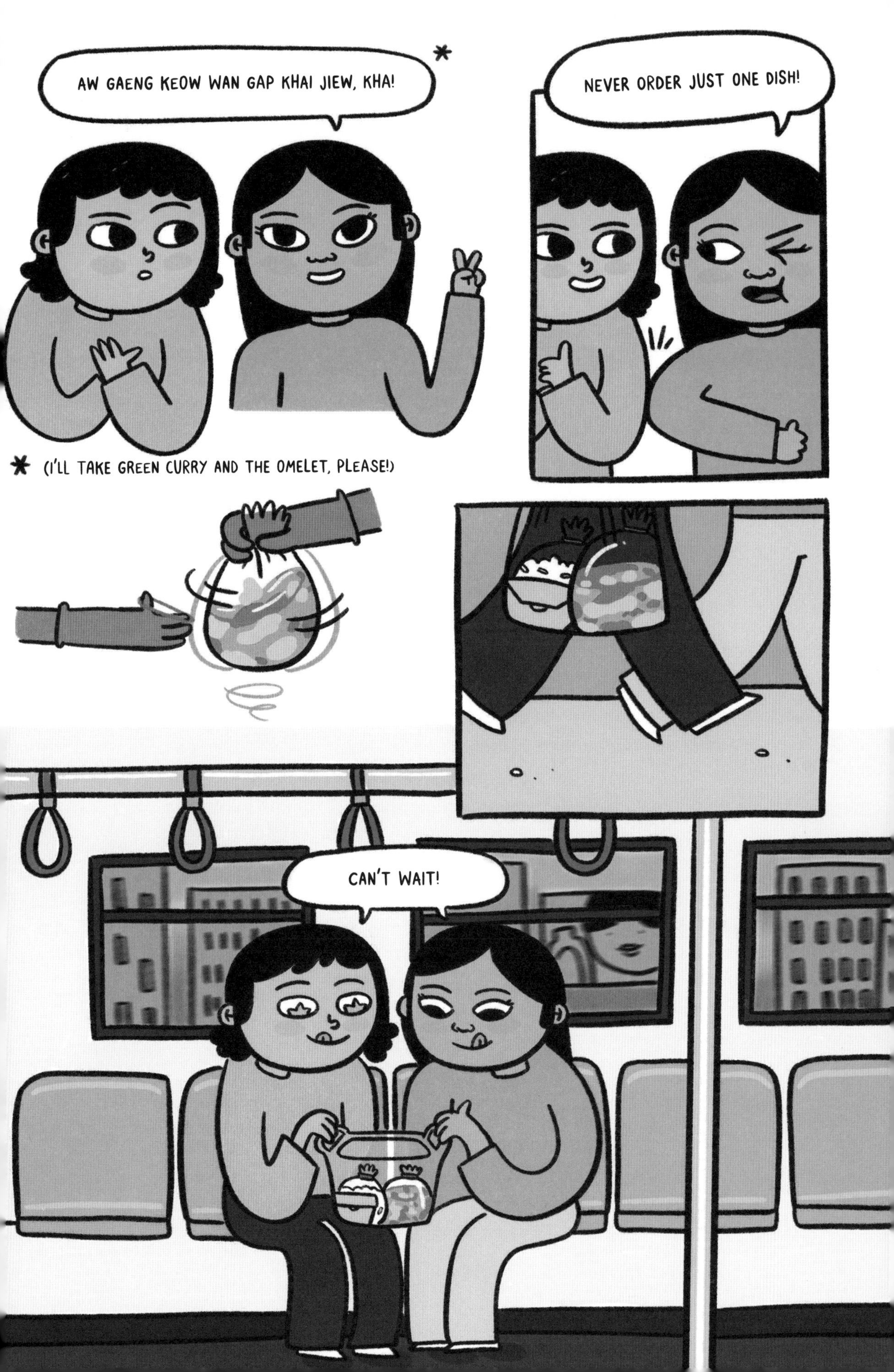
AW GAENG KEOW WAN GAP KHAI JIEW, KHA!
NEVER ORDER JUST ONE DISH!
* (I'LL TAKE GREEN CURRY AND THE OMELET, PLEASE!)
CAN'T WAIT!

GAENG KEOW WAN

FUN FACT: WAN MEANS "SWEET" IN THAI, BUT THE "WAN" IN GAENG KEOW WAN DOES NOT REFER TO THE SWEETNESS OF THE CURRY (GAENG), BUT RATHER THE CURRY'S SHADE OF GREEN (KEOW)! THIS SOUPY CURRY IS TRADITIONALLY SERVED WITH KHAO SUAY (PAGE 170), BUT IT HAS BECOME MORE POPULAR TO SERVE WITH FERMENTED WHITE RICE NOODLES (KHANOM JEEN, SEE PAGE 69) OR RICE VERMICELLI. CHICKEN AND BEEF ARE THE MOST POPULAR MEAT CHOICES, BUT TOFU WORKS GREAT FOR A LIGHTER VEGETARIAN OPTION. THIS CURRY HAS THE WELL-BLENDED FLAVOR OF FRESH HERBS AND SWEET COCONUT MILK, AND THE THAI SWEET BASIL LEAVES ARE A SPECIAL TOUCH. IF YOU LIKE YOUR CURRY WITH A KICK, YOU'LL LOVE THE HEAT OF GREEN CURRY AND THE ADDITION OF SLIGHTLY BITTER THAI ROUND GREEN EGGPLANTS!

MAKES 2 TO 4 SERVINGS AND 1/2 CUP CURRY PASTE

GREEN CURRY PASTE

2 TEASPOONS CORIANDER SEEDS

1 TEASPOON CUMIN SEEDS

4 WHITE PEPPERCORNS

1 WHOLE NUTMEG, OR 1 TEASPOON GROUND NUTMEG

1/2-INCH PIECE GALANGAL, SLICED

1 TABLESPOON SLICED LEMONGRASS

1 FRESH OR FROZEN (THAWED) CILANTRO ROOT, CHOPPED

4 FRESH GREEN SERRANO OR ANAHEIM CHILES OR BANANA PEPPERS (OR ADJUST TO TASTE), STEMMED, SEEDED, AND SLICED

4 FRESH GREEN THAI CHILES (OR ADJUST TO TASTE), STEMMED

4 GARLIC CLOVES, COARSELY CHOPPED

1 TABLESPOON CHOPPED RED SHALLOT OR RED ONION

1 TABLESPOON SHRIMP PASTE

1 1/2 TABLESPOONS STORE-BOUGHT GREEN CURRY PASTE

1/2 TEASPOON FINE SEA SALT

---

4 TABLESPOONS NEUTRAL OIL

1/2 CUP GREEN CURRY PASTE

1 POUND CHICKEN BREASTS OR BONE-IN, SKIN-ON CHICKEN THIGHS, CHOPPED (THROUGH THE BONE) INTO BITE-SIZE PIECES

ONE 14-OUNCE CAN COCONUT MILK

3 1/2 TABLESPOONS GRANULATED SUGAR

2 TEASPOONS FINE SEA SALT

1 TABLESPOON FISH SAUCE

1 1/2 CUPS WATER

10 THAI ROUND EGGPLANTS, STEMMED AND QUARTERED, OR 1/2 POUND GLOBE EGGPLANT, CUBED

2 OUNCES THAI PEA EGGPLANTS, STEMMED, OR 4 OUNCES CANNED BAMBOO SHOOTS, RINSED WITH WATER

2 FRESH RED SERRANO OR ANAHEIM CHILES OR BANANA PEPPERS (OR ADJUST TO TASTE), STEMMED AND THINLY SLICED ON DIAGONAL, PLUS MORE FOR GARNISHING

8 MAKRUT LIME LEAVES, STEMMED

3 CUPS LOOSELY PACKED THAI SWEET BASIL LEAVES, PLUS MORE FOR GARNISHING

1

TO MAKE THE PASTE: IN A SMALL FRYING PAN OVER MEDIUM-HIGH HEAT, COMBINE THE CORIANDER SEEDS, CUMIN SEEDS, AND PEPPERCORNS AND TOAST UNTIL LIGHTLY BROWNED, ABOUT 5 MINUTES.

2

TRANSFER THE TOASTED INGREDIENTS TO A MORTAR AND POUND WITH THE PESTLE UNTIL YOU HAVE A POWDER. TRANSFER THE POWDER TO A SMALL BOWL AND SET ASIDE.

3

IN THE SAME MORTAR, COMBINE THE NUTMEG, GALANGAL, LEMONGRASS, AND CILANTRO ROOT AND POUND WITH THE PESTLE UNTIL COMBINED.

4

ADD THE GREEN SERRANOS, THAI CHILES, GARLIC, SHALLOT, SHRIMP PASTE, STORE-BOUGHT CURRY PASTE, AND SALT TO THE MORTAR AND POUND WITH THE PESTLE UNTIL YOU HAVE A FINE PASTE.

ADD THE TOASTED SPICES TO THE MORTAR AND POUND WITH THE PESTLE TO INCORPORATE. SET ASIDE.

5

IN A MEDIUM SAUCEPAN OVER MEDIUM-HIGH HEAT, WARM THE OIL. ADD THE PASTE TO THE SAUCEPAN AND COOK FOR SEVERAL SECONDS, UNTIL THE PASTE IS GOLDEN BROWN AND FRAGRANT.

6

ADD THE CHICKEN TO
THE SAUCEPAN AND
COOK UNTIL BROWNED,
2 TO 3 MINUTES.

7

SPOON OUT AND RESERVE 2 TABLESPOONS OF THE
COCONUT MILK FOR GARNISH, IF DESIRED. ADD
THE REMAINING COCONUT MILK, SUGAR, SALT, AND
FISH SAUCE INTO THE SAUCEPAN AND MIX WELL.
LOWER THE HEAT TO MEDIUM AND COOK, COVERED,
FOR 5 MINUTES (7 MINUTES IF USING BONE-IN,
SKIN-ON CHICKEN THIGHS), STIRRING OCCASIONALLY.

8

ADD THE WATER, THAI ROUND EGGPLANTS,
AND PEA EGGPLANTS TO THE SAUCEPAN.
MIX WELL AND BRING THE CURRY BACK
TO A BOIL, ABOUT 1 MINUTE.

9

REMOVE THE PAN FROM THE HEAT AND
ADD THE RED SERRANOS, LIME LEAVES,
AND BASIL TO THE SAUCEPAN AND MIX
UNTIL INCORPORATED.

10

TRANSFER THE CURRY
TO A SERVING BOWL AND
GARNISH WITH RED CHILE
SLICES, THAI SWEET BASIL
LEAVES, AND THE RESERVED
COCONUT MILK (IF USING).
SERVE IMMEDIATELY.

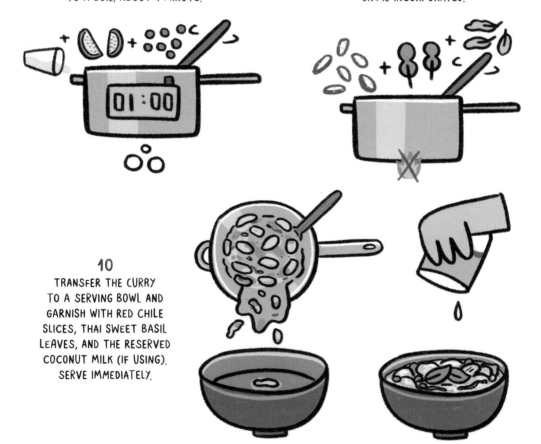

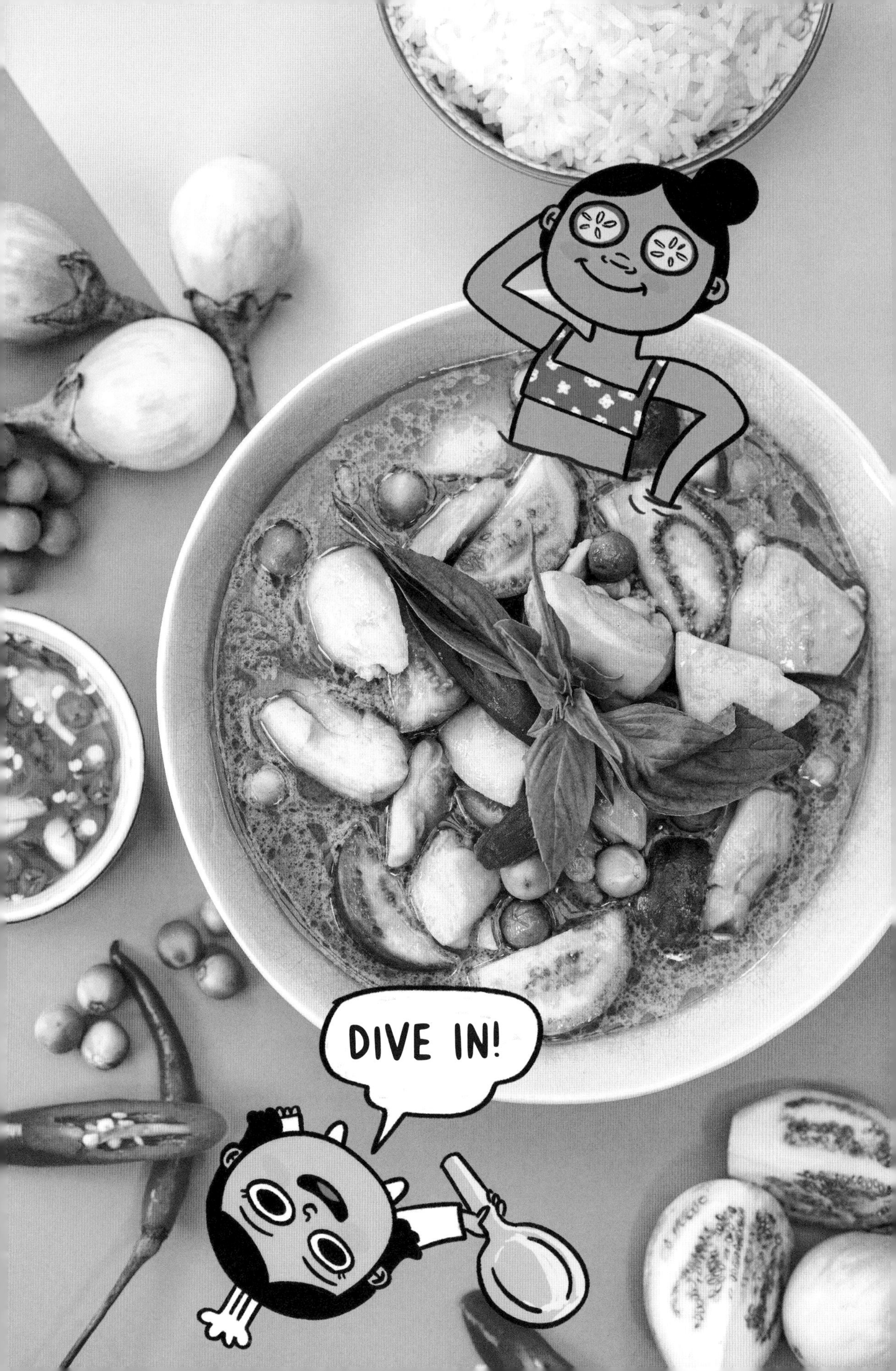
DIVE IN!

GAENG PANANG

PANANG CURRY'S CREAMY, SWEET, SPICY, AND NUTTY FLAVORS ARE GOOD FOR THE SOUL. BELIEVE IT OR NOT, THIS RICH CURRY PAIRED WITH A STEAMING BOWL OF RICE IS A COMMON BREAKFAST CHOICE FOR THAI PEOPLE! THE ZESTY BLEND OF CHILE, MAKRUT LIME, GALANGAL, ROASTED PEANUTS, AND SHRIMP PASTE IS SEAMLESSLY PAIRED WITH THE SWEETNESS OF COCONUT AND SUGAR. IN THIS RECIPE WE WILL USE PORK, BUT FEEL FREE TO MAKE IT HALAL BY USING CHICKEN, SEAFOOD, OR BEEF--OR EVEN GO ALL PLANT-BASED AND OPT FOR TOFU INSTEAD. SERVE WITH KHAO SUAY (PAGE 170).

MAKES 2 TO 4 SERVINGS AND 1/2 CUP CURRY PASTE

PANANG CURRY PASTE

2 TEASPOONS CORIANDER SEEDS

1 TEASPOON CUMIN SEEDS

1/2 TEASPOON GROUND CINNAMON

1/2-INCH PIECE GALANGAL, SLICED

1 TABLESPOON SLICED LEMONGRASS

2 TEASPOONS MAKRUT LIME ZEST

2 FRESH OR FROZEN (THAWED) CILANTRO ROOTS, CHOPPED

10 LARGE DRIED RED THAI CHILES (OR ADJUST TO TASTE), SOAKED IN BOILING WATER FOR 20 MINUTES, DRAINED, STEMMED, AND SEEDED

5 SMALL DRIED THAI CHILES (OR ADJUST TO TASTE), SOAKED IN BOILING WATER FOR 20 MINUTES, DRAINED, AND STEMMED

2 GARLIC CLOVES, COARSELY CHOPPED

2 TABLESPOONS CHOPPED RED SHALLOT OR RED ONION

1/2 TABLESPOON SHRIMP PASTE

1 1/2 TABLESPOONS STORE-BOUGHT PANANG CURRY PASTE

1/2 TEASPOON FINE SEA SALT

1 TABLESPOON GROUND PEANUTS

3 TABLESPOONS NEUTRAL OIL

1/4 CUP PANANG CURRY PASTE

1 POUND PORK COLLAR, CUT INTO BITE-SIZE PIECES

ONE 14-OUNCE CAN COCONUT MILK

3 TABLESPOONS GRANULATED SUGAR

1 TEASPOON FINE SEA SALT

1 TABLESPOON FISH SAUCE

1/2 CUP WATER

2 OUNCES THAI PEA EGGPLANTS, STEMMED, OR GREEN PEAS, PEELED

ONE 8-OUNCE CAN BAMBOO SHOOTS, DRAINED AND RINSED (OPTIONAL)

2 FRESH RED SERRANO OR ANAHEIM CHILES OR BANANA PEPPERS (OR ADJUST TO TASTE), STEMMED AND THINLY SLICED ON DIAGONAL, PLUS MORE FOR GARNISHING

10 MAKRUT LIME LEAVES, STEMMED AND THINLY SLICED, PLUS SHREDDED LEAVES FOR GARNISHING

1

TO MAKE THE PASTE: IN A SMALL FRYING PAN OVER MEDIUM-HIGH HEAT, COMBINE THE CORIANDER SEEDS AND CUMIN SEEDS, AND TOAST UNTIL THEY TURN GOLDEN BROWN, ABOUT 5 MINUTES. (TO PREVENT THE SPICES FROM BURNING, REPEATEDLY REMOVE THE PAN FROM THE HEAT AND SHAKE IT FOR A FEW SECONDS.)

2

TRANSFER THE TOASTED SPICES TO A MORTAR AND POUND WITH THE PESTLE UNTIL YOU HAVE A FINE POWDER. ADD THE CINNAMON AND POUND UNTIL INCORPORATED. TRANSFER THE POWDER TO A SMALL BOWL AND SET ASIDE.

3

IN THE SAME MORTAR, POUND THE GALANGAL, LEMONGRASS, LIME ZEST, AND CILANTRO ROOTS WITH THE PESTLE UNTIL COMBINED.

4

ADD THE DRAINED LARGE AND SMALL DRIED CHILES, GARLIC, SHALLOT, SHRIMP PASTE, STORE-BOUGHT CURRY PASTE, AND SALT TO THE MORTAR AND POUND WITH THE PESTLE UNTIL IT BECOMES A PASTE.

5

ADD THE GROUND PEANUTS AND TOASTED SPICE POWDER TO THE MORTAR AND THEN POUND WITH THE PESTLE TO MIX WELL. SET ASIDE.

6

IN A MEDIUM SAUCEPAN OVER MEDIUM-HIGH HEAT, WARM THE OIL. ADD THE PASTE TO THE SAUCEPAN AND COOK FOR SEVERAL SECONDS, UNTIL THE PASTE IS GOLDEN BROWN AND FRAGRANT.

7

ADD THE PORK TO THE SAUCEPAN, AND COOK UNTIL BROWNED, ABOUT 2 MINUTES.

8

SPOON OUT AND RESERVE 2 TABLESPOONS OF THE COCONUT MILK FOR GARNISH, IF DESIRED. ADD THE REMAINING COCONUT MILK, SUGAR, SALT, AND FISH SAUCE TO THE SAUCEPAN AND MIX WELL. LOWER THE HEAT TO MEDIUM AND COOK, COVERED, FOR 5 MINUTES, STIRRING OCCASIONALLY.

9

ADD THE WATER, PEA EGGPLANTS, AND BAMBOO SHOOTS (IF USING) TO THE SAUCEPAN AND MIX WELL. TURN THE HEAT TO MEDIUM-HIGH AND BRING THE CURRY BACK TO A BOIL, ABOUT 2 TO 3 MINUTES.

10

REMOVE THE PAN FROM THE HEAT, ADD THE FRESH RED CHILES AND LIME LEAVES, AND STIR WELL.

11

TRANSFER THE CURRY TO A SERVING BOWL AND GARNISH WITH RED CHILES, SHREDDED LIME LEAVES, AND THE RESERVED COCONUT MILK (IF USING). SERVE IMMEDIATELY.

GAENG MASSAMAN

WITH ROOTS TRACING ALL THE WAY BACK TO INDIA, MASSAMAN CURRY CAME TO THAILAND MORE THAN TWO HUNDRED YEARS AGO, AND IT IS STILL ONE OF THE MOST LOVED CURRIES EVER. WHAT MAKES THIS ONE DIFFERENT FROM THE REST? MASSAMAN HAS RELATIVELY MILDER OPTIONS, BUT IT'S STILL RICH IN FLAVOR AND THICK IN TEXTURE, LIKE PANANG. THE CURRY PASTE INCORPORATES SPICES SUCH AS CUMIN, CORIANDER, CINNAMON, AND NUTMEG TO SHOWCASE THE INDIAN INFLUENCE, AND THE DISH IS TOPPED WITH PEANUTS TO ROUND OUT THE FLAVOR. IT'S TRADITIONALLY MADE WITH BEEF, BUT WE'LL USE CHICKEN HERE. FEEL FREE TO EXPERIMENT WITH ANY MEAT OR MEAT ALTERNATIVE AND SERVE WITH KHAO SUAY (PAGE 170).

MAKES 2 TO 4 SERVINGS AND 1/2 CUP CURRY PASTE

MASSAMAN CURRY PASTE

2 TEASPOONS CORIANDER SEEDS

1 TEASPOON CUMIN SEEDS

2 WHOLE CLOVES

5 WHITE PEPPERCORNS

1 WHOLE NUTMEG

3 GARLIC CLOVES, PEELED AND HALVED

2 TABLESPOONS COARSELY CHOPPED RED SHALLOT OR RED ONION

1 TABLESPOON SLICED LEMONGRASS

1/2-INCH PIECE GALANGAL, SLICED

1/2-INCH PIECE GINGER, PEELED AND SLICED

10 LARGE DRIED THAI CHILES (OR ADJUST TO TASTE), SOAKED IN BOILING WATER FOR 20 MINUTES, DRAINED, STEMMED, AND SEEDED

3 SMALL DRIED THAI CHILES (OR ADJUST TO TASTE), SOAKED IN BOILING WATER FOR 20 MINUTES, DRAINED, AND STEMMED

1/2 TABLESPOON SHRIMP PASTE

1 TEASPOON GREEN CARDAMOM POWDER

1/2 TEASPOON FINE SEA SALT

2 TABLESPOONS STORE-BOUGHT MASSAMAN CURRY PASTE

2 TABLESPOONS RICE BRAN OR NEUTRAL OIL

4 TABLESPOONS NEUTRAL OIL

1/4 CUP MASSAMAN CURRY PASTE

1 1/2 POUNDS CHICKEN DRUMSTICKS OR BONE-IN, SKIN-ON CHICKEN THIGHS

ONE 14-OUNCE CAN COCONUT MILK

1 CUP WATER

12 OUNCES YUKON GOLD OR OTHER WAXY POTATOES, PEELED AND QUARTERED

1 YELLOW ONION, QUARTERED

2 TABLESPOONS PEANUTS OR CASHEWS, ROASTED

2 STAR ANISE PODS

3 1/2 TABLESPOONS GRANULATED SUGAR

1 TEASPOON FINE SEA SALT

1 TABLESPOON FISH SAUCE

1 TABLESPOON NAM MAKHAM PIAK (PAGE 195)

1

TO MAKE THE PASTE: IN A SMALL FRYING PAN OVER MEDIUM-HIGH HEAT, COMBINE THE CORIANDER SEEDS, CUMIN SEEDS, CLOVES, PEPPERCORNS, AND NUTMEG AND TOAST UNTIL LIGHTLY BROWNED, 5 TO 6 MINUTES. TRANSFER TO A MORTAR AND POUND WITH A PESTLE UNTIL IT IS A POWDER AND SET ASIDE IN A SMALL BOWL.

2

IN THE SAME PAN OVER MEDIUM-HIGH HEAT, COMBINE THE GARLIC, SHALLOT, LEMONGRASS, GALANGAL, AND GINGER, AND TOAST UNTIL FRAGRANT AND DRY, 5 TO 6 MINUTES.

TRANSFER TO A MORTAR AND ADD THE DRAINED CHILES, SHRIMP PASTE, CARDAMOM POWDER, SALT, AND STORE-BOUGHT CURRY PASTE. POUND WITH THE PESTLE UNTIL IT IS A FINE PASTE.

3

TRANSFER THE TOASTED SPICE MIXTURE INTO A MORTAR AND POUND WITH THE PESTLE UNTIL IT IS INCORPORATED. MIX IN THE RICE BRAN OIL AND SET ASIDE.

4

IN A LARGE SAUCEPAN OVER MEDIUM HEAT, WARM THE NEUTRAL OIL. ADD THE PASTE TO THE SAUCEPAN AND COOK FOR SEVERAL SECONDS, UNTIL THE PASTE IS GOLDEN BROWN AND FRAGRANT.

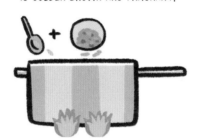

5

ADD THE CHICKEN DRUMSTICKS TO THE SAUCEPAN, AND COOK UNTIL BROWNED, ABOUT 3 MINUTES.

6

ADD 1/2 CUP COCONUT MILK INTO THE SAUCEPAN AND MIX WELL. TURN THE HEAT TO MEDIUM-HIGH AND COOK UNTIL BROWNED, ABOUT 3 MINUTES.

7

SPOON OUT AND RESERVED 2 TABLESPOONS OF THE COCONUT MILK FOR GARNISH, IF DESIRED. ADD THE REMAINING COCONUT MILK, WATER, POTATOES, ONION, PEANUTS, STAR ANISE, SUGAR, SALT, FISH SAUCE, AND NAM MAKHAM PIAK TO THE SAUCEPAN AND MIX WELL. LOWER THE HEAT TO MEDIUM AND LET THE CURRY COOK, COVERED, FOR 15 MINUTES, STIRRING OCCASIONALLY.

8

TURN THE HEAT TO MEDIUM-HIGH AND BRING THE CURRY BACK TO A BOIL, UNCOVERED, FOR ABOUT 5 MINUTES.

9

TRANSFER THE CURRY TO A SERVING BOWL AND TOP WITH THE RESERVED COCONUT MILK (IF USING). SERVE IMMEDIATELY.

TOM YUM GOONG

MAKES 2 SERVINGS

THERE ARE TWO VARIETIES OF THIS MIXED SHRIMP SOUP: CLEAR AND CREAMY. THE CLEAR SOUP IS THE OG ONE, BUT THE CREAMY VERSION HAS NOW BECOME JUST AS POPULAR. IF THIS IS YOUR FIRST TIME TRYING TOM YUM, CONGRATULATIONS! THIS HOT-AND-SOUR SOUP IS ONE OF THOSE DISHES THAT IS SO MIND-BLOWINGLY GOOD THAT WE WISH WE COULD RELIVE TRYING IT FOR THE FIRST TIME. TOM YUM HAS AN UNMISTAKABLE SMELL AND TASTE--THE SOURNESS OF THE LIME AND LEMONGRASS HIT YOUR NOSE RIGHT BEFORE YOU TASTE SPICINESS AND THE SWEETNESS OF THE SHRIMP PASTE. WE KNOW SLURPING HAS BEEN ENCOURAGED ELSEWHERE, BUT A WORD OF WARNING: TAKE IT NICE AND SLOW AND *DON'T* SLURP THIS ONE! TOM YUM IS VERY HOT AND SPICY, SO YOU MIGHT BURN YOUR TONGUE. SERVE WITH KHAO SUAY (PAGE 170).

3 CUPS WATER

1-INCH PIECE GALANGAL, SLICED AND COARSELY CRUSHED

2 STALKS LEMONGRASS, GRASSY TOPS AND TOUGH OUTER LAYER REMOVED, CRUSHED AND CUT INTO 2-INCH PIECES

4 SMALL RED SHALLOTS, HALVED

1/2 TEASPOON FINE SEA SALT

3 TABLESPOONS FISH SAUCE

2 TABLESPOONS NAM PHRIK PHAO (PAGE 196), PLUS OIL FOR GARNISHING (OPTIONAL)

5 OUNCES WHITE BUTTON MUSHROOMS, HALVED, OR WHITE OYSTER AND BEECH MUSHROOMS

8 OUNCES COLOSSAL (U15) WHITE SHRIMP WITH TAILS, UNPEELED OR PEELED AND DEVEINED

1/4 CUP EVAPORATED MILK

1/2 CUP LOOSELY PACKED CILANTRO LEAVES AND STEMS

6 MAKRUT LIME LEAVES, STEMMED

6 SAWTOOTH CILANTRO LEAVES, CUT INTO 1/2-INCH LENGTHS (OPTIONAL)

6 FRESH RED THAI CHILES (OR ADJUST TO TASTE), STEMMED AND DIAGONALLY SLICED

10 PHRIK KHUA (OR ADJUST TO TASTE), (PAGE 187)

3 TABLESPOONS FRESH LIME JUICE

1

IN A MEDIUM SAUCEPAN OVER MEDIUM-HIGH HEAT, COMBINE THE WATER, GALANGAL, LEMONGRASS, AND SHALLOTS, AND BRING TO A BOIL.

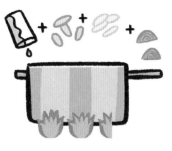

2

ADD THE SALT, FISH SAUCE, NAM PHRIK PHAO, AND MUSHROOMS TO THE SAUCEPAN. STIR TO MIX AND RETURN TO A BOIL.

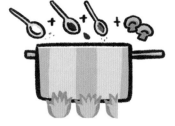

3

ADD THE SHRIMP TO THE PAN, PRESSING DOWN WITH A LADLE TO FULLY SUBMERGE IN THE SOUP, BUT DO NOT STIR.

LET THE SOUP BOIL FOR ABOUT 30 SECONDS, SO THE SHRIMP DO NOT OVERCOOK.

4

ADD THE EVAPORATED MILK, CILANTRO, LIME LEAVES, SAWTOOTH CILANTRO LEAVES (IF USING), CHILES, PHRIK KHUA, AND LIME JUICE TO THE SOUP. MIX WELL.

5

TRANSFER THE SOUP TO A SERVING BOWL AND GARNISH WITH DRIPS OF NAM PHRIK PHAO OIL (IF USING). SERVE IMMEDIATELY.

CHEF MALLIKA SAYS:

IF YOU WANT TO MAKE A CLEAR TOM YUM SOUP, OMIT THE NAM PHRIK PHAO AND EVAPORATED MILK, BUT ADD A KNORR BOUILLON CUBE (PORK OR CHICKEN FLAVOR) FOR AN EXTRA BOOST.

OF COURSE, YOU CAN SUBSTITUTE 1/2 POUND TO 1 POUND OF CHICKEN FOR THE SHRIMP AND MAKE TOM YUM GAI INSTEAD!

PHRIK KHUA IS NOT SPICY AND IS USED TO ADD A TOASTED AROMA TO THE DISH. HOWEVER, THESE TOASTED DRIED CHILES WILL UNLEASH THEIR SPICE IF THEY ARE CRUSHED.

TOM KHA GAI

THIS CHICKEN GALANGAL SOUP IS VERY SIMILAR TO TOM YUM GOONG, BUT THE BIGGEST DIFFERENCE HERE IS COCONUT MILK. AS THE NAME GIVES AWAY, CHICKEN IS PREFERRED, BUT FEEL FREE TO SUBSTITUTE YOUR CHOICE OF PROTEIN. THE STAR OF THIS DISH IS GALANGAL ROOT AND, TRUST US, IT *DOES* MAKE A DIFFERENCE. TOM KHA GAI'S CHARMING APPEAL IS IN ITS WELL-BLENDED MELLOW FLAVOR THAT WILL LINGER LONG AFTER YOU HAVE FINISHED YOUR MEAL. IT'S PERFECT FOR THOSE WHO ENJOY A MILDER EXPERIENCE WITH THAI FOOD. HOWEVER, YOU CAN ALWAYS KICK UP THE SPICE WITH THE DRIED CHILES IF THAT'S MORE YOUR SPEED. SERVE WITH KHAO SUAY (PAGE 170).

2½ CUPS WATER

2-INCH PIECE GALANGAL, SLICED AND COARSELY CRUSHED

2 STALKS LEMONGRASS, GRASSY TOPS AND TOUGH OUTER LAYER REMOVED, CRUSHED AND CUT INTO 2-INCH PIECES

3 SMALL RED SHALLOTS, OR 1 MEDIUM RED ONION, HALVED AND COARSELY CRUSHED

7 MAKRUT LIME LEAVES

6 FRESH RED THAI CHILES (OR ADJUST TO TASTE), STEMMED AND DIAGONALLY SLICED

1 TEASPOON FINE SEA SALT

ONE 14-OUNCE CAN COCONUT MILK

1 POUND CHICKEN BREASTS OR BONE-IN, SKIN-ON CHICKEN THIGHS, CHOPPED (THROUGH THE BONE) INTO BITE-SIZE PIECES

4 OUNCES WHITE BUTTON MUSHROOMS, HALVED, OR WHITE OYSTER OR BEECH MUSHROOMS

4 OUNCES GREEN CABBAGE, CUT INTO 1-INCH SQUARES (OPTIONAL)

2 TABLESPOONS FRESH LIME JUICE

2 TABLESPOONS FISH SAUCE

1½ TABLESPOONS GRANULATED SUGAR

½ TABLESPOON NAM MAKHAM PIAK (PAGE 195; OPTIONAL)

½ CUP LOOSELY PACKED 1-INCH-LONG CUT CILANTRO STEMS AND LEAVES, PLUS MORE FOR GARNISHING

PHRIK KHUA (PAGE 187) FOR GARNISHING (OPTIONAL)

1
IN A MEDIUM SAUCEPAN OVER MEDIUM-HIGH HEAT, COMBINE THE WATER, GALANGAL, LEMONGRASS, SHALLOTS, LIME LEAVES, CHILES, AND SALT AND BRING TO A BOIL.

2
ADD THE COCONUT MILK TO THE SAUCEPAN AND CONTINUE TO BOIL.

3

ADD THE CHICKEN TO THE SAUCEPAN,
TURN THE HEAT TO MEDIUM, AND COOK,
UNCOVERED AND WITHOUT STIRRING,
UNTIL BROWNED, ABOUT 5 MINUTES.

4

WHEN THE CHICKEN IS COOKED THROUGH, MIX
IN THE MUSHROOMS, CABBAGE (IF USING), LIME
JUICE, FISH SAUCE, SUGAR, AND NAM MAKHAM
PIAK (IF USING). RETURN TO A BOIL AND COOK
FOR 3 MINUTES. REMOVE FROM THE HEAT.

5

GENTLY
STIR IN THE
CILANTRO.

6

TRANSFER THE SOUP TO
A SERVING BOWL AND
GARNISH THE SOUP
WITH CILANTRO
AND PHRIK KHUA
(IF DESIRED).
SERVE IMMEDIATELY.

SUPER!

GAI TOM KHAMIN

TURMERIC LOVERS CAN UNITE IN CELEBRATION OF THIS CHICKEN SOUP WITH TURMERIC BECAUSE IT WILL HIT THE SPOT. GAI TOM KHAMIN, A LESSER KNOWN SOUTHERN DISH, DOES NOT TYPICALLY CONTAIN CHILES--WHICH IS SURPRISING AS SOUTHERN FOOD IS KNOWN FOR BEING SUPER-SPICY. THIS LIGHT CHICKEN SOUP IS BURSTING WITH FRAGRANT HERBS AND FRESH TURMERIC ROOT, AND YOU CAN TOP IT OFF WITH A SQUEEZE OF FRESH LIME JUICE, A DASH OF FISH SAUCE, AND BIRD'S EYE CHILES. THIS IS A SIMPLE YET FILLING MEAL THAT'S ALSO EASY TO MAKE FOR YOURSELF, BY YOURSELF: JUST TOSS THE INGREDIENTS IN A POT, LET SIMMER, AND YOU'RE READY TO GO! SERVE WITH KHAO SUAY (PAGE 170).

SERVE WITH KHAO SUAY (PAGE 170).

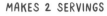

MAKES 2 SERVINGS

3½ CUPS WATER

2-INCH PIECE GALANGAL, SLICED AND COARSELY CRUSHED

2 STALKS LEMONGRASS, GRASSY TOPS AND TOUGH OUTER LAYER REMOVED, CRUSHED AND CUT INTO 2-INCH PIECES

10 GARLIC CLOVES, CRUSHED

3 SMALL RED SHALLOTS, OR 1 MEDIUM RED ONION, HALVED AND COARSELY CRUSHED

1½-INCH PIECE TURMERIC ROOT, COARSELY CRUSHED

1 TEASPOON FINE SEA SALT

1 POUND CHICKEN BREASTS OR BONE-IN AND SKIN-ON CHICKEN THIGHS, CHOPPED (THROUGH THE BONE) INTO BITE-SIZE PIECES

1 TABLESPOON FISH SAUCE, PLUS MORE FOR GARNISHING (OPTIONAL)

1 TEASPOON GRANULATED SUGAR

FRESH RED AND GREEN BIRD'S EYE CHILES OR THAI CHILES, COARSELY CRUSHED, FOR GARNISHING (OPTIONAL)

FRESH LIME JUICE FOR GARNISHING (OPTIONAL)

1
IN A MEDIUM SAUCEPAN OVER MEDIUM-HIGH HEAT, COMBINE THE WATER, GALANGAL, LEMONGRASS, GARLIC, SHALLOTS, TURMERIC, AND SALT AND BRING TO A BOIL.

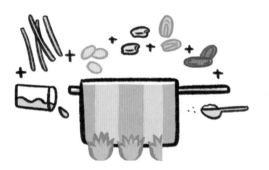

2
ADD THE CHICKEN TO THE SAUCEPAN, TURN THE HEAT TO MEDIUM, AND LET COOK, UNCOVERED, FOR ABOUT 8 MINUTES, STIRRING HALFWAY THROUGH.

3
ADD THE FISH SAUCE AND SUGAR TO THE SAUCEPAN, STIR TO MIX, AND THEN REMOVE FROM THE HEAT.

4
TRANSFER THE SOUP TO A LARGE SERVING BOWL AND GARNISH WITH FISH SAUCE, CRUSHED CHILES, AND LIME JUICE (IF DESIRED). SERVE IMMEDIATELY.

GOOD SOUP

CHEF MALLIKA SAYS

WANT EVEN MORE FLAVOR AND HEAT? ADD ADDITIONAL CHILES, LIME JUICE, AND FISH SAUCE TO YOUR OWN BOWL RIGHT BEFORE YOU POUR THE SOUP.

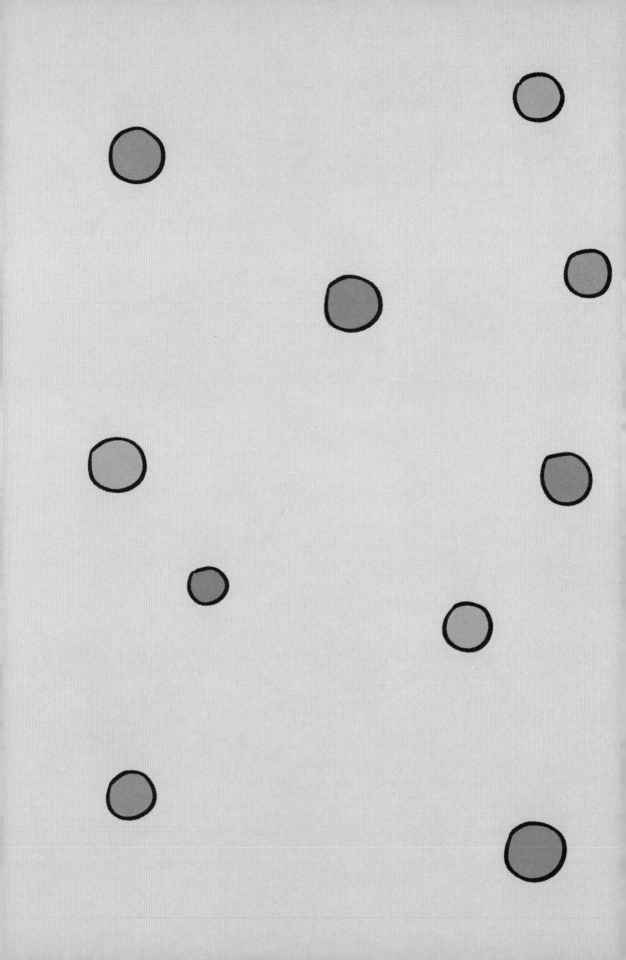

DESSERTS & DRINKS

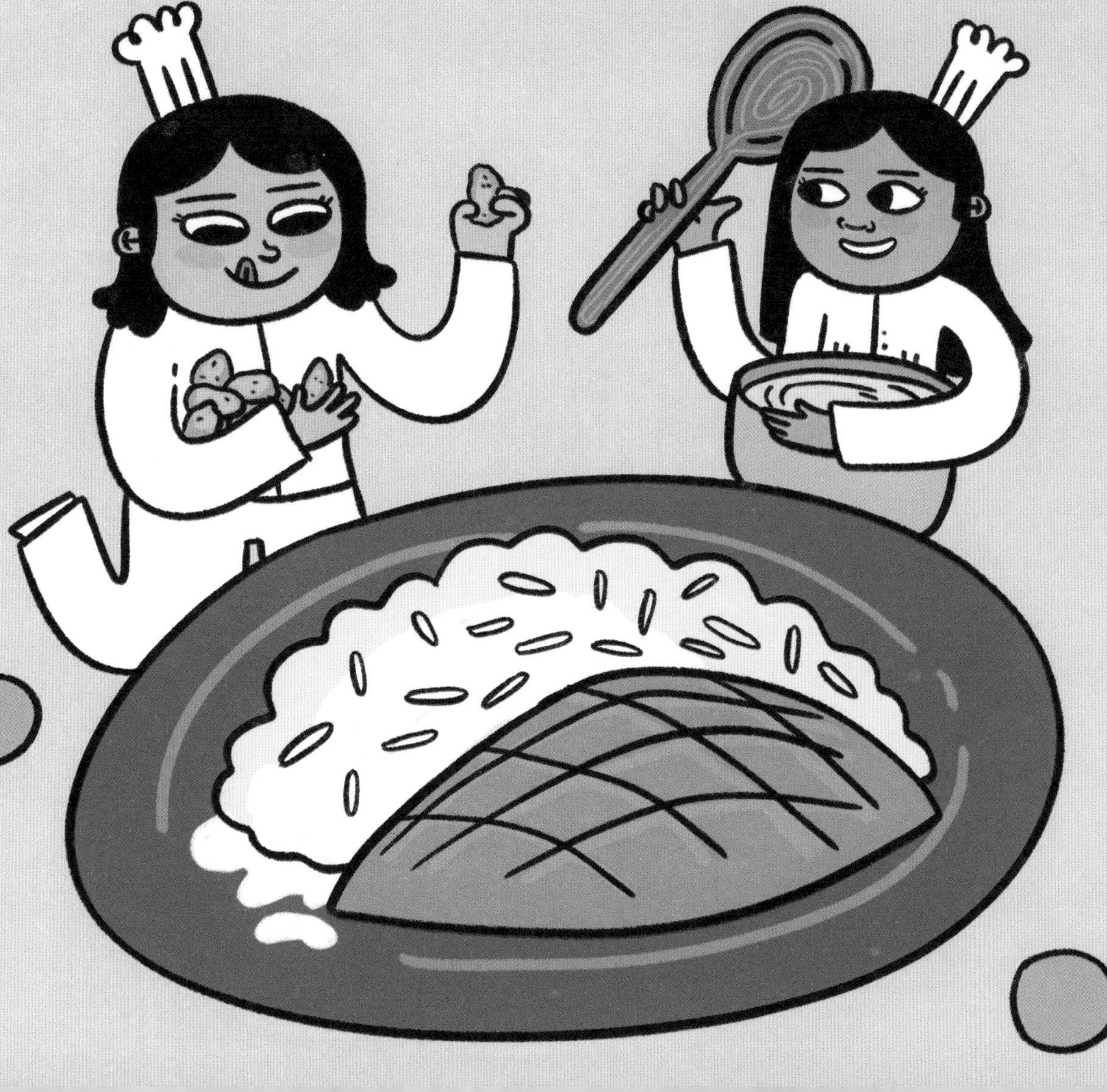

IN THE EARLY DAYS, TRADITIONAL THAI DESSERTS USUALLY CONSISTED OF ONLY RICE FLOUR, COCONUT MILK, AND SUGAR. THEN, THAIS LEARNED TO USE EGGS IN THEIR SWEETS DUE TO THE PORTUGUESE INFLUENCE DURING THE AYUTTHAYA PERIOD (1350–1767). NOW, COCONUT AND PANDAN LEAVES ARE THE MOST TYPICAL CONFECTIONERY FLAVORS.

MARIA GUYOMAR DE PINHA INTRODUCED THAILAND TO SWEET EGG-YOLK DESSERTS, SUCH AS THONG YOT AND FOI THONG, WHICH ARE MADE BY DROPPING EGG-YOLK BATTER INTO BOILING SUGAR SYRUP (*THONG* MEANING "GOLD" IN REFERENCE TO THE BRIGHT YELLOW-ORANGE COLOR OF THE DESSERT; *YOT* MEANING "DROPS" AND *FOI* MEANING "THREADS" TO DESCRIBE THE DIFFERENT FORMS). DURING HER TIME IN THE ROYAL COURT IN THE AYUTTHAYA KINGDOM, MARIA IS CREDITED WITH INVENTING A NUMBER OF NEW DESSERTS, INCLUDING A SAVORY-SWEET CUSTARD KHANOM MO KAENG, THE PERFECT ICE-CREAM ACCOMPANIMENT KHAO NIAW SANGKHAYA (PAGE 157), AND DELICIOUS CRUNCHY BISCUITS CALLED KHANOM PHING. KHOP KHUN KHA, MARIA!*
*THANK YOU, MARIA!

QUEEN OF THAI DESSERTS, MOTHER OF FOI THONG. DAUGHTER OF PORTUGUESE-JAPANESE-BENGALI DESCENT

SINCE THAI DESSERTS ARE A DELICACY THAT REQUIRE TOP-NOTCH INGREDIENTS AND THE UTMOST CARE IN PREPARATION, THE RESULTS WILL BE SOMETHING BREATHTAKINGLY BEAUTIFUL TO LOOK AT.

DESSERT PLAYS A VITAL ROLE IN LOCAL FESTIVALS AND CEREMONIES ACROSS THE WHOLE COUNTRY. THAIS CONSIDER IT TO BE VERY MEANINGFUL; THEREFORE, THEY'LL CAREFULLY SELECT AN OPTION BASED ON ITS NAME AND MEANING TO PERFECTLY FIT EVERY OCCASION. FOR EXAMPLE, FOI THONG ("GOLDEN THREADS"), THONG YOT ("GOLDEN DROPS"), AND THONG YIP ("PINCHED GOLD EGG YOLK") REPRESENT PROSPERITY, THUS THEY ARE A MUST-HAVE IN THAI WEDDINGS AS A WISHING SYMBOL TO THE HAPPY COUPLE.

MALLIKA'S FAVORITE AND MOST MEMORABLE DESSERT IS BUA LOY, SINCE IT'S THE FIRST THAI DESSERT THAT SHE LEARNED TO MAKE AT A YOUNG AGE.

FROM DOUGH TO DELIGHT: BUA LOY

KIDS! DO YOU WANT TO MAKE BUA LOY TOGETHER?

WHICH SHAPE ARE YOU GOING FOR?

BALLS

FLOWER

BUFFALO

RICE FLOUR

DO YOU ACTUALLY KNOW WHAT "BUA LOY" MEANS?
FLOATING LOTUS.
BUA LOY
A FAMILY FAVE!

BUA LOY

BUA LOY LITERALLY MEANS "FLOATING LOTUS," AND EVEN THOUGH THERE ARE NO REAL LOTUS FLOWERS INVOLVED, THERE ARE STILL SOME BEAUTIFUL FLOATING COLORS. THIS DESSERT IS MADE OF GLUTINOUS RICE-FLOUR BALLS, NATURALLY COLORED WITH TARO, PUMPKIN, PURPLE YAM, AND SWEET POTATO, THEN SERVED IN WARM COCONUT MILK WITH KHAI WAAN (SWEET EGG). WHEN YOU BOIL THE RICE-FLOUR BALLS IN WATER, YOU KNOW THEY ARE FINISHED COOKING WHEN THEY START RISING TO THE SURFACE. THE RESULT? A GORGEOUS BOWL OF SEEMINGLY FLOATING LOTUSES. THAI KIDS LEARN HOW TO MAKE BUA LOY AT A YOUNG AGE BY HELPING TO ROLL THE MANY COLORFUL DOUGH BALLS. AS A CHILD, MALLIKA ENJOYED MOLDING THE BALLS INTO DIFFERENT ANIMAL SHAPES, FLOWERS, AND HEARTS. HAVE FUN WITH YOUR SHAPES!

MAKES 8 SERVINGS

½ CUP PEELED AND CUBED FRESH OR FROZEN (THAWED) TARO ROOT

½ CUP PEELED AND CUBED FRESH SWEET POTATO OR PUMPKIN

6 FRESH OR FROZEN (THAWED) PANDAN LEAVES; 3 CUT INTO ½-INCH PIECES, 3 FOLDED AND KNOTTED

½ CUP WATER, PLUS MORE AS NEEDED

1½ CUPS GLUTINOUS RICE FLOUR, PLUS MORE FOR SPRINKLING

2 CUPS COCONUT MILK (PREFERABLY AROY-D BRAND)

¼ CUP GRATED PACKED PALM SUGAR (ABOUT 1 PIECE)

3 TABLESPOONS GRANULATED SUGAR

½ TEASPOON FINE SEA SALT

¾ CUP CANNED COCONUT MEAT IN SYRUP, DRAINED (OPTIONAL)

KHAI WAAN FOR SERVING (PAGE 159) (OPTIONAL)

1

IN THE BOTTOM LEVEL OF A STEAMER POT, BRING 2 INCHES OF WATER TO A BOIL OVER HIGH HEAT.

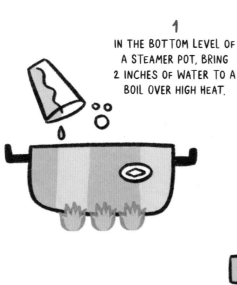

2

PUT THE TARO ROOT AND SWEET POTATO IN INDIVIDUAL SMALL STEAMER-SAFE BOWLS. PLACE THE BOWLS IN THE UPPER SECTION OF THE STEAMER POT AND CLOSE THE LID. TURN THE HEAT TO MEDIUM AND LET STEAM FOR 20 MINUTES.

3

FOLD AND KNOT 3 OF THE PANDAN LEAVES AND SET ASIDE. CUT THE REMAINING 3 PANDAN LEAVES INTO ½-INCH PIECES. IN A BLENDER, COMBINE THE CUT PANDAN LEAVES WITH ¼ CUP OF THE WATER. BLEND AT HIGH SPEED UNTIL WELL EMULSIFIED.

4

POUR THE PANDAN WATER THROUGH CHEESECLOTH INTO A MEDIUM BOWL. SQUEEZE THE CLOTH TO MAKE SURE ALL THE WATER IS SEPARATED FROM THE PANDAN PULP. DISCARD THE PULP AND RESERVE THE PANDAN WATER.

5

DIVIDE THE GLUTINOUS RICE FLOUR AMONG THREE LARGE BOWLS.

6

ADD THE PANDAN WATER TO ONE BOWL OF FLOUR AND KNEAD WITH YOUR HANDS UNTIL IT BECOMES AN EVENLY COLORED DOUGH, ABOUT 3 MINUTES. COVER WITH DAMP CHEESECLOTH OR A LID.

7

ADD THE STEAMED TARO ROOT AND REMAINING ¼ CUP WATER TO THE SECOND BOWL OF FLOUR AND KNEAD WITH YOUR HANDS UNTIL IT BECOMES AN EVENLY COLORED DOUGH, ABOUT 3 MINUTES. COVER WITH DAMP CHEESECLOTH OR A LID.

ADD THE STEAMED SWEET POTATO TO THE THIRD BOWL OF FLOUR AND KNEAD WITH YOUR HANDS INTO AN EVENLY COLORED DOUGH, ABOUT 3 MINUTES. COVER WITH DAMP CHEESECLOTH OR A LID.

8

SPRINKLE A LAYER OF GLUTINOUS RICE FLOUR OVER A LARGE BAKING SHEET.

9

STARTING WITH THE PANDAN DOUGH, PINCH OFF A PEA-SIZE PIECE OF DOUGH AND ROLL IT INTO A SMOOTH BALL BETWEEN YOUR PALMS. SMOOTH DOWN ANY POINTS WITH YOUR THUMB AND INDEX FINGER AND MOLD THEM INTO ANY PREFERRED SHAPE; FOR EXAMPLE, IF YOU'D LIKE TO MAKE A FLOWER, ENCIRCLE ONE BALL WITH A NUMBER OF OTHER BALLS TO FORM THE PETALS.

10

FILL A LARGE POT OR WOK WITH 10 CUPS OF WATER, SET OVER HIGH HEAT, AND BRING TO A BOIL.

11

DROP THE SHAPED DOUGH ONTO THE PREPARED BAKING SHEET AND REPEAT UNTIL ALL THREE DOUGHS ARE FORMED. ADD ALL THE FORMED DOUGH TO THE BOILING WATER AND TURN THE HEAT TO MEDIUM. COOK, UNCOVERED, UNTIL ALL THE SHAPES HAVE FLOATED TO THE SURFACE; STIR TO MAKE SURE THAT NONE HAVE STUCK TO THE BOTTOM. CONTINUE TO COOK FOR 2 MINUTES MORE.

12

USING A SKIMMER, TRANSFER THE COOKED BUA LOY TO A LARGE BOWL OF COLD WATER AND LET SIT FOR 2 MINUTES. DRAIN AND SET ASIDE.

13

IN A LARGE SAUCEPAN OVER MEDIUM HEAT, COMBINE THE COCONUT MILK, REMAINING 3 KNOTTED PANDAN LEAVES, THE PALM SUGAR, GRANULATED SUGAR, AND SALT AND MIX WELL UNTIL THE SUGARS AND SALT HAVE DISSOLVED.

14

WHEN THE COCONUT MILK BEGINS TO STEAM, ADD THE BUA LOY AND COCONUT MEAT (IF USING). LET SIMMER FOR 2 TO 3 MINUTES, MAKING SURE THE MIXTURE DOESN'T BOIL, AND THEN REMOVE FROM THE HEAT.

15

SPOON THE BUA LOY AND COCONUT MILK INTO BOWLS AND TOP WITH A KHAI WAAN IN THE CENTER (IF DESIRED). SERVE IMMEDIATELY.

CHEF MALLIKA SAYS:

IF YOU WANT A PINK OR RED COLOR, USE THAI SALA (PALM FRUIT) SYRUP. HALE'S BLUE BOY BRAND IS THE BEST!

IF YOUR BUA LOY DOUGH BECOMES TOO DRY WHILE KNEADING, ADD ROOM-TEMPERATURE WATER, UP TO 1 TABLESPOON AT A TIME TO AVOID MUSHY DOUGH.

THE YIELD IS FOR 8 SERVINGS, BUT IF YOU WANT TO MAKE HALF AT A TIME, COOK ONLY HALF OF THE DRAINED DOUGH BALLS AND HALF OF THE COCONUT MILK. THE REMAINING DRAINED DOUGH BALLS AND COCONUT MILK (IF ALREADY OPEN) CAN BE REFRIGERATED IN SEPARATE AIRTIGHT CONTAINERS IN A FRIDGE FOR UP TO 2 DAYS, OR FROZEN FOR UP TO 6 MONTHS.

KHAI WAAN
(PAGE 159)

BUA LOY
(PAGE 150)

KHAO NIAW MAMUANG

THE MOST ACCESSIBLE THAI DESSERT HAS TO
BE THIS MANGO STICKY RICE. IT'S VERY EASY TO
MAKE AT HOME SINCE THERE ARE BARELY MORE
THAN TWO MAIN INGREDIENTS: MANGO AND, YOU
GUESSED IT, SWEET STICKY RICE (KHAO NIAW
MOON). THE SUGAR RUSH FROM THE RIPE MANGO
COMBINED WITH THE SWEET COCONUT MILK AND
THE GLUTINOUS TEXTURE OF STICKY RICE IS
WHAT MAKES THIS TREAT SO HIGHLY COMPELLING.
IF YOU WANT TO SERVE A SHOW-STOPPING
HOMEMADE DESSERT WITHOUT SWEATING IN
THE KITCHEN FOR HOURS, KHAO NIAW MAMUANG
IS YOUR GO-TO OPTION. IF MANGOES ARE OUT OF
SEASON OR A VIRAL VIDEO LEADS TO A WORLD-
WIDE MANGO SHORTAGE, CONSIDER EATING THE
SWEET COCONUT STICKY RICE ON ITS OWN WITH
TOASTED WHITE SESAME SEEDS OR THUA THONG
(DEEP-FRIED SPLIT MUNG BEANS).

MAKES 4 SERVINGS

KHAO NIAW MOON

ONE 14-OUNCE CAN COCONUT MILK
(PREFERABLY AROY-D BRAND)

3 FRESH OR FROZEN (THAWED) PANDAN LEAVES,
TIED TOGETHER IN A SINGLE KNOT

4 1/2 TABLESPOONS GRANULATED SUGAR

1/2 TEASPOON FINE SEA SALT

1 CUP STICKY OR GLUTINOUS RICE, SOAKED
IN ROOM-TEMPERATURE WATER FOR 4 HOURS,
DRAINED, AND COOKED (SEE PAGE 172)

3/4 CUP COCONUT CREAM (PREFERABLY
AROY-D BRAND)

2 TABLESPOONS GRANULATED SUGAR

1 TEASPOON RICE FLOUR

1/2 TEASPOON FINE SEA SALT

2 FULLY RIPE, SWEET MANGOES, PEELED, PITTED,
AND SLICED 1/2 INCH THICK

THUA THONG (RECIPE FOLLOWS) FOR TOPPING
(OPTIONAL)

TOASTED WHITE SESAME SEEDS FOR TOPPING
(OPTIONAL)

MINT LEAVES FOR GARNISHING (OPTIONAL)

1

TO MAKE THE KHAO NIAW MOON: IN A MEDIUM
SAUCEPAN OVER MEDIUM-HIGH HEAT, COMBINE
THE COCONUT MILK, PANDAN LEAVES, SUGAR,
AND SALT AND BRING TO A BOIL.

2

REMOVE FROM THE HEAT AT ONCE.

3

TRANSFER THE
SWEET COCONUT
MILK TO A
LARGE BOWL.

4

ADD THE COOKED
STICKY RICE TO THE
SWEET COCONUT
MILK AND MIX UNTIL
INCORPORATED.

5

USING A LID OR A PLATE, COVER
THE BOWL AND LET THE RICE
REST FOR 10 MINUTES.

6

IN THE SAME SAUCEPAN, COMBINE THE
COCONUT CREAM, SUGAR, RICE FLOUR,
AND SALT AND STIR UNTIL COMBINED.

7

PLACE THE SAUCEPAN OVER MEDIUM HEAT
AND STIR CONTINUOUSLY AS THE COCONUT
CREAM STARTS TO HEAT UP. DO NOT
ALLOW IT TO BOIL. REMOVE FROM THE
HEAT AND SET ASIDE.

8

USING A SPOON, FLUFF THE
STICKY RICE IN THE BOWL.

9

RE-COVER THE BOWL AND LET
REST FOR 10 MINUTES.

10

PLACE THE MANGO SLICES ONTO A PLATE AND
SCOOP THE STICKY RICE NEXT TO THEM. POUR
THE COCONUT CREAM MIXTURE OVER THE RICE
OR SERVE IN A SEPARATE CUP FOR INDIVIDUAL
POURING PREFERENCE. TOP WITH THUA TONG
OR SESAME SEEDS AND GARNISH WITH MINT
LEAVES (IF DESIRED). SERVE IMMEDIATELY.

THUA THONG

GOLDEN BEANS

MAKES 2 TABLESPOONS

2 TABLESPOONS PEELED SPLIT MUNG BEANS, RINSED THREE TIMES, SOAKED IN BOILING WATER FOR 20 MINUTES, AND DRAINED

1/4 CUP NEUTRAL OIL

1/4 TEASPOON FINE SEA SALT

1

PLACE THE DRAINED MUNG BEANS IN A STEAMER-SAFE SERVING BOWL.

2

IN THE BOTTOM LEVEL OF A STEAMER POT, BRING 2 INCHES OF WATER TO A BOIL OVER HIGH HEAT. PLACE THE BOWL OF MUNG BEANS IN THE UPPER SECTION OF THE STEAMER POT.

TURN THE HEAT TO MEDIUM, COVER, AND LET STEAM FOR 20 MINUTES. REMOVE FROM THE HEAT AND SET ASIDE.

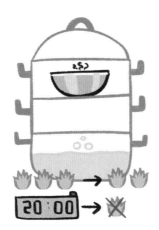

3

LINE A PLATE WITH PAPER TOWELS. IN A SMALL SAUCEPAN OVER MEDIUM HEAT, WARM THE OIL.

4

WHEN THE OIL IS SHIMMERING, ADD THE MUNG BEANS AND COOK, STIRRING CONSTANTLY, UNTIL THEY TURN GOLDEN, UP TO 3 MINUTES. USING A SKIMMER OR TONGS, TRANSFER TO THE PREPARED PLATE TO DRAIN AND SET ASIDE.

5

ADD THE SALT AND MIX WELL. TRANSFER TO AN AIRTIGHT CONTAINER AND STORE AT ROOM TEMPERATURE FOR UP TO 1 MONTH.

KHAO NIAW SANGKHAYA

THIS STICKY RICE WITH STEAMED CUSTARD, ANOTHER TRADITIONAL THAI DESSERT HEAVILY INFLUENCED BY THE PORTUGUESE, DATES BACK TO THE AYUTTHAYA PERIOD. BECAUSE THAI PEOPLE DID NOT CONSUME DAIRY BACK THEN, MARIA GUYOMAR DE PINHA, THE QUEEN OF THAI DESSERTS DURING THAT TIME, CREATED SANGKHAYA WITH COCONUT MILK. SANGKHAYA IS ALSO AVAILABLE IN THE FORM OF A BEAUTIFUL PANDAN-GREEN CUSTARD DIP OR SPREAD FOR EATING WITH BREAD, AND THIS STEAMED VERSION, WHICH IS BEST EATEN WITH SWEET COCONUT STICKY RICE.

MAKES 8 SERVINGS

4 EGGS

1/2 CUP PACKED GRATED PALM SUGAR (ABOUT 2 PIECES)

1 TEASPOON FINE SEA SALT

2 FRESH OR FROZEN (THAWED) PANDAN LEAVES, CUT CROSSWISE INTO 2-INCH RIBBONS

1 CUP COCONUT MILK

1 CUP KHAO NIAW MOON (PAGE 154)

1

CRACK THE EGGS INTO A LARGE STEAMER-SAFE BOWL AND ADD THE PALM SUGAR, SALT, AND PANDAN LEAVES. USING A SPOON, BREAK UP ANY LUMPS OF PALM SUGAR AND STIR UNTIL THE EGGS ARE WELL MIXED AND SUGAR IS DISSOLVED.

2

REMOVE THE PANDAN LEAVES FROM THE MIXTURE. THEN ADD THE COCONUT MILK TO THE BOWL AND USE A WHISK OR FORK TO MIX WELL.

3

IN THE BOTTOM LEVEL OF A STEAMER POT, BRING 2 INCHES OF WATER TO A BOIL OVER HIGH HEAT.

CHEF MALLIKA SAYS:

IT'S TRADITIONAL TO MAKE THE SANGKHAYA USING DUCK EGGS FOR BRIGHTER COLOR, IF YOU'RE ABLE TO ACCESS THEM!

4

PLACE THE BOWL OF SANGKHAYA IN THE UPPER SECTION
OF THE STEAMER, TURN THE HEAT TO MEDIUM-LOW,
AND CLOSE THE LID. LET STEAM FOR 20 MINUTES.

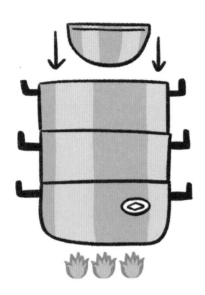 

5

REMOVE THE BOWL FROM THE
STEAMER AND LET COOL TO
A ROOM TEMPERATURE.

HOT!

6

SCOOP TWO SPOONFULS OF KHAO NIAW MOON
ONTO INDIVIDUAL SERVING PLATES. (IT IS
TRADITIONALLY SERVED ON BANANA LEAVES.)
THEN TOP EACH MOUND WITH A LAYER OF
SANGKHAYA. SERVE IMMEDIATELY.

SWEET!!

KHAI WAAN

SWEET EGG

MAKES 4 EGGS

2 CUPS WATER

2-INCH PIECE FRESH GINGER, PEELED AND THINLY SLICED

3 TABLESPOONS GRANULATED SUGAR

4 EGGS

1

IN A MEDIUM SAUCEPAN OR WOK OVER HIGH HEAT, COMBINE THE WATER, GINGER, AND SUGAR AND BRING TO A BOIL TO FORM A SYRUP.

2

CAREFULLY CRACK THE EGGS INTO A LARGE BOWL.

3

ONCE THE SYRUP IS BOILING, TURN THE HEAT TO MEDIUM-HIGH AND GENTLY POUR IN THE EGGS (OR USE A LADLE TO GENTLY DROP IN EACH EGG TO KEEP THEM INTACT).

4

COOK UNTIL THE WHITES ARE THICKENED, ABOUT 2 MINUTES FOR MEDIUM-BOILED OR 3 MINUTES FOR HARD-BOILED EGGS. REMOVE FROM THE HEAT. DRAIN AND SET ASIDE.

AI TIM GATHI

FORGET WHAT YOU THOUGHT YOU KNEW ABOUT COCONUT ICE CREAM, IT'S TIME TO TALK *TOPPINGS*. DO YOU CHOOSE COCONUT JELLY, SUGAR PALM SEEDS, OR BOTH? JACKFRUIT OR CORN? WHAT ABOUT STICKY RICE? DO YOU LIKE YOUR ICE CREAM IN A CUP OR SERVED ON TOP OF HOT-DOG BUNS? THAT'S RIGHT, IT'S TIME TO LEVEL UP THAT BORING TUB OF COCONUT ICE CREAM BY MAKING YOUR OWN AND UNLOCKING THE SECRETS TO THIS SIMPLE THAI DESSERT.

ICE CREAM

4 CUPS COCONUT MILK

3/4 CUP GRANULATED SUGAR

2 TABLESPOONS CORNSTARCH OR TAPIOCA FLOUR

1 TEASPOON FINE SEA SALT

2 TEASPOONS VANILLA EXTRACT

4 HOT DOG BUNS

FILLINGS

KHAO NIAW MOON (PAGE 154; OPTIONAL)

COCONUT JELLY, CANNED IN SYRUP (OPTIONAL)

SUGAR PALM SEEDS, CANNED IN HEAVY SYRUP (OPTIONAL)

SLICED JACKFRUIT, CANNED (OPTIONAL)

FRESH OR FROZEN (THAWED) CORN KERNELS (OPTIONAL)

1/4 CUP UNSALTED ROASTED PEANUTS

EVAPORATED MILK (PREFERABLY CARNATION BRAND) FOR DRIZZLING

1

TO MAKE THE ICE CREAM:
IN A MEDIUM SAUCEPAN, COMBINE THE COCONUT MILK, SUGAR, CORNSTARCH, SALT, AND VANILLA. STIR OR WHISK UNTIL INCORPORATED.

2

PLACE THE SAUCEPAN OVER MEDIUM HEAT AND STIR CONTINUOUSLY UNTIL THE COCONUT MIXTURE STARTS TO STEAM, 10 TO 15 MINUTES. BE CAREFUL TO PREVENT THE MIXTURE FROM BOILING.

CHEF MALLIKA SAYS:

IF YOU ARE A WHIPPED CREAM LOVER, TRY USING 2 CUPS OF COCONUT MILK AND 2 CUPS OF WHIPPED CREAM IN THE FIRST STEP.

3

REMOVE THE SAUCEPAN FROM THE HEAT
AND LET THE MIXTURE COOL TO ROOM
TEMPERATURE. (IF YOU ARE SHORT
ON TIME, PLACE THE SAUCEPAN IN AN
ICE BATH.) THE MIXTURE WILL BECOME
SLIGHTLY THICKENED.

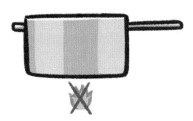

4

TRANSFER THE MIXTURE TO
A RESEALABLE CONTAINER,
CLOSE THE LID, AND FREEZE
FOR 4 HOURS.

5

REMOVE THE ICE CREAM FROM THE FREEZER
AND TRANSFER TO A BLENDER. PROCESS ON
HIGH SPEED UNTIL BLENDED EVENLY,
1 TO 2 MINUTES. (IF YOU DON'T HAVE
A BLENDER, USE A HAND-HELD MIXER.)

6

TRANSFER BACK TO THE CONTAINER, CLOSE
THE LID, AND FREEZE FOR 10 HOURS MORE,
OR UP TO OVERNIGHT.

7

WHEN READY TO SERVE, LET THE ICE CREAM
SIT AT ROOM TEMPERATURE UNTIL IT IS SOFT
ENOUGH TO SCOOP, 5 TO 10 MINUTES.

8

SPLIT OPEN THE HOT DOG BUNS AND LAYER WITH
THE FILLINGS OF YOUR CHOICE, FOLLOW WITH A FEW
SCOOPS OF THE COCONUT ICE CREAM, AND THEN
TOP WITH THE ROASTED PEANUTS AND A DRIZZLE
OF EVAPORATED MILK. SERVE IMMEDIATELY.

NAM PAN

THERE'S NOTHING BETTER THAN REFRESHING FRUIT ON A HOT SUMMER DAY, SO LET'S TALK SMOOTHIES! THESE TWO FLAVOR OPTIONS--NAM TANGMO PAN (WATERMELON) AND NAM MANAO PAN (LIME)--CAPTURE THAT SUMMER BEACHY FEELING SO WELL, AND NOW YOU CAN ENJOY THEM LITERALLY ANYWHERE. SMOOTHIES ARE AN EFFORTLESS WAY TO PACK A BUNCH OF NUTRITIOUS INGREDIENTS INTO ONE PORTABLE CONTAINER, MAKING IT EASY TO STAY HYDRATED ALONG THE WAY TOO.

MAKES 2 SERVINGS

NAM TANGMO PAN

2 TABLESPOONS GRANULATED SUGAR (OR ADJUST TO TASTE)

2 TABLESPOONS WATER

2½ CUPS COLD WATERMELON CHUNKS, SEEDED, PLUS WATERMELON SLICES FOR GARNISHING (OPTIONAL)

¼ TEASPOON FINE SEA SALT (OPTIONAL)

2 CUPS ICE, CRUSHED OR CUBED

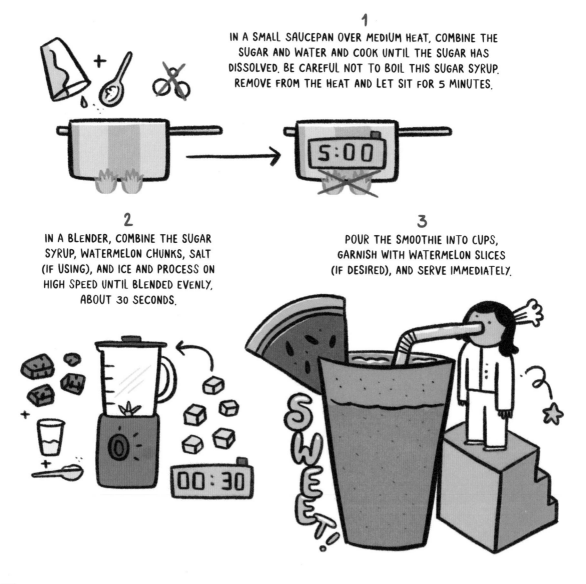

1

IN A SMALL SAUCEPAN OVER MEDIUM HEAT, COMBINE THE SUGAR AND WATER AND COOK UNTIL THE SUGAR HAS DISSOLVED. BE CAREFUL NOT TO BOIL THIS SUGAR SYRUP. REMOVE FROM THE HEAT AND LET SIT FOR 5 MINUTES.

2

IN A BLENDER, COMBINE THE SUGAR SYRUP, WATERMELON CHUNKS, SALT (IF USING), AND ICE AND PROCESS ON HIGH SPEED UNTIL BLENDED EVENLY, ABOUT 30 SECONDS.

3

POUR THE SMOOTHIE INTO CUPS, GARNISH WITH WATERMELON SLICES (IF DESIRED), AND SERVE IMMEDIATELY.

SWEET!

NAM MANAO PAN

1/2 CUP FRESH LIME JUICE, PLUS LIME SLICES FOR GARNISHING (OPTIONAL)

1/3 CUP GRANULATED SUGAR (OR ADJUST TO TASTE)

1/4 CUP WARM (ABOUT 140°F) WATER

1/4 TEASPOON FINE SEA SALT

2 CUPS ICE, CRUSHED OR CUBED

1

IN A SMALL BOWL, COMBINE THE LIME JUICE, SUGAR, WATER, AND SALT AND STIR UNTIL THE SUGAR HAS DISSOLVED.

2

IN A BLENDER, COMBINE THE ICE AND THE LIME JUICE MIXTURE AND PROCESS ON HIGH SPEED UNTIL BLENDED EVENLY, ABOUT 30 SECONDS.

3

POUR THE SMOOTHIE INTO CUPS, GARNISH WITH LIME SLICES (IF DESIRED), AND SERVE IMMEDIATELY.

SOUR!

CHA YEN

CHA YEN ACCURATELY TRANSLATES TO "COLD TEA." KNOWN AROUND THE WORLD AS SIMPLY THAI TEA, THIS STRONG-BREWED BEVERAGE IS ALREADY VERY AROMATIC ON ITS OWN, BUT IT'S ONLY COMPLETE WHEN MIXED WITH SWEETENED CONDENSED MILK AND, OF COURSE, WE CAN'T FORGET THE ICE. THIS REFRESHINGLY SWEET AND ENERGIZING (HELLO, SUGAR RUSH!) DRINK IS BOTH A LOCAL AND TOURIST FAVE, ENJOYED WHILE WALKING AROUND THAILAND IN THE BOILING HEAT.

MAKES 2 SERVINGS

4 TABLESPOONS THAI TEA MIX
(PREFERABLY CHATRAMUE BRAND)

2 CUPS BOILING WATER

4 TABLESPOONS GRANULATED SUGAR
(OR TO TASTE)

2 TABLESPOONS SWEETENED CONDENSED MILK (PREFERABLY CARNATION BRAND) OR SWEETENED NONDAIRY CREAMER

CRUSHED ICE OR ICE CUBES FOR SERVING

1/4 CUP EVAPORATED MILK
(PREFERABLY CARNATION BRAND)

1
PLACE A REUSABLE CLOTH FILTER BAG OVER A SMALL PITCHER, ADD THE TEA MIX AND BOILING WATER, AND MIX WELL. COVER AND LET THE TEA STEEP FOR 5 MINUTES.

2
REMOVE THE FILTER BAG. ADD THE SUGAR AND CONDENSED MILK TO THE PITCHER AND MIX WELL.

3
COVER THE PITCHER (OR TRANSFER THE TEA TO A RESEALABLE CONTAINER) AND REFRIGERATE FOR AT LEAST 2 HOURS.

4
ADD ICE TO TWO GLASSES. EVENLY DIVIDE THE TEA AMONG THE GLASSES AND TOP WITH THE EVAPORATED MILK. SERVE IMMEDIATELY.

IF YOU DON'T HAVE A SPECIFIC REUSABLE THAI TEA STRAINER BAG, A COTTON TEA BAG OR COFFEE FILTER BAG DOES THE JOB.

UNFORTUNATELY, IF THE TEA MIX IS NOT IMPORTED FROM THAILAND, IT MIGHT NOT RESULT IN THE ICONIC BRIGHT ORANGE COLOR.

CHON GAEW!*

*CHEERS!

EGGS, RICE... WHAT ELSE DO WE NEED FROM THE STORE?

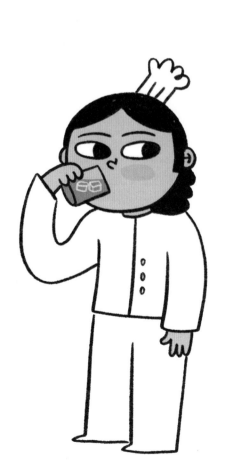

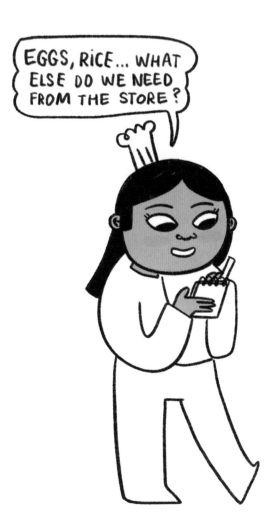

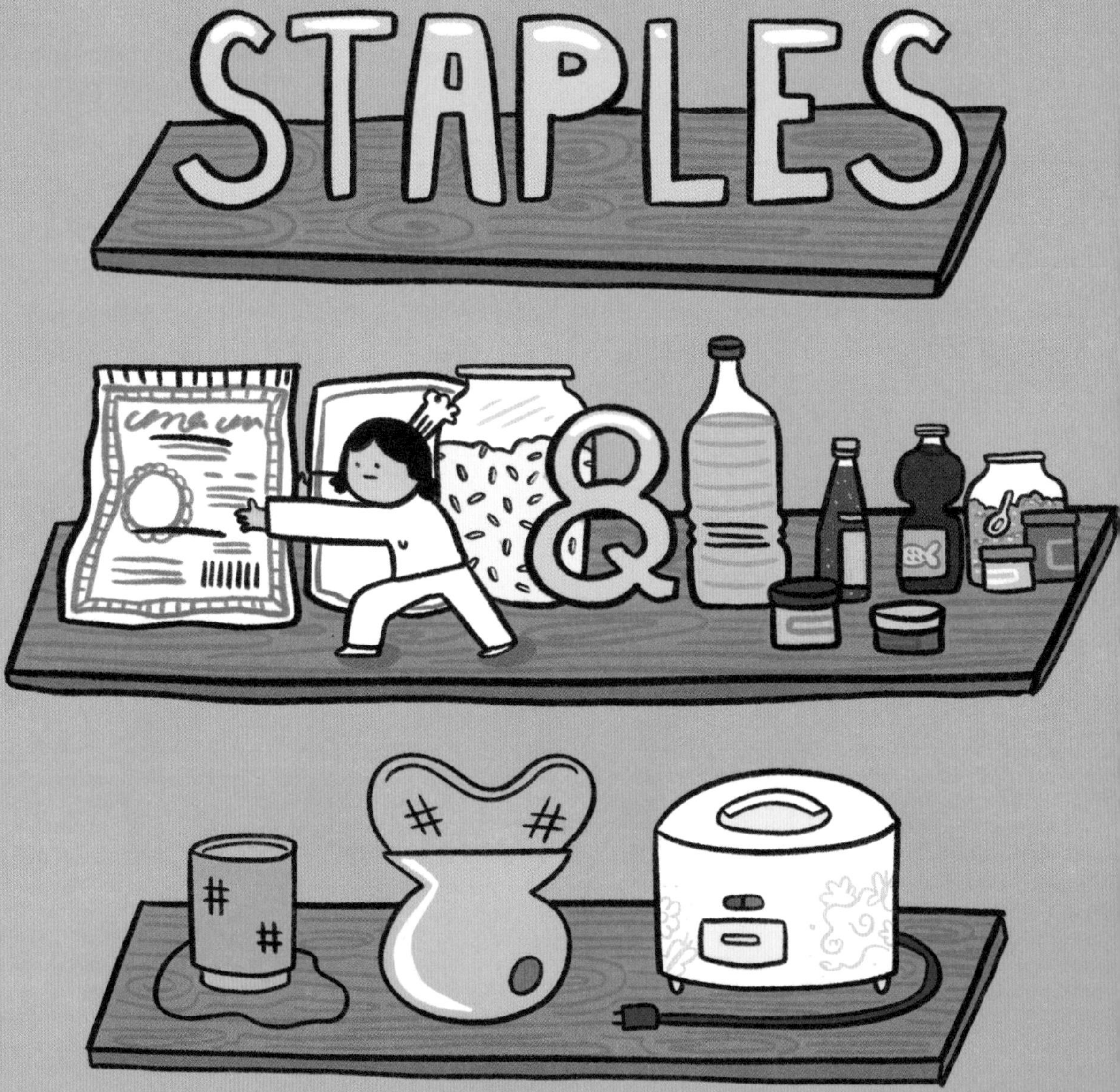
STAPLES
&

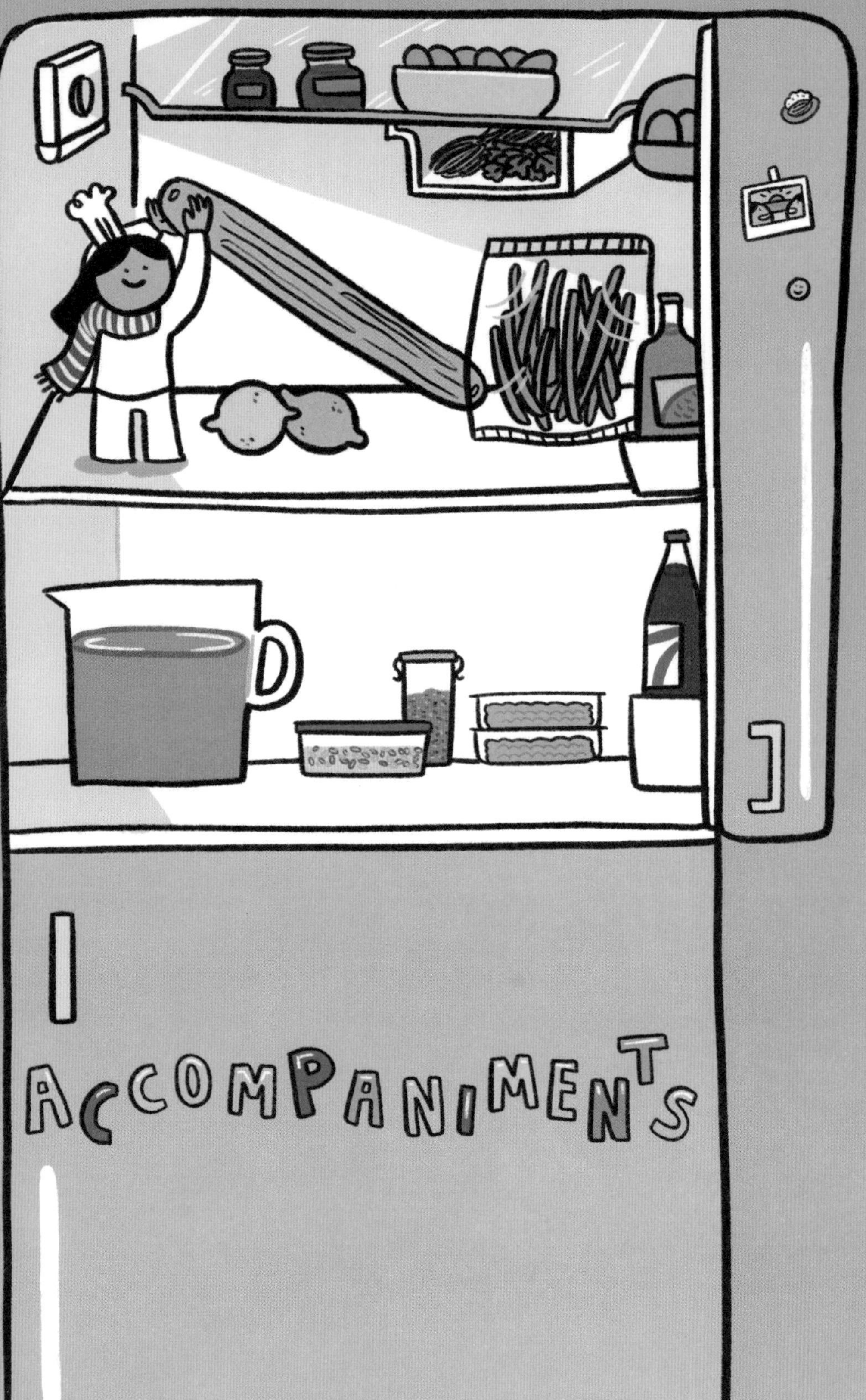
ACCOMPANIMENTS

THIS CHAPTER DIVES INTO THE EXTRA ELEMENTS AND SPECIAL FLAVORS THAT YOU CAN ADD TO ALL THAI DISHES. THESE ARE THE THAI PANTRY STAPLES YOU SHOULD ALWAYS HAVE ON HAND, SUCH AS A PHRIK NAM PLA FOR ADDING A SPICY TANGY BOOST TO YOUR NOODLES, OR GRATHIAM JIEW FOR ADDING A CRUNCHY GARLICKY KICK TO YOUR STIR-FRY.

WE'LL SHOW YOU HOW TO MAKE THE DELICIOUS ACCOMPANIMENTS THAT WILL SUPPORT YOUR DISH, SUCH AS THE PERFECT FRIED EGG OR STICKY RICE--THE EASY WAY.

BECAUSE EGGS ARE SO AFFORDABLE AND VERSATILE, THEY ARE OFTEN SERVED AS A SIDE DISH OR EVEN AS A COMPLETE MEAL WHEN PAIRED WITH RICE. THERE'S AN ENDLESS NUMBER OF EGG RECIPES, BUT TODAY WE'RE SHARING THE MOST EXCITING CLASSICS.

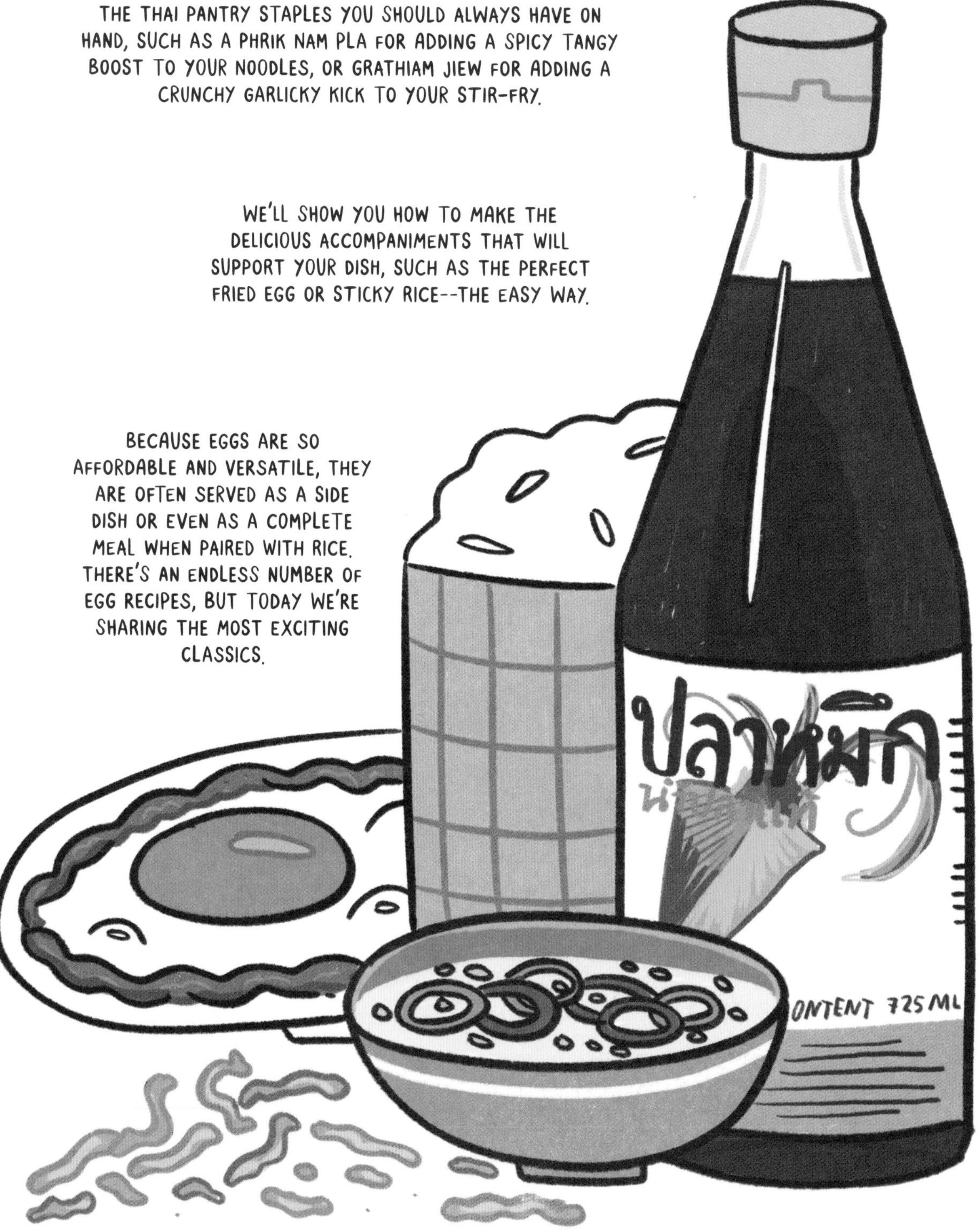
ปลาหมึก
ONTENT 725 ML

AND SINCE RICE IS A VERY IMPORTANT ELEMENT IN THAI CUISINE, IT IS A GOOD IDEA TO LEARN HOW TO MAKE SOME *REALLY GOOD* JASMINE AND STICKY RICE, JUST LIKE THE THAIS.

THE BEST PART IS THESE STAPLES AND ACCOMPANIMENTS ARE STRONG ENOUGH TO STAND ON THEIR OWN! WITH ONLY EGGS, RICE, AND ONE SAUCE OF YOUR CHOICE, YOU ALREADY HAVE A COMPLETE AND HAPPY MEAL.

KHAO SUAY

KHAO SUAY LITERALLY TRANSLATES TO "BEAUTIFUL RICE." CUTE, ISN'T IT? ANOTHER WORD FOR KHAO SUAY IS *KHAO HOM MALI,* WHICH MEANS "JASMINE RICE," AND IT OFTEN REFERS TO THE UNCOOKED VERSION. IT'S PRETTY COMMON FOR THAI PEOPLE TO EAT RICE THREE TIMES A DAY. AT MALLIKA'S HOUSE, THEY HAVE A THREE-MEAL PORTION OF RICE COOKED AND READY IN THE KITCHEN FROM MORNING UNTIL DUSK!

MAKES 4 CUPS

2 CUPS JASMINE RICE
2 CUPS WATER

1

PUT THE RICE INTO A MEDIUM SAUCEPAN AND ADD ENOUGH WATER TO COVER. USING YOUR HAND, GENTLY STIR THE RICE AROUND AND WATCH AS THE WATER GETS CLOUDY WITH SEDIMENT.

2

DRAIN THE RICE IN A FINE-MESH STRAINER OVER THE SINK, THEN TRANSFER BACK TO THE SAUCEPAN. REPEAT THE RINSING PROCESS TWICE, OR UNTIL THE WATER IS CLEAR.

CHEF MALLIKA SAYS:

TO REHEAT COOKED RICE STRAIGHT FROM THE FRIDGE IN THE MICROWAVE, SPRINKLE SOME WATER OVER THE TOP TO LIGHTLY MOISTEN THE RICE AND MIX WELL. HEAT 1 CUP OF COOKED RICE FOR 60 SECONDS AND 2 CUPS FOR 90 SECONDS.

3

PLACE THE SAUCEPAN WITH CLEANED RICE OVER MEDIUM HEAT AND ADD THE 2 CUPS WATER. MIX WELL.

TURN THE HEAT TO HIGH. STIR THE RICE CONSTANTLY SO IT DOES NOT STICK TO THE BOTTOM OF THE PAN AND BRING TO A BOIL.

4

WHEN THE WATER COMES TO A BOIL, TURN THE HEAT TO MEDIUM AND COVER. LET COOK, UNDISTURBED, FOR 10 MINUTES.

5

REMOVE THE LID AND, USING A SPOON, FLUFF UP THE RICE.

6

RE-COVER THE RICE AND CONTINUE COOKING FOR 5 MINUTES MORE. THEN REMOVE THE PAN FROM THE HEAT TO PREVENT THE RICE FROM BURNING ON THE BOTTOM.

7

LET THE RICE REST FOR 5 TO 10 MINUTES BEFORE SERVING.

SUAY!

*PRETTY!

KHAO NIAW

THIS STICKY RICE, WHICH CAN ALSO BE CALLED "SWEET" OR "GLUTINOUS" RICE, IS PERFECT WITH FINGER FOODS SUCH AS DEEP-FRIED OR GRILLED MEATS AND PAPAYA SALAD OR AS THE MAIN INGREDIENT IN MANY DESSERTS. IT'S NOT *REALLY* SWEET, NOR DOES IT CONTAIN GLUTEN, BUT IT IS A BIT SWEETER THAN JASMINE RICE, YES, AND PRIZED FOR ITS CHEWY, STICKY, GOOEY TEXTURE. THAI KIDS *ADORE* STICKY RICE, AND THEY SOMETIMES CARRY AROUND A TINY WOVEN BASKET WITH A KID-SIZE PORTION. EVEN CHRISTINA REMEMBERS HAVING HER OWN PERSONAL LITTLE BASKET IN BELGIUM. ENJOY YOUR RICE WITH FAVORITES SUCH AS SOM TUM (PAGE 46), SUEA RONG HAI (PAGE 50), AND LARB MOO (PAGE 116).

MAKES 4 CUPS

2 CUPS STICKY RICE
8 CUPS WATER, PLUS MORE FOR SOAKING

1

IN A MEDIUM BOWL, COMBINE THE RICE AND 3½ CUPS OF WATER AND LET SOAK FOR 1 TO 2 HOURS. (THE LONGER YOU SOAK, THE SOFTER THE RICE.)

2

DRAIN THE RICE IN A FINE-MESH STRAINER OVER THE SINK, THEN TRANSFER BACK TO THE BOWL, COVER WITH FRESH WATER, AND GENTLY STIR WITH YOUR HAND TO CLEAN. REPEAT THIS PROCESS UNTIL THE WATER IS CLEAR.

3

PLACE THE DRAINED RICE IN A STEAMER-SAFE SERVING BOWL.

CHEF MALLIKA SAYS:

SHORT ON TIME? YOU CAN ACHIEVE THE SAME RESULTS BY MAKING STICKY RICE IN A MICROWAVE! PLACE SOAKED AND DRAINED STICKY RICE IN A MICROWAVE-SAFE BOWL, ADD 1¼ CUPS WATER TO THE RICE, COVER, AND MICROWAVE ON FULL POWER FOR 5 MINUTES. FLUFF THE RICE, COVER, AND HEAT FOR 3 MINUTES MORE. LET THE RICE REST FOR A FEW MINUTES BEFORE SERVING.

TO REHEAT 1 CUP OF COOKED STICKY RICE IN A MICROWAVE, START BY HEATING IT FOR 1 MINUTE. IF IT'S STILL COLD, PUT IT BACK IN FOR 20 SECONDS. THERE'S NO TURNING BACK ONCE YOU'VE OVERCOOKED THE RICE, SO BE MINDFUL AND KEEP CHECKING.

COOKED STICKY RICE SHOULD BE COVERED AT ALL TIMES DURING A MEAL, OTHERWISE IT WILL GET DRY AND HARD FROM EXPOSURE TO THE AIR.

4

IN THE BOTTOM OF A STEAMER POT OVER HIGH HEAT, BRING THE 8 CUPS WATER TO A BOIL.

5

TURN THE HEAT TO MEDIUM, PLACE THE SERVING BOWL OF RICE IN THE UPPER SECTION OF THE STEAMER POT, COVER, AND STEAM THE RICE FOR 15 MINUTES.

6

REMOVE THE LID AND, USING A SPOON, FLUFF UP THE RICE.

7

RE-COVER THE STEAMER POT AND CONTINUE COOKING FOR 5 MINUTES MORE.

8

REMOVE THE STEAMER POT FROM THE HEAT. LET THE RICE REST UNTIL THE STEAM HAS DISSIPATED, 5 TO 10 MINUTES.

9

USING A KITCHEN TOWEL, LIFT THE BOWL FROM THE STEAMER POT. (IF YOU HAVE A TRADITIONAL BAMBOO BASKET, TRANSFER THE RICE TO THE BASKET.) COVER THE RICE WITH PLASTIC WRAP OR ALUMINUM FOIL TO KEEP IT FROM DRYING OUT. SERVE IMMEDIATELY.

BLENDING TRADITIONS:
THE VERSATILE OMELET

MALLIKA LEARNED TO COOK
WHEN SHE WAS SEVEN.

THE KITCHEN WAS PROBABLY THE
ONE PLACE IN HER HOME WHERE
SHE SPENT THE MOST TIME, EVER.

HER FIRST DISH WAS KHAI JIEW BECAUSE
THAI OMELETS ARE SO QUICK AND EASY—
BUT OH, SO GOOD.

(THEY WERE ESPECIALLY FUN TO MAKE
WHEN HER PARENTS WEREN'T HOME...)

THE OMELET THAT SHE LEARNED TO
MAKE FEATURED A **LOT** OF FISH SAUCE.

WHEN SHE MOVED TO BANGKOK, SHE DISCOVERED THAT PEOPLE IN THE CITY PREFERRED TO USE SOY SAUCE INSTEAD!

AT FIRST, SHE WAS SELF-CONSCIOUS: "DID I DO IT THE WRONG WAY MY WHOLE LIFE?"

...

SO NATURALLY SHE STARTED USING SOY SAUCE FOR HER OMELETS AS WELL...

...BUT LATER SHE REALIZED THAT SHE DIDN'T HAVE TO GIVE UP HER CHILDHOOD PREFERENCES JUST BECAUSE OTHERS HAD THEIR OWN. THE BEAUTY OF FOOD IS THAT YOU CAN TRY NEW THINGS AND APPRECIATE THEM—BUT YOU DON'T HAVE TO CHANGE YOURSELF.

KHAI JIEW

KHAI JIEW LITERALLY TRANSLATES TO "FRIED EGG," BUT IT'S ACTUALLY AN OMELET. THIS IS OFTEN THE VERY FIRST DISH THAT MOST THAI KIDS LEARN HOW TO MAKE BECAUSE IT'S SO SIMPLE, AND YOU CAN ADD ANY INGREDIENTS YOU LIKE. SERVE WITH RICE AND NAM JIM JAEW (PAGE 184), OR PAIR WITH OTHER MAIN DISHES, SUCH AS GAENG PANANG (PAGE 134), GAENG KEOW WAN (PAGE 130), PAD GAPRAO (PAGE 98), AND PAD PHAK BUNG (PAGE 97).

MAKES 1 SERVING

2 EGGS

1/4 TEASPOON SEASONING POWDER, OR 1/2 TEASPOON GRANULATED SUGAR

1 TEASPOON THIN SOY SAUCE OR FISH SAUCE

2 TABLESPOONS CHOPPED VEGETABLES OR MEAT (CHIVES, CARROTS, FRESH SWEET BASIL LEAVES, GROUND PORK, OR FINELY CHOPPED SHRIMP; OPTIONAL)

2 TABLESPOONS NEUTRAL OIL

1
CRACK THE EGGS INTO A MEDIUM BOWL.

2
ADD THE SEASONING POWDER AND THIN SOY SAUCE TO THE EGGS AND BEAT WELL.

3
ADD THE VEGETABLES OR MEAT (IF USING) TO THE EGGS AND MIX WELL.

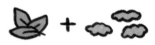

4
IN A LARGE FRYING PAN OVER HIGH HEAT, WARM THE OIL.

CHEF MALLIKA SAYS:

IF YOU PLAN TO PAIR THIS WITH A STIR-FRIED WOK DISH (PAD PHAK BUNG, FOR EXAMPLE), MAKE THE OMELET FIRST. THEN YOU CAN FINISH THE REST OF THE MEAL IN THE SAME PAN RIGHT AFTER!

5

WHEN THE OIL IS LIGHTLY SMOKING, TURN THE HEAT TO MEDIUM-HIGH AND IMMEDIATELY POUR THE BEATEN EGGS INTO THE CENTER OF THE PAN.

6

USING A SPATULA, SPREAD THE EGGS EVENLY.

7

WHEN THE EDGES AND BOTTOM OF THE EGGS START TO SET, USE THE SPATULA TO GENTLY PUSH IN THE EDGES TO LET THE UNCOOKED EGG FROM THE TOP SURFACE RUN DOWN TO THE BOTTOM.

8

ONCE THE SURFACE OF THE EGG IS NO LONGER RUNNY AND YOU SEE SMALL BUBBLES BEGINNING TO FORM, INSERT THE SPATULA UNDER THE EGGS AS FAR AS POSSIBLE AND FLIP THE OMELET TO REVEAL A PERFECTLY BROWNED BOTTOM.

FLIP!

CRISPY!

9

WHEN THE SECOND SIDE OF THE OMELET IS EQUALLY BROWNED, REMOVE FROM THE HEAT.

10

SERVE THE OMELET IMMEDIATELY.

KHAI DAO

KHAI DAO, WHICH TRANSLATES TO "STAR EGG," IS INDEED THE BEAUTIFUL FRIED-EGG STAR TO TOP EVERY DISH. CRAVING A PERFECT EGG BUT YOU'RE IN A HURRY? TRY THIS ONE. TRUST US. WHAT'S SO GOOD ABOUT THE THAI STYLE OF MAKING FRIED EGGS IS THAT THE WHITE EDGES OF THE EGG GET SUPER-CRISPY AND THE YOLK IS THE PERFECT DEGREE OF RUNNINESS. SERVE WITH KHAO SUAY (PAGE 170) AND YOUR PREFERRED HOT SAUCE, OR PHRIK NAM PLA (PAGE 185). THIS IS A CLASSIC TOPPER TO SPICY STIR-FRY DISHES SUCH AS PAD GAPRAO (PAGE 98).

MAKES 1 SERVING

3 TABLESPOONS NEUTRAL OIL
1 EGG

1
IN A SMALL FRYING PAN OVER MEDIUM-HIGH HEAT, WARM THE OIL.

2
WHEN THE OIL IS LIGHTLY SMOKING, GENTLY CRACK THE EGG INTO THE CENTER OF THE PAN.

CHEF MALLIKA SAYS:

IF COOKING MORE THAN ONE EGG IN A PAN AT A TIME, ADJUST THE AMOUNT OF NEUTRAL OIL TO MATCH.

ARE YOU A HUGE FAN OF FRIED EGGS? YOU CAN MAKE YUM KHAI DAO (FRIED EGG SALAD) AS WELL! FOLLOW ALL THE INGREDIENTS AND STEPS OF YUM WOON SEN (PAGE 52), BUT USE SIX OR SEVEN FRIED EGGS, QUARTERED, IN PLACE OF THE PORK ROLL AND GLASS NOODLES.

3

USING A SPATULA, SCOOP THE OIL ONTO THE EGG YOLK.
REPEAT UNTIL THE YOLK BECOMES LIGHTER IN COLOR
AND THE EDGES OF THE EGG WHITES ARE BROWN
AND CRISPY, ABOUT 1 MINUTE.

1:00

4

IF YOU PREFER A WELL-COOKED EGG,
OR IF YOU DON'T HAVE ENOUGH OIL
LEFT IN THE PAN TO SCOOP, GENTLY
FLIP THE EGG. REMOVE FROM THE
HEAT ONCE THE EGG IS COOKED
TO YOUR LIKING.

FLIP

PERFECT!

5

SERVE THE EGG
IMMEDIATELY.

KHAI TOM

THE IDEAL THAI BOILED EGG IS SIMPLY MEDIUM-BOILED AND SERVES AS THE PERFECT ACCOMPANIMENT TO MANY RICE DISHES AND NOODLES, SUCH AS NAM PHRIK ONG (PAGE 118), GAENG KEOW WAN (PAGE 130) WITH KHANOM JEEN, AND GAENG PANANG (PAGE 134). HOWEVER, KHAI TOM IS ALSO GREAT ON ITS OWN WHEN TOPPED WITH PHRIK NAM PLA--A DELICIOUS SAUCE THAT COMBINES LIME, FISH SAUCE, SUGAR, CHILES, GARLIC, AND SHALLOTS--TO CREATE MINI FLAVOR BOMBS! SERVE WITH RICE OR PAIR WITH YOUR FAVORITE MAIN DISHES.

MAKES 4 EGGS

4 EGGS

PHRIK NAM PLA (PAGE 185) FOR SERVING

1

IN A SMALL SAUCEPAN OVER HIGH HEAT, COMBINE THE EGGS AND WATER TO COVER AND BRING TO A BOIL.

2

TURN THE HEAT TO MEDIUM-HIGH AND COOK THE EGGS FOR 7 TO 8 MINUTES FOR MEDIUM-BOILED OR FOR 12 MINUTES FOR HARD-BOILED.

CHEF MALLIKA SAYS:

THE EASIEST WAY TO PEEL A HARD-BOILED EGG? PUT IT IN A SMALL GLASS, THEN COVER THE TOP WITH YOUR HAND AND SHAKE VIGOROUSLY ABOUT TWENTY TIMES. THE SHELL WILL BE CRACKED ENOUGH TO BE EASILY AND BEAUTIFULLY REMOVED.

3

ONCE THE BOILED EGGS ARE READY, POUR OUT THE HOT WATER AND ADD COLD WATER. LEAVE FOR 2 MINUTES AND THEN PEEL THE EGGS.

4

USING THREAD OR A KNIFE, CUT THE EGGS IN HALF LENGTHWISE.

5

PLACE THE EGGS FACE UP ON A SERVING PLATE. TOP WITH PHRIK NAM PLA AND SERVE.

EGGCELLENT!

KHAI TOON

STEAMED EGG IS YET ANOTHER FAVORITE EGG DISH. WHEN MALLIKA WAS YOUNGER, SHE DIDN'T LIKE STEAMED EGGS AT ALL BECAUSE OF THE "INTERESTING" TEXTURE AND RELATIVELY BLAND FLAVOR THAT OFTEN COMES WITH STEAMING. HOWEVER, WHEN HER AUNT CAME UP WITH HER OWN RECIPE THAT INCLUDED FRIED SHALLOTS AS A TOPPING, MALLIKA BECAME AN INSTANT FAN--AND YOU WILL TOO! SERVE WITH KHAO SUAY (PAGE 170) OR PAIR WITH MAIN DISHES, SUCH AS PAD PHAK BUNG (PAGE 97), PAD GAPRAO (PAGE 98), OR PAD SATOR (PAGE 100).

MAKES 2 SERVINGS

4 EGGS

1 TEASPOON SEASONING POWDER OR GRANULATED SUGAR

1 TABLESPOON THIN SOY SAUCE OR FISH SAUCE

3/4 CUP WATER

5 TABLESPOONS NEUTRAL OIL

1/2 CUP HOM JIEW (PAGE 188)

1
CRACK THE EGGS INTO A LARGE STEAMER-SAFE BOWL.

2
ADD THE SEASONING POWDER AND THIN SOY SAUCE TO THE EGGS, THEN BEAT VERY WELL.

3
ADD THE 3/4 CUP WATER TO THE EGGS AND MIX WELL.

4
IN THE BOTTOM LEVEL OF A STEAMER POT, BRING 2 INCHES OF WATER TO A BOIL OVER HIGH HEAT.

CHEF MALLIKA SAYS:

AS WITH A KHAI JIEW (SEE PAGE 176), YOU CAN ALSO MIX IN OTHER INGREDIENTS, SUCH AS GROUND PORK AND VEGETABLES, WHEN BEATING THE EGGS.

5

PLACE THE BOWL OF EGGS IN THE UPPER SECTION OF
THE STEAMER POT. (THIS IS TO PREVENT FROM GETTING
BURNED BY HOT STEAM WHEN YOU'RE LOWERING THE BOWL
OVER THE BOILING POT!) LOWER THE HEAT TO MEDIUM,
COVER, AND ALLOW THE EGGS TO STEAM FOR 20 MINUTES.

6

REMOVE THE STEAMER POT FROM
THE HEAT AND SET ASIDE UNTIL
THE STEAM HAS DISSIPATED.

7

USING A KITCHEN TOWEL,
LIFT THE BOWL FROM THE
STEAMER POT.

HOT!

8

TOP THE EGGS WITH
THE HOM JIEW AND
SERVE IMMEDIATELY.

WAW!

NAM JIM JAEW

NAM JIM JAEW IS A SPICY DIPPING SAUCE, ORIGINATING FROM THE ISAAN REGION. THERE ARE SEVERAL DIFFERENT RECIPES FOR THIS ONE, BUT WE'RE STICKING TO THE ORIGINAL WITH THE KEY INGREDIENTS OF TAMARIND PASTE AND ROASTED RICE POWDER. NAM JIM JAEW IS THE PERFECT ADDITION TO GRILLED MEAT, SEAFOOD, VEGETABLES, AND STICKY RICE BECAUSE IT COMBINES ALL THE SPICY AND TANGY FLAVORS FOR WHICH THAI CUISINE IS FAMOUS. THE TOASTED RICE POWDER ADDS NUTTINESS AND CRUNCH, SO DON'T OMIT IT!

MAKES ABOUT 1/3 CUP

1 1/2 TABLESPOONS GRATED PALM SUGAR (ABOUT 1/2 PIECE) OR GRANULATED SUGAR

1 TABLESPOON NAM MAKHAM PIAK (PAGE 195)

3 TABLESPOONS FISH SAUCE

2 1/2 TEASPOONS FRESH LIME JUICE

1 TABLESPOON PHRIK PON (PAGE 192; ADJUST TO TASTE)

1 1/2 TABLESPOONS KHAO KHUA (PAGE 190)

2 TABLESPOONS CHOPPED CHIVES OR GREEN ONIONS (WHITE AND GREEN PARTS)

1 TABLESPOON THINLY SLICED RED SHALLOT OR RED ONION

1

IN A SMALL BOWL, COMBINE THE PALM SUGAR, NAM MAKHAM PIAK, FISH SAUCE, LIME JUICE, PHRIK PON, AND KHAO KHUA.

2

ADD THE CHIVES AND SHALLOT TO THE BOWL AND MIX WELL.

3

NAM JIM JAEW CAN BE STORED IN THE FRIDGE IN AN AIRTIGHT CONTAINER FOR UP TO 3 DAYS.

AMMMMAZING!

PHRIK NAM PLA

MAKES ABOUT 1/3 CUP

PHRIK NAM PLA IS A CLASSIC CHILE FISH SAUCE THAT CAN BE COMBINED WITH ANY DISH FOR A SPICY, SWEET, AND UMAMI KICK. YOU'VE PROBABLY NOTICED A SMALL JAR OF IT PLACED ON EVERY TABLE AT THAI STREET RESTAURANTS--IT'S A STAPLE! THAIS, ESPECIALLY MALLIKA, CAN GET CRANKY IF THERE'S NO PHRIK NAM PLA, SO BETTER BE PREPARED IF YOU HAVE YOUR THAI FRIENDS COMING OVER.

- 6 FRESH RED AND GREEN THAI CHILES (OR ADJUST TO TASTE), STEMMED AND THINLY SLICED CROSSWISE
- 4 GARLIC CLOVES, SLICED PAPER-THIN
- 1/4 CUP FRESH LIME JUICE
- 1 TEASPOON GRANULATED SUGAR
- 1/4 CUP FISH SAUCE
- CHOPPED CILANTRO LEAVES AND STEMS FOR GARNISHING (OPTIONAL)

1

IN A SMALL BOWL, COMBINE THE CHILES, GARLIC, AND LIME JUICE. LET STAND FOR 3 MINUTES TO PREVENT THE CHILE SEEDS FROM TURNING BLACK QUICKLY.

2

ADD THE SUGAR AND FISH SAUCE TO THE BOWL AND MIX WELL. GARNISH WITH CILANTRO (IF DESIRED).

3

PHRIK NAM PLA CAN BE STORED IN THE FRIDGE IN AN AIRTIGHT CONTAINER FOR UP TO 7 DAYS.

PHRIK NAM SOM

PHRIK NAM SOM IS JUST SLICED FRESH CHILES SOAKED IN VINEGAR, BUT IT'S A PERMANENT MEMBER OF THE THAI SEASONING SET. ONE SPOONFUL IS GUARANTEED TO ELECTRIFY ANY NOODLE DISH WITH A SALTY, SOUR ZING!

MAKES ABOUT 1/2 CUP

2 FRESH RED OR GREEN (OR BOTH) SERRANO OR ANAHEIM CHILES OR BANANA PEPPERS, STEMMED AND SLICED

1/4 TEASPOON FINE SEA SALT

1/2 CUP DISTILLED WHITE VINEGAR

1

IN A MEDIUM BOWL OR A JAR, COMBINE THE CHILES, SALT, AND VINEGAR. THIS CAN BE USED IMMEDIATELY, BUT IT IS BEST TO LET IT SOAK FOR UP TO 3 DAYS.

2

PHRIK NAM SOM CAN BE STORED IN AN AIRTIGHT CONTAINER IN THE FRIDGE FOR MONTHS.

PHRIK KHUA

MAKING PHRIK KHUA IS THE PROCESS OF TOASTING DRIED CHILES. WHY DO WE NEED TO DO THIS EXTRA STEP OF SLOWLY TOASTING CHILES THAT ARE ALREADY DRIED? IT ADDS ANOTHER LEVEL OF DEEP HERBAL, SMOKY (ALMOST TOBACCO-LIKE) FLAVOR TO YOUR DISH. PHRIK KHUA IS OFTEN USED AS A GARNISH FOR SOUPS.

MAKES 10 CHILES

2 TABLESPOONS NEUTRAL OIL

10 DRIED RED THAI CHILES (OR ADJUST TO TASTE), STEMMED

1
IN A SMALL PAN OVER MEDIUM HEAT, WARM THE OIL.

2
WHEN THE OIL IS SHIMMERING, ADD THE DRIED CHILES AND TOAST, TURNING FREQUENTLY, UNTIL THEY ARE BROWNED, 2 TO 3 MINUTES. IF IT LOOKS LIKE THE CHILES ARE ABOUT TO BURN, REMOVE FROM THE HEAT AT ONCE.

3
PHRIK KHUA CAN BE STORED IN AN AIRTIGHT CONTAINER IN A COOL, DRY PLACE FOR UP TO 3 MONTHS.

GRATHIAM JIEW
OR HOM JIEW

BOTH FRIED GARLIC AND FRIED SHALLOT ARE CRUCIAL TOPPINGS IN THAI CUISINE. WE SPRINKLE ONE (OR BOTH) ON TOP OF OUR DISHES TO DECORATE AND ENHANCE THE TEXTURE AND TASTE. FRIED GARLIC AND SHALLOTS ARE OFTEN ADDED TO STIR-FRIED DISHES, STEAMED EGGS, NOODLE SOUPS, AND ANYTHING ELSE YOU CAN GET YOUR HANDS ON.

MAKES ABOUT 1/2 CUP

2 GARLIC HEADS, CLOVES SEPARATED BUT UNPEELED, OR 10 SMALL RED SHALLOTS OR 3 MEDIUM RED ONIONS, PEELED AND SLICED PAPER-THIN

1/3 CUP NEUTRAL OIL

1/4 TEASPOON FINE SEA SALT

1
IN A MORTAR AND USING THE PESTLE, FINELY CRUSH THE GARLIC.

2
LINE A PLATE WITH PAPER TOWELS. IN A SMALL SAUCEPAN OR FRYING PAN OVER MEDIUM-HIGH HEAT, WARM THE NEUTRAL OIL.

CHEF MALLIKA SAYS:

IF YOU DON'T HAVE A MORTAR AND PESTLE, MINCE THE GARLIC WITH A KNIFE OR GRATE IT WITH A MICROPLANE GRATER.

3

WHEN THE OIL IS SHIMMERING, ADD THE GARLIC OR SHALLOTS
AND SALT AND FRY UNTIL GOLDEN AND CRISP, 3 TO 4 MINUTES
FOR GARLIC AND 10 MINUTES FOR SHALLOTS.

4

USING TONGS OR A SKIMMER,
TRANSFER THE GARLIC OR
SHALLOTS TO THE PREPARED
PLATE AND LET DRAIN.

5

ONCE DRAINED, TRANSFER
TO A SMALL BOWL AND
LET COOL.

6

GRATHIAM JIEW OR HOM
JIEW CAN BE STORED IN AN
AIRTIGHT CONTAINER
IN THE FRIDGE FOR UP
TO 3 MONTHS.

CRISPY!

KHAO KHUA

KHAO KHUA IS CRUSHED TOASTED RICE ENHANCED
WITH THE AROMA OF MAKRUT LIME LEAVES.
IT'S A KEY INGREDIENT OF ISAAN CUISINE FOR
DISHES SUCH AS LARB AND SAUCES SUCH AS
NAM JIM JAEW (PAGE 184). KHAO KHUA IS QUITE
SIMPLE TO MAKE. IT JUST TAKES A LITTLE
TIME AND EFFORT TO TOAST AND POUND,
BUT IT'S DEFINITELY WORTH IT.

MAKES ABOUT 1/3 CUP

1/4 CUP UNCOOKED STICKY RICE OR JASMINE
RICE (PREFERABLY STICKY RICE)

5 MAKRUT LIME LEAVES, STEMMED AND
TORN INTO SMALL PIECES

1
IN A MEDIUM FRYING PAN OVER
MEDIUM HEAT, COMBINE THE RICE
AND LIME LEAVES AND TOAST,
STIRRING OCCASIONALLY,
UNTIL EVENLY BROWNED,
20 TO 25 MINUTES.

20:00

2
WHILE TOASTING, REPEATEDLY
REMOVE THE PAN FROM THE HEAT
AND SHAKE IT FOR A FEW SECONDS
TO PREVENT THE RICE FROM
BURNING.

SHAKE

SHAKE

CHEF MALLIKA SAYS:

YOU CAN USE A BLENDER OR FOOD PROCESSOR TO MAKE TOASTED RICE POWDER
IN LESS THAN A MINUTE, BUT THE PERFECTION OF TOASTED RICE POWDER COMES
FROM HOW MUCH TIME YOU'VE SPENT ROASTING AND POUNDING IT WITH A
MORTAR AND PESTLE. THE MORE TIME YOU SPEND, THE BETTER THE RESULT.
TO ACHIEVE THE PERFECT TEXTURE IN A SHORTER TIME, USING A
STONE MORTAR AND PESTLE IS RECOMMENDED!

TO MAKE YOUR TOASTED RICE POWDER MORE FRAGRANT,
ADD A FEW THIN SLICES OF GALANGAL AND LEMONGRASS
BEFORE TOASTING.

3

TRANSFER THE TOASTED RICE AND
LIME LEAVES TO A MORTAR AND
LET COOL FOR 3 MINUTES.

4

USING THE PESTLE, POUND THE TOASTED RICE AND LIME
LEAVES GENTLY TO PREVENT THE RICE FROM FLYING OUT
OF THE MORTAR. CAREFULLY INCREASE YOUR POUNDING
SPEED TO CRUSH THE RICE INTO A POWDER; THIS CAN
TAKE UP TO 40 MINUTES (IF USING A CLAY MORTAR).

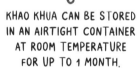

5

THE TEXTURE SHOULD BE
SOMEWHAT LIKE SAND.

6

KHAO KHUA CAN BE STORED
IN AN AIRTIGHT CONTAINER
AT ROOM TEMPERATURE
FOR UP TO 1 MONTH.

TEXTURE CHECK:

PHRIK PON

PHRIK PON IS A TOASTED GROUND CHILE THAT
BELONGS IN THE ICONIC SEASONING SET, WHERE
YOU CAN FIND ITS SIBLINGS: PHRIK NAM PLA
(PAGE 185), GRANULATED SUGAR, AND PHRIK
NAM SOM (PAGE 186). THIS HOMEMADE CHILE
POWDER IS A GREAT WAY TO AMP UP THE SPICE
LEVEL BECAUSE IT IS USUALLY SPICIER THAN
ANY STORE-BOUGHT OPTION. BE CAREFUL WITH
YOUR MEASUREMENTS WHEN ADDING TO A DISH.
REMEMBER: YOU CAN ALWAYS ADD MORE, BUT
YOU CAN'T TURN BACK!

MAKES ABOUT 1/3 CUP

1 1/2 OUNCES DRIED THAI CHILES, STEMMED
1/2 TEASPOON FINE SEA SALT

1
IN A SMALL FRYING PAN OVER
MEDIUM HEAT, COMBINE THE DRIED
CHILES AND SALT AND TOAST,
STIRRING OCCASIONALLY,
UNTIL WELL BROWNED,
15 TO 20 MINUTES.

15:00

2
WHILE TOASTING, REPEATEDLY
REMOVE THE PAN FROM THE HEAT
AND SHAKE IT FOR A FEW SECONDS
TO PREVENT THE CHILES
FROM BURNING.

SHAKE
SHAKE

CHEF MALLIKA SAYS:

YOU CAN USE A BLENDER OR FOOD PROCESSOR TO GRIND THE CHILES IN
LESS THAN A MINUTE, BUT IT TAKES ABOUT 5 MINUTES TO POUND WITH
A MORTAR AND PESTLE.

3

TRANSFER THE TOASTED
CHILES TO A MORTAR AND
LET IT COOL FOR 3 MINUTES.

4

USING THE PESTLE, POUND
THE TOASTED CHILES
INTO A POWDER, ABOUT
5 MINUTES (IF USING A
CLAY MORTAR).

5

THE TEXTURE SHOULD BE
FLAKY AND POWDERY.

SPICE!

6

PHRIK PON CAN BE STORED IN AN
AIRTIGHT CONTAINER AT ROOM
TEMPERATURE FOR UP TO 3 MONTHS.

PHRIK PON THORD

MAKES ABOUT ⅓ CUP

¼ CUP NEUTRAL OIL

6 TABLESPOONS PHRIK PON (PAGE 192)

3 TABLESPOONS GRATHIAM JIEW (PAGE 188)

PHRIK PON THORD IS VERY SIMILAR TO PHRIK PON, BUT PAN-FRYING THE CHILE POWDER IN OIL GIVES IT A SMOKY FRAGRANCE AND ENHANCES THE SAVORY FLAVOR IN ANY DISH. THAIS OFTEN USE THIS IN NOODLE DISHES; THEREFORE, IT CAN SOMETIMES BE FOUND IN THE SEASONING SET AS WELL.

1

IN A SMALL SAUCEPAN OVER MEDIUM-HIGH HEAT, WARM THE OIL. WHEN THE OIL IS LIGHTLY SMOKING, ADD 5 TABLESPOONS OF THE PHRIK PON AND ALL OF THE GRATHIAM JIEW.

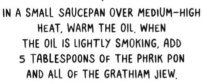

2

STIR THE CHILE OIL FOR 15 SECONDS, THEN IMMEDIATELY REMOVE FROM THE HEAT.

3

ADD THE REMAINING 1 TABLESPOON PHRIK PON TO THE OIL AND CONTINUE TO STIR FOR 15 SECONDS. LET COOL.

4

PHRIK PON THORD CAN BE STORED IN AN AIRTIGHT CONTAINER IN THE FRIDGE FOR UP TO 1 MONTH.

NAM MAKHAM PIAK

NAM MAKHAM PIAK, WHICH DIRECTLY TRANSLATES TO "WET TAMARIND WATER" BUT IS MORE LIKE A PASTE, IS THE EXTRACT FROM TAMARIND PULP MIXED WITH WATER. THIS IS WHAT GIVES THE SOUR FLAVOR PROFILE TO THAI DISHES. IT IS ESPECIALLY USED IN SAVORY DIPPING SAUCES, SOUPS, AND CURRIES. TAMARIND PASTE HAS BEEN FOUND TO BE VERY BENEFICIAL FOR HEALTH, AND IT'S VERY EASY TO MAKE AT HOME.

MAKES ABOUT ½ CUP

1/4 CUP TAMARIND PULP OR SEEDLESS WET TAMARIND

1/2 CUP WARM (ABOUT 140°F) WATER

1
IN A MEDIUM BOWL, COMBINE THE TAMARIND PULP AND WATER AND LET SOAK FOR 3 MINUTES. SET A FINE-MESH STRAINER OVER A MEDIUM SAUCEPAN.

2
USING YOUR HANDS, SQUEEZE THE PULP AND BREAK UP ANY LARGE CLUMPS UNTIL AS MUCH LIQUID AS POSSIBLE IS EXTRACTED.

3
POUR THE SQUEEZED TAMARIND WATER THROUGH THE PREPARED STRAINER.

4
USING THE BACK OF A SPOON, PRESS THE PULP REMAINING IN THE STRAINER AND SCRAPE THE BOTTOM OF THE STRAINER FOR ANY REMAINING TAMARIND WATER. THE TEXTURE SHOULD BE SLIGHTLY THICK, NOT WATERY.

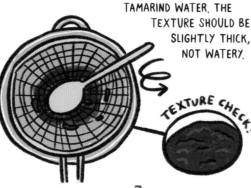

TEXTURE CHECK

5
SET THE SAUCEPAN OVER MEDIUM HEAT AND COOK FOR 5 MINUTES, STIRRING OCCASIONALLY.

6
REMOVE THE SAUCEPAN FROM THE HEAT AND LET COOL.

7
NAM MAKHAM PIAK CAN BE STORED IN AN AIRTIGHT CONTAINER IN THE FRIDGE FOR UP TO 2 WEEKS, OR POUR INTO AN ICE-CUBE TRAY AND FREEZE FOR UP TO 3 MONTHS.

CHEF MALLIKA SAYS:
THE TAMARIND WATER CAN BE USED IMMEDIATELY AFTER STEP 4, BUT CONTINUE ON IF YOU'RE MAKING FOR LONG-TERM STORAGE.

WAW!

NAM PHRIK PHAO

NAM PHRIK PHAO, A THAI CHILE JAM, IS SWEET, SLIGHTLY SOUR, SALTY, SLIGHTLY SPICY, AND SMOKY ALL AT ONCE. THIS CONDIMENT IS PERFECT WITH TOM YUM GOONG (PAGE 138), ANY STIR-FRIED DISH YOU DESIRE, AND EVEN ON ITS OWN WITH FRESH VEGETABLES OR AS A SPREAD ON TOAST. THE CHILE OIL FROM THE JAM CAN ALSO BE DRIZZLED ATOP ANY DISH TO ADD MORE FLAVOR DEPTH.

MAKES ABOUT 1 CUP

8 SMALL RED SHALLOTS, OR 2 MEDIUM RED ONIONS, COARSELY CHOPPED

6 GARLIC CLOVES, COARSELY CHOPPED

1 TABLESPOON SHRIMP PASTE

1/4 CUP NEUTRAL OIL

3 TABLESPOONS DRIED SHRIMP

10 LARGE DRIED THAI CHILES (OR ADJUST TO TASTE), STEMMED AND CUT INTO 1/2-INCH-LONG PIECES

1/2 TEASPOON FINE SEA SALT

1 1/2 TEASPOONS GRANULATED SUGAR

1/4 CUP PACKED GRATED PALM SUGAR

2 TABLESPOONS FISH SAUCE

2 TABLESPOONS NAM MAKHAM PIAK (PAGE 195)

1

SET A SMALL FRYING PAN OVER MEDIUM HEAT. ADD THE SHALLOTS AND GARLIC AND TOAST UNTIL SOFT AND BROWN, 5 TO 6 MINUTES. USING TONGS, TRANSFER TO A PLATE AND SET ASIDE.

2

IN THE SAME PAN OVER MEDIUM HEAT, ADD THE SHRIMP PASTE AND TOAST UNTIL FRAGRANT, ABOUT 2 MINUTES. TRANSFER TO A PLATE AND SET ASIDE.

3

IN THE SAME PAN OVER MEDIUM-HIGH HEAT, WARM THE OIL. WHEN THE OIL IS LIGHTLY SMOKING, ADD THE DRIED SHRIMP AND COOK, STIRRING OCCASIONALLY, UNTIL BROWN AND CRISPY, ABOUT 3 MINUTES. USING THE SKIMMER, TRANSFER THE FRIED SHRIMP TO A PLATE AND SET ASIDE.

4

TURN THE HEAT TO MEDIUM. ADD THE DRIED CHILES TO THE PAN AND COOK FOR 30 SECONDS. TRANSFER THE CHILES TO THE PLATE AND SET ASIDE. TRANSFER THE OIL TO A SMALL BOWL. SET ASIDE.

5

PUT THE FRIED SHRIMP INTO A MORTAR AND POUND WITH THE PESTLE INTO A PASTE. TRANSFER TO A BOWL AND SET ASIDE.

6

IN THE SAME MORTAR, COMBINE THE TOASTED SHALLOTS, GARLIC, AND SHRIMP PASTE AND POUND WITH THE PESTLE INTO A PASTE.

7

ADD THE FRIED DRIED CHILES TO THE MORTAR AND POUND WITH THE PESTLE TO MAKE A CHILE PASTE.

8

SET A SMALL SAUCEPAN OVER MEDIUM HEAT. ADD THE CHILE PASTE, SALT, GRANULATED SUGAR, PALM SUGAR, FISH SAUCE, AND NAM MAKHAM PIAK AND MIX WELL UNTIL INCORPORATED, ABOUT 2 MINUTES.

9

ADD THE POUNDED SHRIMP TO THE PAN AND STIR UNTIL INCORPORATED, ABOUT 1 MINUTE. THE PASTE WILL BECOME THICK AND STICKY.

10

POUR IN THE RESERVED OIL AND MIX WELL UNTIL THE CHILE JAM GENTLY BOILS FOR 10 TO 15 SECONDS. REMOVE FROM THE HEAT AT ONCE AND LET COOL.

11

NAM PHRIK PHAO CAN BE STORED IN AN AIRTIGHT CONTAINER IN THE FRIDGE FOR UP TO 1 MONTH.

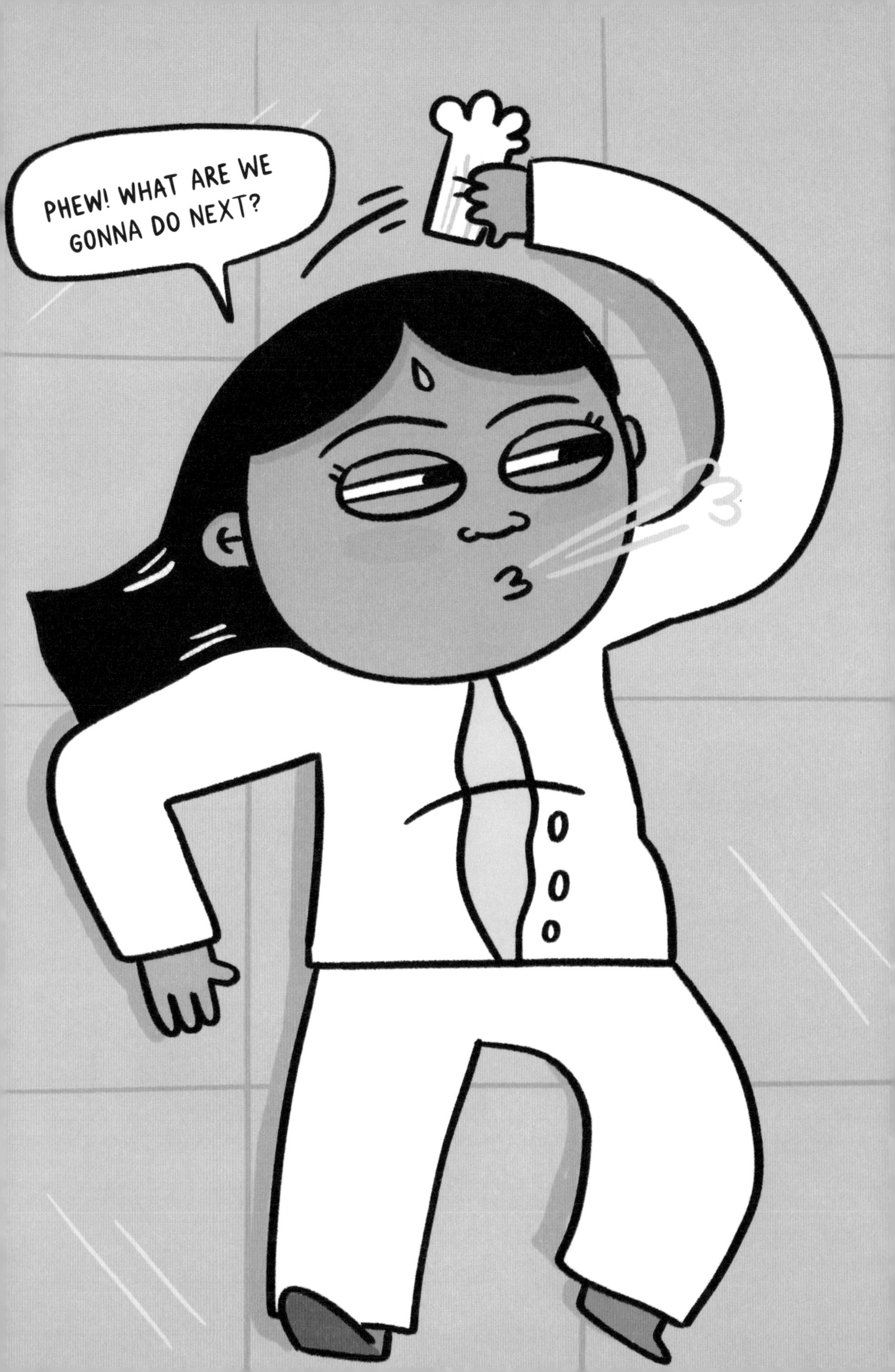
PHEW! WHAT ARE WE GONNA DO NEXT?

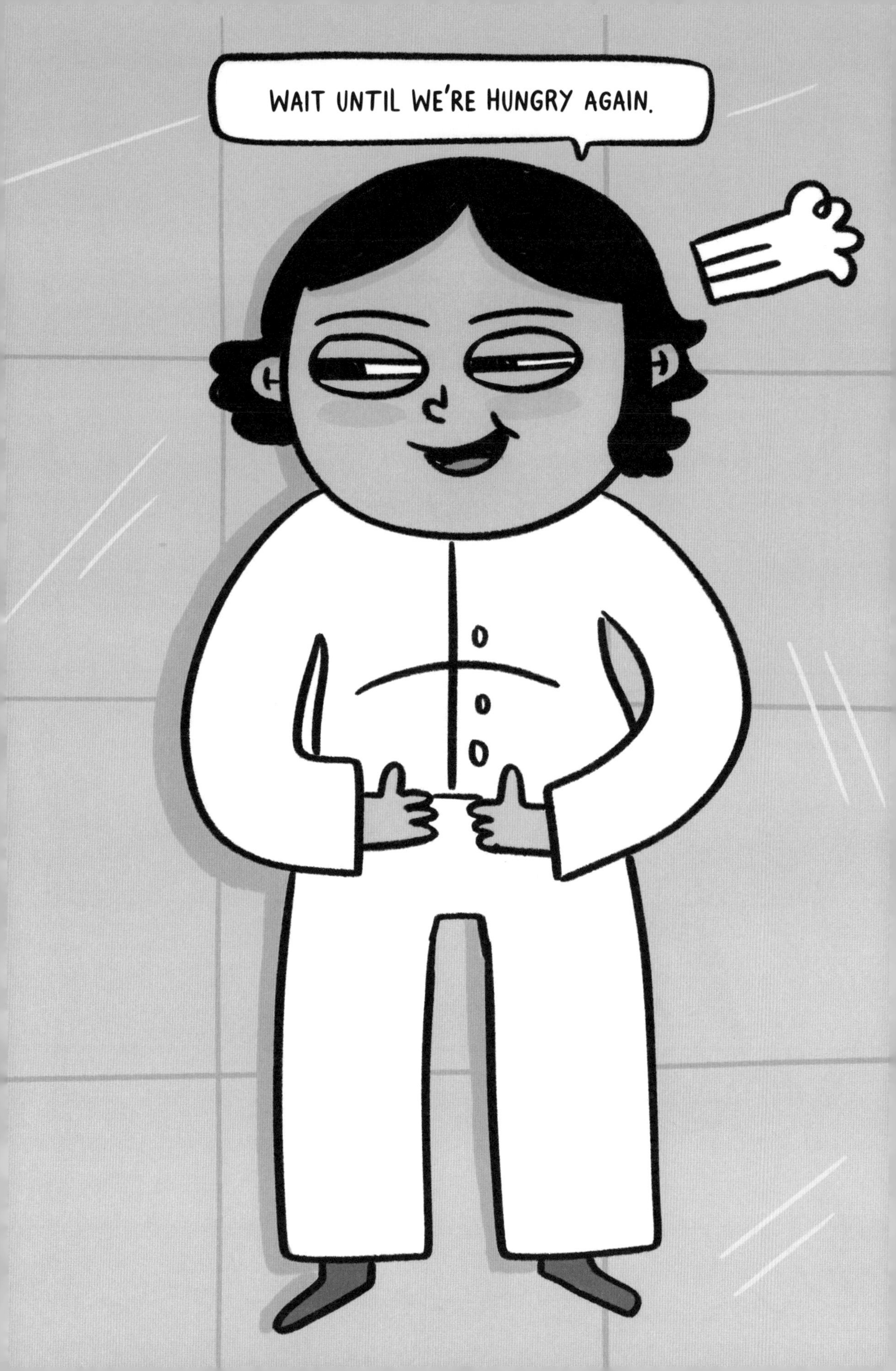
WAIT UNTIL WE'RE HUNGRY AGAIN.

ACKNOWLEDGMENTS

I WOULD LIKE TO THANK THE FOLLOWING PEOPLE.

FIRST, AND PRIMARILY, CHRISTINA, WHO GAVE ME AN INCREDIBLE OPPORTUNITY TO WORK ON THIS BOOK. I FEEL SO GRATEFUL TO BE PART OF THIS EXCITING PROJECT, BUT MORE IMPORTANTLY, TO HAVE HER AS MY PROJECT PARTNER. I REALLY APPRECIATE HER SWEET SUPPORT THROUGHOUT MY DIFFICULT MOMENTS. WITH HER AMAZING TALENT AND SMARTS, WORKING ON THIS BOOK COULD NOT HAVE GONE ANY SMOOTHER.

JINTANA SUKTHAMAPLA, MY BELOVED AUNT WITH WHOM I GREW UP FOR THE FIRST TWENTY-FIVE YEARS OF MY LIFE, BOTH IN OUR HOMETOWN IN THE SOUTH AND IN BANGKOK. SHE'S THE ONE WHO PASSED COOKING SKILLS ON TO ME, BEGINNING WHEN I WAS SEVEN YEARS OLD. MY AUNT WAS ALSO THE BEST CHEF IN OUR VILLAGE AND BECAME THE BEST FOOD VENDOR IN OUR ALLEY IN BANGKOK. NOW I LIVE IN FINLAND, BUT SHE'S STILL AT THE SAME GROCERY STORE IN BANGKOK, AND SHE ALWAYS PICKS UP MY CALLS WHENEVER I HAVE QUESTIONS OR NEED ADVICE.

SUNANTA SUKTHAMAPLA, MY OTHER BELOVED AUNT, WHO SUPPORTED ME THROUGHOUT MY HIGH SCHOOL AND UNIVERSITY EDUCATIONS. WITHOUT HER, I WOULD NOT HAVE BEEN ABLE TO WRITE THE RECIPES IN ENGLISH.

NEXT, OF COURSE, MY PARTNER, TATU KAUPPINEN, AND MY CLOSE FAMILY, WHO SUPPORTED ME DURING THE WHOLE WRITING AND TESTING PROCESS. MY FRIENDS AND NEIGHBORS IN FINLAND, WHO TRIED THE FOODS FROM THE RECIPES AND GAVE CONSTRUCTIVE FEEDBACK TO IMPROVE THE DISHES.

SUMARIN KLANGNOK, A FRIEND I'VE MET IN FINLAND. SHE WAS THE CHEF AND OWNER OF MOOM MUUM NOODLE & RICE CAFÉ IN HUA HIN, THAILAND, FROM 2015 TO 2020. THANK YOU FOR YOUR VALUABLE CONTRIBUTION AND KNOWLEDGE OF THE FOOD AND LIFESTYLE OF NORTHERN THAI PEOPLE.

KANOKWAN FENEL, A STUDENT AND A FRIEND THAT I'VE MET IN FINLAND. SHE HELPED ME WITH THE SHOPPING AND TESTING THE RECIPES. I FEEL SO THANKFUL FOR YOUR FRIENDSHIP, KIND SUPPORT, AND VALUABLE ADVICE.

WANPAPAS PIMDEE, A STUDENT, A FRIEND, AND AN ASSISTANT THAT I'VE MET IN FINLAND. SHE WAS MY GREAT SUPPORT WITH MY TEACHING BUSINESS WHILE I WAS WORKING ON THIS BOOK. ALSO, A BIG THANK-YOU FOR MY PROFESSIONAL HEADSHOT.

—MALLIKA

WHAT A JOY THIS JOURNEY HAS BEEN, BUT ONLY THANKS TO A FANTASTIC TEAM. FIRST AND FOREMOST, MY PARTNER IN CRIME: MALLIKA. I ADMIRE YOUR NEVER-ENDING ENTHUSIASM AND RESILIENCE. I'M VERY PROUD OF YOU AS MY TEACHER, MENTOR, AND FRIEND. A SPECIAL MENTION FOR FARN SAETIA, AN INCREDIBLY TALENTED PHOTOGRAPHER AND FRIEND. I CAN'T WAIT TO SEE WHAT THE FUTURE BRINGS FOR YOU.

A BIG THANK-YOU TO MARK GOTTLIEB, MY LITERARY AGENT. IT'S ALWAYS A PLEASURE AND HONOR WORKING WITH YOU. YOU BELIEVED IN ME FROM THE VERY BEGINNING. TINA DE SOUTER, THANK YOU SO MUCH FOR GUIDING ME THROUGHOUT THE EARLIEST DAYS. WITHOUT YOU, THIS WOULD HAVE BEEN WAY HARDER.

SPECIAL THANKS TO KASPER, SUMMER, AND GHOST FOR ALLOWING US TO COOK AND SHOOT IN THEIR BEAUTIFUL KITCHEN.

SHANNEN, DO YOU REMEMBER OUR TRAM RIDE, WHERE YOU SUDDENLY BURSTED OUT THE TITLE OF THIS BOOK? THANKS FOR THAT, MY BEAN. YOU'RE MORE THAN A MANAGER, YOU'RE FAMILY. A BIG SHOUTOUT TO MOENIA: CHEERS FOR BEING SUCH A GREAT HAND MODEL AND A NEVER-ENDING SOURCE OF (MENTAL) SUPPORT. I'LL NEVER TAKE YOU FOR GRANTED.

SHOKRAN, ADEL. YOU'RE THE BEST PARTNER SOMEONE COULD EVER WISH FOR. YOU'RE SO INCREDIBLY PATIENT, LOVING, AND KIND TO ME. THANK YOU FOR ASSISTING DURING THE SHOOT. SO, HONEYMOON IN THAILAND, THEN?

THANK YOU TO ALL FAMILY, BESTIES, AND READERS. MY DAD, BROTHER, UNCLE, AND GRANDPARENTS FOR CHEERLEADING. TO ALL THE ANTWERP COFFEE BARISTAS WHO MUST HAVE SEEN ME STRUGGLING ENDLESSLY: THANKS FOR LETTING ME STAY DRAWING UNTIL WAY PAST CLOSING HOURS.

I'M GRATEFUL FOR ANYONE WHO HAS SUPPORTED, CHEERED ME ON, OR PROVIDED FOR ME IN WHICHEVER WAY. MAKING A BOOK IS OFTEN TIMES A LONELY JOB, BUT THIS BOOK IS A DIRECT RESULT OF COMMUNITY WORK. THIS ONE IS FOR THE CULTURE.

OENIA, CHEERS FOR BEING SUCH A GREAT HAND MODEL.

–CHRISTINA

WE WOULD LIKE TO EXPRESS OUR BIGGEST GRATITUDE TO KIMMY TEJASINDHU AND CHLOE RAWLINS FROM TEN SPEED PRESS. YOU CAME ON OUR PATHS AT THE RIGHT TIME AND ALWAYS PROVIDED THE SPACE FOR ABSOLUTE CREATIVE FREEDOM. KIMMY, THE UNIVERSE MADE THIS THAI FEMALE TEAM HAPPEN, AND WE'RE FOREVER GRATEFUL FOR THAT. CHLOE, THANK YOU SO MUCH FOR YOUR ENDLESS PATIENCE AND GUIDANCE THROUGHOUT THE WHOLE PROCESS.

BIG SHOUT-OUT TO OUR COPYEDITOR, ANDREA CHESMAN, AND PRODUCTION EDITORS, DOUG OGAN AND SERENA WANG! WE CAN'T IMAGINE HAVING TO PLOW THROUGH OUR FIRST MANUSCRIPT. WHAT A MESS IT MUST HAVE BEEN. OUR ENDLESS GRATITUDE FOR THOSE TIRELESS EAGLE EYES.

AND LAST, BUT DEFINITELY NOT LEAST, WE'D LIKE TO THANK EACH AND EVERY ONE OF OUR READERS, FOLLOWERS, BUYERS, CHEERLEADERS . . . EVERYONE WHO, IN ONE WAY OR ANOTHER, HAS SUPPORTED CHROSTIN AND MALLIKIELI. YOU MAKE THESE THINGS HAPPEN, YOU KNOW? WITHOUT YOU, THERE'S NO US. SO, THANK YOU.

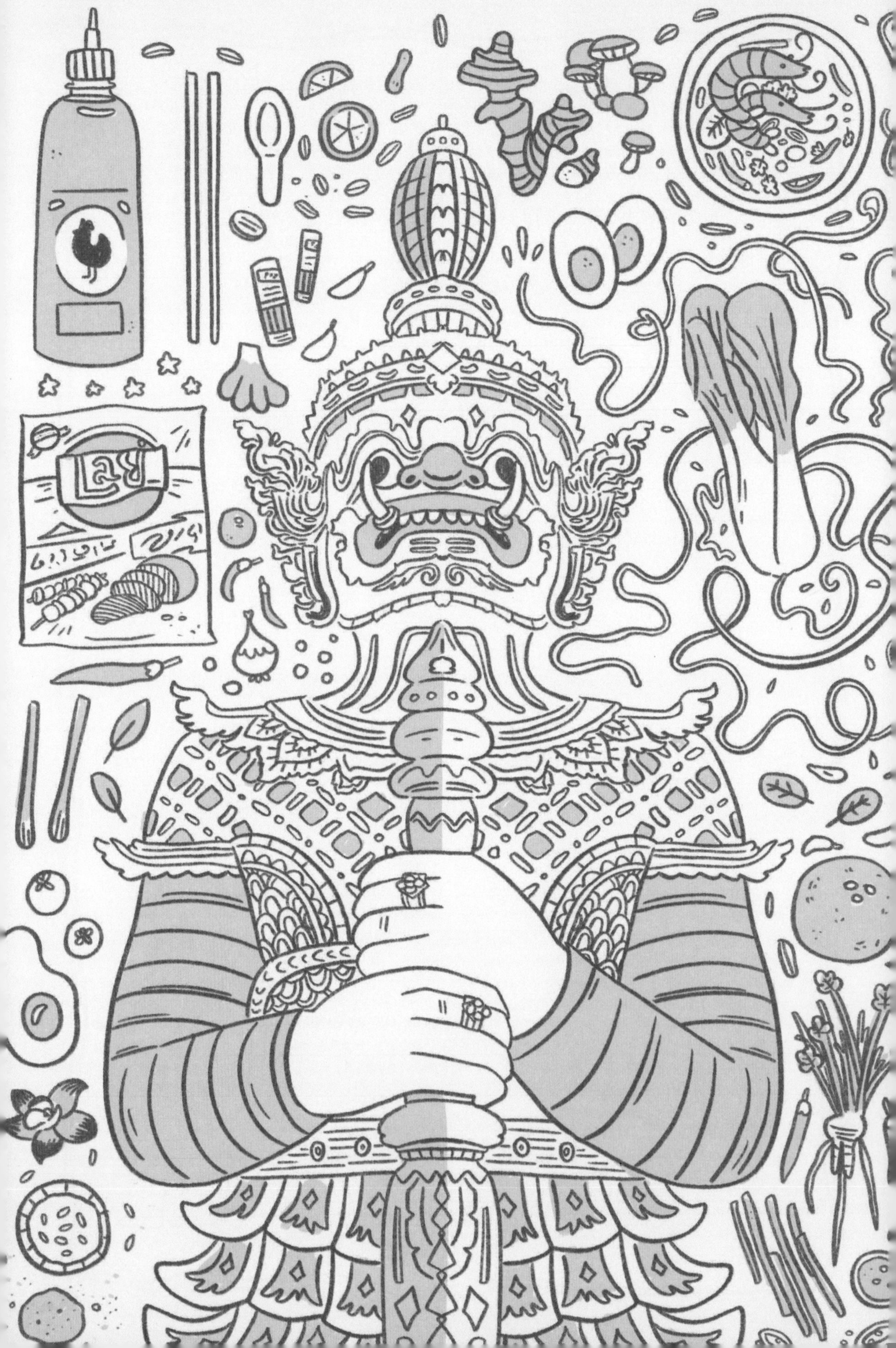

ABOUT THE CONTRIBUTORS

CHRISTINA DE WITTE COMBINES HER DAILY LIFE AS A CARTOONIST WITH OWNING A SECOND-HAND AND UPCYCLING STORE IN BELGIUM. HER ROOTS LAY IN UDON THANI, THE ISAAN REGION OF THAILAND. SHE STARTED MAKING COMICS PROFESSIONALLY WHEN SHE WAS NINETEEN AND PUBLISHED HER DEBUT BOOK, *THE ULTIMATE SURVIVAL GUIDE TO BEING A GIRL*, IN 2018. AFTER FIVE YEARS OF WORKING FOR A BELGIAN MAGAZINE, SHE DECIDED IT WAS TIME TO FOLLOW *HER* DREAMS. YOU'RE CURRENTLY HOLDING ONE OF THEM. THAT, AND WRITING A GRAPHIC NOVEL. MANIFESTING!

MALLIKA KAUPPINEN GREW UP IN A BIG FAMILY IN A REMOTE AREA IN THE SOUTHERN PART OF THAILAND. SHE CAME INTO CONTACT WITH COOKING AT THE AGE OF SEVEN. AT TEN YEARS OLD, SHE MOVED TO BANGKOK TO PURSUE A BETTER EDUCATION. SHE STARTED TUTORING OTHER STUDENTS IN FOREIGN LANGUAGES AT SEVENTEEN, BUT SHE DID NOT REALIZE THAT A LANGUAGE-TEACHING PATH WAS HER FULFILLING CAREER UNTIL SHE MOVED TO FINLAND IN 2015. SHE STILL LIVES THERE WITH HER HUSBAND AND SON. TODAY, SHE TEACHES FINNISH AND THAI ONLINE, AND SHE IS THE FOUNDER OF HER OWN TEACHING COMPANY, MALLIKIELI. SHE PUBLISHED HER FIRST BASIC FINNISH STUDY BOOK, *OPITAAN SUOMEA THAIKSI 1*, FOR THAI AUDIENCES IN 2022.

INDEX

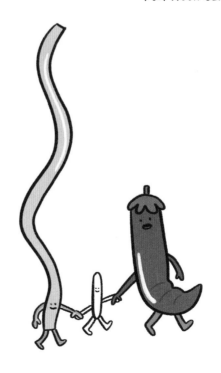

PUBLISHED IN THE UNITED STATES BY TEN SPEED PRESS, AN IMPRINT OF THE
CROWN PUBLISHING GROUP, A DIVISION OF PENGUIN RANDOM HOUSE LLC, NEW YORK.
TENSPEED.COM

TEN SPEED GRAPHIC AND COLOPHON ARE TRADEMARKS OF PENGUIN RANDOM HOUSE LLC.

LIBRARY OF CONGRESS CATALOGING-IN-PUBLICATION DATA
NAMES: WITTE, CHRISTINA DE, AUTHOR. | KAUPPINEN, MALLIKA, 1990- AUTHOR.
TITLE: NOODLES, RICE, AND EVERYTHING SPICE : A THAI COMIC BOOK COOKBOOK /
   CHRISTINA DE WITTE AND MALLIKA KAUPPINEN. IDENTIFIERS: LCCN 2022042556
   (PRINT) | LCCN 2022042557 (EBOOK) | ISBN 9781984861603 (TRADE PAPERBACK) |
   ISBN 9781984861610 (EBOOK) SUBJECTS: LCSH: COOKING, THAI. | LCGFT: COOKBOOKS.
   CLASSIFICATION: LCC TX724.5.T5 W68 2023 (PRINT) | LCC TX724.5.T5 (EBOOK) |
   DDC 641.59593--DC23/ENG/20220923
LC RECORD AVAILABLE AT HTTPS://LCCN.LOC.GOV/2022042556
LC EBOOK RECORD AVAILABLE AT HTTPS://LCCN.LOC.GOV/2022042557

TRADE PAPERBACK ISBN: 978-1-9848-6160-3
EBOOK ISBN: 978-1-9848-6161-0

PRINTED IN CHINA

EDITOR: KIMMY TEJASINDHU | PRODUCTION EDITORS: DOUG OGAN AND SERENA WANG
ART DIRECTOR AND DESIGNER: CHLOE RAWLINS | CO-COVER DESIGNER: MEGGIE RAMM
PRODUCTION DESIGNER: NICK PATTON
PRODUCTION MANAGER: DAN MYERS
FOOD AND PROP STYLIST, DIGITECH, AND PHOTO RETOUCHER: FARN SAETIA
PHOTO AND PROP STYLIST ASSISTANT: ADEL SETTA
COPYEDITOR: ANDREA CHESMAN | PROOFREADER: KATE BOLEN
INDEXER: STEPHEN CALLAHAN
PUBLICIST: MAYA BRADFORD | MARKETER: JOEY LOZADA

10 9 8 7 6 5 4 3 2 1

FIRST EDITION